W9-BCM-427

Citizenship, Gender, and Work

Citizenship, Gender, and Work

Social Organization of Industrial Agriculture

Robert J. Thomas

UNIVERSITY OF CALIFORNIA PRESS
Berkeley   Los Angeles   London

University of California Press
Berkeley and Los Angeles, California

University of California Press, Ltd.
London, England

Copyright © 1985 by The Regents of the University of California

Library of Congress Cataloging in Publication Data

Thomas, Robert J.
  Citizenship, gender, and work.

  Bibliography: p. 233
  Includes index.
  1. Lettuce industry—Southwestern States—Employees.
I. Title.
HD8039.L452U67   1985   305'.9633   84–8626
ISBN 0–520–05310–9

1 2 3 4 5 6 7 8 9

This book is dedicated to Paul and Rita Thomas. They taught me the meaning and the value of hard work.

Contents

Acknowledgments

The people who enabled me to complete this study are conspicuous in my memory, though only a few of their names will appear in these pages. Foremost among them are the men and women with whom I worked and talked during those torturously long days in the field and the evenings of replenishment that followed. Their willingness to spend time with a curious, imposing, and often confused *gabacho* infused my research with greater insight and purpose than it would otherwise have had. Although I must preserve their anonymity because of the vulnerable positions they occupy, their lives and their work are chronicled in this study. I am sure that some of them still wonder how anyone can become a doctor by cutting lettuce. This is the evidence.

Appreciation must also be offered to the union officials, growers, and executives who provided information valuable to the study. Union and management alike questioned my purpose but their cooperation allowed me to more accurately weigh competing arguments and interpretations concerning the dynamics of lettuce production and industrial agriculture.

During the field portion of the research, Juana Franklin, Rich Carbajal, Frank Bardacke, Julie Miller, and Bob Buttner were invaluable in helping me cope with the hardest work I had ever done. Their kind advice and condolence made it possible to keep going—even when my back and feet said it was time to quit.

Intellectually, my debts are varied and numerous. First in
line is Arnold S. Feldman. Much beyond what was called for,
Ackie enlightened, endured, encouraged, and ignored me at
all the right times. His prophecies—"you *will* get a grant, you
will finish the study, you *will* get a job"—have all been borne
out, though I tended to disbelieve him all along the way.
Without doubt his incredibly high standards in training and
his demands for excellence have made those achievements
possible. I know I cannot discharge my debt to him, just as I
am sure I will continue to ask for favors.

My debt to Bill Friedland is a long-standing one. Through
Bill, I came to appreciate the sociological perspective as an
undergraduate. This was no small accomplishment since I
took only one sociology course. His tutelage, always centered
on the need to develop a praxis of sociology, captured my
interest and guided me through a number of fascinating
studies. I also thank Bill for his advice to "get out of California
if you're going to go to graduate school." I did, but decided
after several Chicago winters to renew my research on southwestern agriculture.

I was fortunate in having the manuscript read in its entirety
by John Walton, Allan Schnaiberg, and Howie Becker. They
all provided a great deal of criticism, support, and professional socialization along the way. I would also like to thank
William J. Wilson, Michael Burawoy, Paul Lubeck, Bob Al-
ford, Chuck Tilly, Mayer Zald, and Michael Kearney for their
help at various stages of the research and writing. Many of
my friends listened, criticized, questioned, and complained
while I went through this process. In particular, I toast Whit
Soule, William Finlay, Sam Gilmore, Ann Fredricks, Tim
Kappel, and Joy Charlton. Another reason for listing them
here is so that I can say later that I knew them when they
were just graduate students. Sheila Wilder undertook the
enormously difficult task of word-processing the manuscript
and did it with the dispatch, patience, and good humor that
is her trademark. However, a certain computer company,
which for reasons of legal liability shall go unnamed, has lost
me forever as a customer due to the last-minute destruction
of several disks by one of its expensive machines.

The National Science Foundation (NSF #78–25914) and the Graduate School of Northwestern University aided enormously with grants to support this study. Of course, neither those institutions nor the people listed above are responsible for the evidence or conclusions presented in this work. I alone take responsibility for them.

Finally, the writing and revision process could not have been completed without the steadfast support of my best friend, Rosanna Hertz. She persistently argued that I could not overlook the salience of gender and family in the organization of work and labor markets and pushed me in the direction of a literature which I, as a "class-first" analyst, had succeeded in ignoring. The evidence for how convincing (and right) she was is clear throughout this study.

1

Citizenship and Labor Supply

INTRODUCTION

In a lush field of green extending off to the horizon, a harvest crew plods steadily along narrow irrigation furrows. Toward the front of the group, a line of men walks bent at the waist, their arms extended to the ground. Each man repeats the same motion: he grasps a single lettuce head, digs his fingers into the floppy leaves that surround the solid core like enormous green flower petals, and tilts the plant slightly to expose its thick taproot. A quick plunge of his broad knife cleanly severs the root a fraction of an inch above the pebbly clay soil. Lifting the plant with a hand that seems hardly big enough to hold the head securely, he deftly trims the upturned trunk and, with a sharp twist of the wrist, sends the detached wrapper leaves flying in all directions. In a fluid motion, he lays the trimmed lettuce gently on the carpet of discarded leaves and then reaches for the next head. The cycle takes four seconds; it will be repeated more than 5,000 times that day. Trailing behind the leaders, other members of the harvest crew pack and seal the lettuce in cardboard cartons. Their movements are rapid but controlled. In the crew's wake, leaves lie flattened as if mowed by some enormous machine.

Reaching the end of their rows, two men straighten and stare momentarily across the asphalt county road in the direc-

1

tion of another immense green field. Removing his baseball cap slowly and drawing a soiled red bandana across his sweaty brow, Cruz speaks slowly to his companion: "It looks like we'll be over there next week, Miguelito. That is, if it doesn't rain." Miguel, at thirty the younger of the two, rubs the small of his back and nods. "Yeah," he responds, "we'll cut that field and the next one and then next year we'll be back to cut them both again. Only next year it'll be harder. My back will hurt more and my knife won't be as sharp. And," he adds, "the year after that I'll be thirty-two and an old man like you." Laughing in response to the remark, Cruz shifts his gaze to his companion and raises his eyebrows: "Do you think Mexicans wear out faster than other people? Or do we just start out tired?" Cruz acknowledges Miguel's silence with a nod of his own and, donning his cap, turns around to face a new row of lettuce.

Two months earlier in a field not far from the one picked by Cruz, Miguel, and their co-workers, a different harvest crew was at work. They, too, were harvesting lettuce. Unlike Cruz and Miguel's crew, these workers trailed behind a lumbering mechanical contraption called a "wrapping machine." The machine, little more than a sophisticated mobile conveyor belt, makes it possible for some workers to sit and wrap heads of lettuce in plastic wrap before they are packed and shipped. It changes the division of labor employed by Cruz and Miguel to one paced and controlled by gears and motors.

Differences between the crews, however, are more than mechanical: the wrap crew is more than half female and the men are either young (in their teens) and trying to break into the lettuce harvest or much older (mid-forties to sixties) and looking to earn enough to keep themselves and their families going. The men tend not to stay in the crew very long; many of the women, however, have worked in this crew or company for five or more years.

As the wrap machine bounces lazily through the field, its huge tractor tries churning up precisely contoured irrigation furrows, a platoon of workers walks behind cutting the lettuce heads and handing them to the wrappers seated on the machine. The cutters are men and the wrappers women.

Several of the women teasingly grill a recent addition to the crew. "Are you sure you're not Mexican?" they asked. "Maybe we'll call you Guero just so you have a Spanish name. 'Bob' isn't a good name for a *lechugero* (lettuce worker)," offered another woman, La Señora, as everyone called her. The younger men, boys really, and the aging men laughed but did not add anything; several looked away as Guero looked around for some clue about how to respond to the gentle ribbing.

Apparently unable to resist the temptation to continue questioning the embarrassed Guero, La Señora finally discovers he is Anglo and a student who wants to learn about lettuce harvesting. "A student?" she laughs, adding, "The only Anglos I've ever seen out here have been bosses or Communists!" That comment draws a chorus of snickers. Several days later Guero approached La Señora during a break and asked why she thought Anglos didn't work in the fields. "Why?" she snorted and then answered herself, "Because there are always enough Mexicans to go around. They just whistle across the border and here come ten thousand more hungry people." But, Guero wondered aloud, there are many unemployed people in the United States, too. To that La Señora responded: "But, unemployed Anglos won't work for what they pay us women and they won't work for what illegals get paid. All the ranchers know that."

These comments point to a paradox in work organization found in an important set of agribusiness enterprises in the southwestern United States. Where the trend in recent years has been toward the substitution of harvesting machinery for seasonal labor, producers of head lettuce have persisted in organizing production in a highly labor-intensive fashion. Despite the perishability of the crop, its extreme vulnerability to minute variations in climate, and a seemingly unpredictable market, the lettuce industry hires thousands of farm worker men and women each year to bend, stoop, and cut their way through the fields in a fashion more reminiscent of nineteenth-century farming than twentieth-century agribusiness.

Were the lettuce industry populated by small-scale, marginal enterprises, these observations would not be so striking. However, lettuce production in California and Arizona is no marginal business: in 1980 firms in the two states grossed nearly $500 million in total revenues. In an inflationary period in which such gross figures are hard to comprehend, another factor must be taken into account: between 40 and 60 percent of the national market in lettuce has been cornered by four firms (Friedland, Barton, and Thomas, 1981:49; and other calculations provided in chap. 3). Leading firms in the industry obviously are not marginal family enterprises. Instead, they represent examples of some of the most advanced of modern business organizations. As later evidence will suggest, the top lettuce producers are highly profitable, financially prosperous, bureaucratically administered capitalist enterprises. They bear as little resemblance to the prototypical family farm as the corner grocery does to the A&P or Safeway supermarket chains. In fact, the two "giants" of the lettuce (and, for that matter, vegetable) business are organizational extensions of multinational corporations into the fields.

Lettuce, under the guidance of large corporate capital, has ceased to be a seasonal venture. Lettuce is a manufactured commodity grown year-round and channeled to national and international markets. Cultivation and harvesting are scheduled on a long-term basis. Computers monitor output and assist in inventory control. Batteries of telephones and advanced communications equipment connect corporate officers with production supervisors, planning offices, and distant markets. Company planes whisk busy executives from company landing strips in sweltering rural valleys to air-conditioned headquarter complexes. Gone is the farm family, the lettuce patch, and the few "hired hands."

Yet, for all the organizational sophistication surrounding the lettuce business, the harvest labor process remains remarkably "backward." While production orders may emanate from distant corporate offices and sales contracts may be negotiated in plush restaurants, crews of lechugeros push themselves through blistering heat and physical torture to prepare the "green gold" for market. The physical demands of the work alone are reason enough to evoke images of nineteenth-century sweatshops. In the "ground-pack" harvest (the predominant form of harvest work organization) nearly all the work is done by hand. Lechugeros frequently walk stooped through the fields for ten hours a day, six days a week, completing the equivalent of 2,500 toe-touches a day in order to earn a living and get the crop in. Not surprisingly, the ground-pack labor process takes its toll: "careers" in the industry are short and painful, with even the most ardent and committed lechugeros lasting less than fourteen years (on average) in the job.

The economic rewards hardly compensate for the physical destructiveness of the work. On average, even the most productive workers earn less than 30 percent of the average annual wage for manufacturing operatives. Though some lechugeros can earn upward of $500 a week during peak periods, most earn much less. But even those inflated figures fail to take into account important costs: the physical drain of cutting lettuce that prevents full-year employment; the high costs of transportation, food, and shelter accompanying migration between production areas; the expenses of travel from home to work (often a thousand miles between a worker's pemanent residence and some of the work sites); and the nonmonetary but significant costs of separation from home and family while on *la corrida* (the trail of work in the lettuce harvest).

Despite the fact that lechugeros (especially those who work in the ground-pack harvest) tend to earn more than other farm workers and often proclaim themselves the "champagne of farm labor," higher wages establish a claim for social status only within the farm worker community. The low status of the lechugero and other farm workers is itself the product of a complex interaction among class, ethnic, and organizational factors. In spite of the economic success of the organizations that employ them, lettuce workers face a hostile and discriminatory environment when they seek housing, police and government services, and, most directly, better wages and working conditions.

For many, the glaring contrast in economic position and

social status between agribusiness corporations and farm laborers is not a startling finding. After all, John Steinbeck's *Grapes of Wrath*, Carey McWilliams's *Factories in the Fields*, and Edward R. Murrow's documentary "Harvest of Shame" painted similar pictures in the 1930s, 1940s, and 1950s. More recently, the strikes and boycott campaigns marshalled by the United Farm Workers (UFW) union and its leader, Cesar Chavez, brought the plight of southwestern farm workers to national attention in the late 1960s and early 1970s. Even in the lettuce industry—a major focal point of union organizing for over a decade—*campesinos* (farm workers) continue to struggle for basic economic and political rights and protections.

The paradoxical success of agribusiness in the lettuce industry is further underscored when one looks closer at the labor process. For, although the work is arduous, careers short, and rewards relatively meager, ground-pack harvest crews (which hereafter I will refer to as "ground crews") are remarkably productive and *skilled*. A ground crew of thirty-six workers can, under normal conditions, cut, pack, and load 3,500 cartons of lettuce per day, that is, enough to fill 3½ railroad cars (the equivalent of 84,000 heads of lettuce). The efficiency of the crew resides in the precise and controlled division of labor among crew members: workers perform coordinated tasks in such a way as to minimize extraneous movement and thereby establish a high level of synchronization. Since crew members are most often paid on a crew-based piece-rate (so many cents per carton completed), the "collective" skill of the crew unit determines group *and* individual earnings.

Ground crews in the lettuce harvest therefore present a sharp contrast to the general conception of farm work as unskilled, casual employment. Since the speed and efficiency of the harvest is a function of the skills *both* of individuals and the collective, the crew-based labor process more closely resembles the traditional organization of work in many mining, construction, lumbering, and longshoring settings. In other words, the organization of lettuce harvesting places considerable emphasis on the stability and experience of crew members in their jobs and in their relations with one another. And, as I will suggest later, the emphasis on stability and experience comes from both the company and the crew: workers derive economic and social gains from cohesiveness; companies get higher output from experienced crews. Ground crews are, quite literally, extremely productive "social" harvesting machines whose performance is critical to the timely production and marketing of a highly valuable crop.

In combination, these characteristics of the ground crews suggest that individual and, more directly, *crew* skills are highly valuable to lettuce firms. The centrality of these crews to the harvest of a profitable but perishable crop suggests that lechugeros should occupy a strong labor market position. And, to some extent, they do; according to UFW sources, nearly 70 percent of the lettuce industry is unionized. However, thousands of lettuce workers and nonunionized farm laborers in the Southwest lack the organizational means by which to negotiate effectively over wages, work rules, and the conditions of employment.

The situation encountered by the ground crews of the lettuce industry raises a number of important questions: How can agribusiness firms in the lettuce industry avail themselves of such valuable labor at so low a price? How can workers organized into skilled crews be denied the ability to claim the status and reward commonly associated with skill? What factors account for managerial control and worker consent?

The preceding questions capture but half the problem. The ground-crew harvest accounts for nearly 80 percent of the lettuce cut and packed in the Southwest; the remaining 20 percent is harvested under different conditions, in the process described earlier as wrapping. This method of harvesting exhibits characteristics of the ground crew: a group of workers (usually 33 to a crew) cuts, packs, and loads lettuce using only the most rudimentary tools. In contrast to the ground-pack, however, the "wrap-pack" inserts a new activity—enveloping heads of lettuce in individual plastic packages—and a new source of coordination—a large, mobile conveyor apparatus. The wrap-pack harvest removes from the crew the critical element of mutual coordination: the pace and coordination of work is controlled not by crew members but by the mobile conveyor (see chap. 3 for a diagram). In other words, though the machine does not do anything to the

lettuce other than move it from one work station to another
(and is therefore *not* a harvesting machine), the machine coordinates cutting, wrapping, packing, and loading and regulates
the work pace.

With the breaking down of the skill of the ground crew
(especially the collective dimension of skill), harvest workers
participate in a different kind of labor process. In contrast to
a crew-based piece-rate, wrap crew workers are paid an hourly
wage rate much lower than the potential hourly equivalent in
the ground crew. Individual proficiency in a job or crew skill
do not constitute a basis for appreciably higher earnings.
Workers need have nothing more than a passing acquaintance
with one another and a few hours practice at their individual
tasks for the crew to achieve near-average productivity. Yet,
the continued appearance of an adequate supply of workers
to fill crew positions is no less important in the wrap crew
than it is in the ground crew. And, even though the work has
been "deskilled" (to use Braverman's term) through the introduction of capital investments in machines and auxiliary
equipment, employers in the lettuce industry seek to achieve
continuity in the makeup of the wrap crews. That is, for
the agribusiness employer as for the owner-manager of a
McDonald's fast-food franchise, there is an organizational
advantage in having the same workers performing, day in
and day out, the mindless and repetitive tasks of cutting lettuce and frying Big Macs (Boas and Chain, 1976:41–43).

The situation encountered in the wrap-pack harvest thus
raises another set of important questions: How can these
machine-paced crews operate productively if, as is generally
presumed, labor is casual and uncommitted? Alternatively,
how can the firms that employ those machines to harvest this
valuable crop be assured that labor (even the same workers)
will show up consistently?

STRATIFICATION IN THE WORKPLACE
AND IN SOCIETY

Although the preceding questions are drawn from the case
of the lettuce industry, they are connected to a number of

important issues in the study of work and stratification. Most important among those issues, especially in light of recent developments in Marxian and neo-Marxian labor market and labor process theories, is the relationship between stratification in the workplace and stratification in society. The corpus of research on dual and segmented labor markets (Edwards, Reich, and Gordon, 1975; Gordon, Edwards, and Reich, 1982) has stimulated much greater concern with the consequences of change in economic organizations for how work is organized, how jobs are structured, and, ultimately, how the working class is divided economically and politically. Likewise, recent studies of the labor process under capitalism (Braverman, 1975; Edwards, 1979; and Burawoy, 1979) have focused considerable attention on how the dynamics of technological development and class relations in the workplace affect the contours of stratification in society. Yet both approaches have shown a measure of insensitivity to the interactive character of problems of work organization and control in the labor process and problems of social and political inequality outside the enterprise. The lesser emphasis or, in some cases, lack of emphasis on the manner in which social and political institutions can shape the labor process derives largely from a general adherence to a unidirectional theory of determination that sees economic structural arrangements as molding or shaping the "rest of society." This approach, I will argue, distracts us from the way in which labor process and labor markets, on the one side, and social and political institutions, on the other, *structure one another*. That is, rather than rest with the argument that class relations embedded in the labor process determine the structure of social and political institutions—and with them the conditions necessary for the reproduction of those class relations—I will contend that the structure of the labor process can be influenced by social relations and social processes external to it.

   More concretely, I will argue that theories of labor market segmentation and labor process organization often fail to account for historically persistent inequalities by race, gender, and citizenship precisely because they rely upon a strict economic determination of social and political inequality. By looking primarily to the workplace to explain stratification in society and thereby promoting a "class-first" (Hartmann and Markusen, 1980) analysis, these theories find it difficult to deal with inequality built around categories of race, gender, and citizenship as anything other than functions or functional aspects of class relations. By limiting political economy in this fashion, institutional arrangements such as are found in the welfare state, the family, and national state systems are transformed into dependent entities consigned theoretically to "superstructure," the "sphere of reproduction," or the "social structure of accumulation" and are made visible only when needed to drive home a point about structural issues.

In an effort to rectify these shortcomings, I will emphasize the interactive character of labor processes, labor markets, and social structure and point to a reformulation of the argument which allows for a more systematic integration of nonclass categories of inequality.

Before proceeding, however, it is necessary to show more directly the linkage between the questions posed at the beginning of this chapter and the issues raised regarding labor market and labor process theories.

INITIAL CONSIDERATIONS

In undertaking this study, I had the benefit of prior exposure to research on work organization in agriculture—specifically, the processing tomato industry (Friedland and Barton, 1975: chap. IV) and other segments of agricultural production in California (Thomas, 1977). The tomato industry study and a later work focusing more directly on the lettuce industry (Friedland, Barton, and Thomas, 1981) sought to uncover the conditions leading up to and resulting from harvest mechanization. In both studies, labor market and labor supply issues seemed directly connected to the organization of work. In the tomato industry, a remarkably rapid shift to mechanical harvesting appeared to be precipitated by a reduction in the supply of braceros (contract laborers from Mexico), even though the technology for mechanical harvesting had been unpopular and seen as too cumbersome by many agricultural employers (Friedland and Barton, 1975:20–34). In the lettuce industry, the technology for mechanical harvesting had been (and continues to be) in place, ready to be employed as an alternative to a highly labor-intensive harvesting system. Yet for all the turmoil surrounding unionization efforts and lettuce boycotts (Levy, 1975; Jenkins and Perrow, 1977; Friedland and Thomas, 1974; and Thomas and Friedland, 1982, for analyses of the battles for unionization of lettuce workers in California)[1], the mechanical alternative has yet to be deployed. In assessing the conditions that might lead to harvest mechanization, Friedland, Barton, and Thomas (1981: chap. 3) pointed to the importance of labor supply considerations for analyzing methods of work organization. However, an important question remained: what was it about the labor system that made managerial control over the harvest labor process unproblematic, even in the wake of high levels of unionization?

For many readers, it might seem that two obvious factors provide the explanation: (1) that the geographic proximity of the American Southwest and Mexico offers a pool of cheap labor making possible the paradoxical coincidence of profitable firms and low-wage labor; and/or (2) that something about the business of agriculture sets it apart from the conditions, and therefore the explanations, of industrial organization. To some extent these factors will be shown to be important; after all, the unique setting of southwestern agriculture, especially with respect to labor supply issues, is not the same as one encounters in the New England region. However, these factors provide only a very partial answer to the questions I have asked.

In the first case, the geographic proximity of Mexico would seem a logical explanation for why Mexican workers have played an important role in the historical development of the southwestern agricultural economy. Taylor and Vasey (1936a and 1936b), London and Anderson (1970), and Galarza (1964, 1971) have documented the general significance of alien workers to the region's agricultural history. But arguments about geographic proximity do not inherently explain why Mexicans, for example, should have been more "attractive" workers than other disadvantaged or negatively privileged workers (e.g., blacks or women). Nor does this argument explain why, in different historical periods, Chinese, Japanese, Filipino, and U.S. workers competed with Mexicans as the principal source of farm labor. Moreover, it does not explain why women have numerically dominated some segments of agricultural production while men dominated in others.

Macrostructural analyses provided by Portes (1978), Jenkins (1978), Cornelius (1976), and others have moved to overcome the shortcomings of this explanation by emphasizing the economic disparities between the United States and Central and South America which give rise to an important "push" complement to the "pull" factors of employment in U.S. agriculture. These arguments are helpful in understanding how uneven development contributes to the formation of labor pools. However, they only explain how uneven development makes *possible* the employment of foreign workers, not why those workers show up in the jobs they do, what the effect of their presence is, or whether the actual demand for labor is as undifferentiated as the supply would seem to be. And, equally important for our concern with issues of stratification in the workplace and in society, neither this argument nor the one based on geographic proximity attempts to more systematically analyze the relationship between citizenship status and labor supply—even though both refer implicitly to issues of citizenship. This is especially the case when undocumented immigrants ("illegal aliens") are seen to play an important role in the contemporary setting.

The second explanation, based on considerations about agriculture as an exceptional system of production, argues that characteristics of agricultural production distinguish it so greatly from other economic sectors and production processes that efforts to analyze it using industrial categories prove fruitless. Factors such as the perishability of the product, the time gap between the principal production activities (e.g., planting, cultivating, and harvesting), the relative immobility of agricultural firms, and the greater uncertainties brought on by plant biology and weather have historically been used by agricultural interests as an argument against their inclusion under generic policies, such as coverage under the stipulations of the National Labor Relations Act (Friedland and Thomas, 1974:52–54). Though on the surface this characterization would seem to have little to do with explaining the relationship between labor processes and labor markets, it does by virtue of giving the appearance that analyses of agricultural enterprises, labor processes, and labor markets ought to be made *apart from* industry. Even Carey McWilliams's (1977) stirring imagery of "factories in the fields" could not budge many policy makers (or rural sociologists, for that matter) from believing that agriculture was indeed different. Until recent developments in the political economy and the sociology of agriculture (Buttel and Newby, 1980; Friedland, 1979; Friedmann, 1981; and Buttel, Ehrensaft, and Friedland, forthcoming), such a characterization went largely unchallenged.

In the wake of these studies, however, two implications must be considered. First, a number of agricultural enterprises and commodity groups have been shown to be characterized by organizational structures and labor processes that very closely approximate relations of production and employment found in industrial settings (Friedland, Barton, and Thomas, 1981; Hightower, 1972; Mines and Anzaldua, 1982; and Scheuring and Thompson, 1978). Second, comparative works by Friedland, Barton, and Thomas (1981) and Mann and Dickinson (1980) have pointed to considerable variation by enterprise and commodity group. Moreover, Friedmann (1981) has called for distinctions between industrial agriculture and simple commodity production—reflecting more and less direct involvement in capitalist relations of production and exchange. These studies not only question the exceptional character of agriculture as a production system and the undifferentiated character of agricultural enterprises; they further argue for sensitivity to the differentiation among segments of agriculture in terms of demands for labor. With regard to the latter point in particular, they argue that differential needs for labor have developed within agriculture which cannot be satisfied through a homogeneous supply of

unskilled workers. If, indeed, there is a differentiated demand for labor according to levels of skill, degrees of stability,
or other characteristics, how are those jobs filled? Moreover,
their research has the practical implication of questioning
whether theories of sectoral splits in the economy and corre-
sponding labor market segmentation are capable of providing
an explanation for the coincidence of large-scale firms and
low-paid labor—for example, as found in the case of the
lettuce industry. That is, sectoral theories have tended to
categorize agriculture as part of the "competitive" sector of
the economy (see, e.g., Beck, Horan, and Tolbert, 1978;
Oster, 1979; O'Connor, 1973; and Edwards, 1979) when, in
fact, segments of it, like the lettuce industry, may be dominated by firms whose characteristics appear much more consistent with "monopoly" or "core" organizations than with
"competitive" or "peripheral" firms.

SEGMENTED LABOR MARKET APPROACHES

Since the concern here is to analyze the connections between
organizational structure, labor process, and labor market, it
is instructive to turn to theories of segmentation in labor
markets and labor processes for aid in the development of an
explanatory framework. Works on segmentation by Gordon,
Edwards, and Reich (1982) and on labor processes by Braverman (1975), Edwards (1979), and Burawoy (1979), though
differing in terms of focus and conclusions, share a number
of analytic concerns useful to this study: (1) the effect of
changes in the economic structure for the organization of
work and labor markets; (2) the factors underlying differentiation in labor processes and labor markets; and (3) to a
varying degree, the political aspects of industrial organization,
especially the sources of differential amounts of power between workers and managers and its effect on control over
work. In this section I will turn to a consideration of the
strengths and weaknesses of segmented labor market theory;
in the section that follows I will undertake a parallel consideration of labor process theory.

In recent years, labor market theory has been expanded in an attempt to develop explanations for a number of problems long ignored by neoclassical economics: for example, the persistence of poverty, differential levels and types of employment for different population groups (especially blacks, women, and Latinos), creation of different career trajectories for members of the traditional working class, and variation in employment opportunities and jobs by organizational type (Gordon, 1972). The effort to link labor market processes to social stratification began with the pioneering efforts of Averitt (1968), Bluestone (1970), Doeringer and Piore (1975), and Gordon (1972). Their investigations into the linkage between opportunity structures (as represented in job openings in different types of organizations) and poverty were built on sectoral analyses of the economy. Averitt and Bluestone proposed dual and tripartite models of economic organization, claiming that the division of the economy into different kinds of enterprises—differentiated along the lines of size, market share, and capitalization—had resulted in radically different opportunity structures for workers. They counterposed, for example, the relative affluence of workers in heavily unionized, large-scale firms with the low wages and unprotected positions of workers employed by less substantial, nonunion enterprises.

Doeringer and Piore (1975), looking much more closely at the employment and training practices developed by those large-scale firms, argued that the traditional notions of labor market operation had been undercut by the appearance of a division between internal and external labor markets. Internal labor markets, they contended, had evolved within many large enterprises, especially those located in basic industries like steel and auto, into administrative structures designed to shelter firms from the vagaries of external labor market operation (especially fluctuations in supply and demand and the difficulties of acquiring skilled labor in the external labor market) and to provide workers with a measure of protection from competition with outside labor market participants. They further noted that internal labor markets resulted from the construction of durable relationships between management

and organized labor, that is, collective bargaining and seniority systems had pushed for the creation of bureaucratic rules
and procedures for the allocation of union members into slots
within the organization. The upshot of internal labor market
construction was the creation of barriers to entry into some
of the most prosperous and highly rewarded occupations
within the overall economy. Entry-level positions were concentrated at the lower ranks of the blue-collar hierarchy and
reward systems (especially in terms of nonwage benefits such
as insurance and pensions) were oriented toward maximizing
stability in the individual firm's labor force.

   Though theories of internal labor market existence and
operation had predated the work of Doeringer and Piore
(Kerr, 1954) and Marxist economists such as Baran and
Sweezy (1968) and Dobb (1963) had drawn attention to the
bifurcation of the economy into monopoly and competitive
sectors, the combination of these approaches, particularly in
the work of Gordon (1972), Edwards, Reich, and Gordon
(1975), Edwards (1975, 1979), and Gordon, Edwards, and
Reich (1982), resulted in a new body of research and a new
theoretical approach to the relationship between economic
organizations and labor markets. "Dual labor market" and
later "segmented labor market" theories sought to draw attention to the relationship between economic segmentation
among firms, segmentation in labor markets, and divisions
within the working class. This approach, posing an alternative to the traditional Marxist model of a homogeneous
or homogenizing working class, gained popularity in part
because it offered a common framework for discussing economic processes and social stratification. Sociologists, in particular, began using the language, if not always the meaning,
of dual and segmented labor market theory to reorient traditional approaches to numerous topics, for example, income
determination analyses (Beck, Horan, and Tolbert, 1978;
Bibb and Form, 1977; Wright and Perrone, 1977; Baron and
Bielby, 1980). Such a reorientation meant that many more
sociologists looked to these neo-Marxian theoretical formula-
tions and away from the neoclassical assumptions of competition within labor markets and market determination of

wages and opportunities (see Kalleberg and Sorenson, 1979, for a review of the breadth and impact of dual/segmented labor market theory on sociology, and Gordon, 1972, and Cain, 1976, for reviews of the debate engendered within economics).

In response to critics who argued that dual labor market theory did not deserve status as a theory (see Cain's defense of neoclassical approaches, 1976:1235–1257), Edwards (1979) and Gordon, Edwards, and Reich (1982), in particular, extended the original arguments into a historical analysis of the interaction of organizational structure (among economic enterprises), organization of the labor process and attendant systems of control, and segmentation in labor markets. The thrust of their argument can be summarized in the following propositions:

(1) that the segmentation of the economy into core (large-scale, highly capitalized, and oligopolistic) enterprises and peripheral (small-scale, less capitalized, and competitive) enterprises represented the working out of capitalist economic development proceeding through the combined concentration and centralization of capital as a means by which to avoid a declining rate of profit;

(2) that the concentration and centralization of capital in core enterprises had been brought about in part by their increasing market shares and in part by the development of more and more productive forms of work organization;

(3) that processes of concentration and centralization and the introduction of more productive forms of work organization had resulted in higher levels of concentration of workers in large, mechanized firms and a greater capacity on the part of workers not only to view themselves as collectivities but also to express common interests in the form of unions and union contracts;

(4) that the size and scale of core enterprises, combined with the increasing militance of workers, necessitated the development of new forms of control within those

organizations, that traditional mechanisms of control ("simple forms of control" manifested in paternalism, strong foremen, and coercion) had been undermined by the increasing size and complexity of the organizations, and had to be replaced by "technical" forms of control, manifested in greater subdivision of tasks and machine-pacing coupled with wage increases tied to increased productivity;

(5) that increasing internalization of business-related functions and the growing complexity of work processes and products resulted in the development of new hybrid occupations within these organizations (e.g., engineers, staff functions such as sales, marketing, research and design, labor relations and personnel) which, along with growth within the services sector (especially in financial institutions, retail and wholesale trade, education and government), resulted in the establishment of a new set of positions to be filled by labor market participants—particularly in secretarial, clerical, and other so-called white-collar jobs;

(6) that the increasingly organizationally specific character of many of these occupations within the core enterprises, the higher level of educational training (or credentialing) required to fill white-collar positions, and the creation of new, service-oriented enterprises (e.g., specializing in the production of "soft" products such as computer software, basic technological research, etc.) required not only new techniques for management but also new forms of control over employees—resulting in the rise of "bureaucratic" control systems, organized principally around the administrative structures for labor allocation Doeringer and Piore describe as internal labor markets;

(7) these factors in combination have resulted in an economic landscape characterized by one hill and a number of hillocks—with core enterprises constituting the hill in terms of their economic leverage, their share of the labor force, and their impact on the economy, and semiperipheral and peripheral firms constituting the

hillocks, with their lesser levels of organizational complexity, fewer numbers of employees, lesser technological sophistication, and less rewarding (in terms of
pay, job security, and promotional possibilities) job
opportunities.

Their cumulative impact, according to Edwards (1979), has
been a segmentation in labor market structure brought about
by a segmentation in demand. Thus, in a broad historical
sweep, this approach appears to have brought together
models of economic, organizational, and social change.

In their later work, Gordon, Edwards, and Reich elaborate
this view by bringing in arguments concerning development
stages of capitalism and long swings in the capitalist economy.
Their most important addition from the point of view of our
analysis, however, is a broad conception of the arrangement
of social, political, and market institutions necessary to sustain
the process of capital accumulation: what they refer to as the
"social structure of accumulation" (1982:9–10, 22–26). The
integration of a social structure of accumulation is a critical
amendment to the model inasmuch as it allows that social and
political institutions and structures may potentially influence
the process of capital accumulation itself. In earlier formula-
tions (especially Edwards, Reich, Gordon, 1975, and to a lesser
but still significant extent, Edwards, 1979) it appeared that
the structure of the economy massively determined the shape
of the "rest of society." The analysis of social structure and
its constituent elements (e.g., family, religious institutions,
and community forms) and political structure (i.e., the state
and governing apparatus) was reduced to an assessment of
their functionality with respect to capital accumulation.

In practice, however, specifying that a social structure of
accumulation exists somewhat apart from the accumulation
process does not proceed far enough. That is, unless the
analysis of capitalist economic development is accompanied
by a systematic study of social structure under capitalism,
then such important and historically visible forms of inequality as racial, sexual, and political stratification tend to revert
to their functional form. This is particularly critical in the

stage of segmentation where race, gender, and citizenship play a particularly important role in the division of the working class.

The stage of segmentation, charted by Gordon, Edwards, and Reich as roughly beginning in the 1920s (1982:chap. 5), is depicted as the period in which differentiation in economic enterprises, labor processes, and labor markets emerges with greatest strength. It is a stage marked by the development of three analytically separable labor market structures (primary, subordinate primary, and secondary) and, significantly, by a disproportional representation of disadvantaged members of society—blacks, women, Latinos, and immigrants—in the lowest paying, lowest status, and least stable (secondary) jobs. While the empirical evidence provided by Gordon et al. and others is substantial, what continues to be unclear is why those workers should show up in those jobs. Or, more generally, we are led to ask: where in the social structure of accumulation—what set of processes and institutions, what set of historical developments, and in what relation to the accumulation process—do we locate the process and the purpose behind the creation of those disadvantaged statuses? Without a more systematic and simultaneous analysis of the interaction between social and economic structures, the appearance of these disadvantaged categories of labor seems *conjunctural* (i.e., entirely circumstantial) or *functional* (i.e., entirely determined in form and content by the accumulation process).

WORK AND CONTROL IN CAPITALIST INDUSTRY

Recent analyses of the organization of work in advanced capitalist industry have succeeded in breathing life back into the sociology of work and stratification, particularly in the United States. Three major efforts, in particular, have opened new avenues of inquiry. First, Harry Braverman's *Labor and Monopoly Capital* (1975) presented a sweeping analysis of the social and organizational forces mediating technological change ("the degradation of work" of the book's subtitle) in the twentieth century. With an emphasis on how the control over work is made possible through the separation of conception and execution, Braverman made a significant attempt to extend Marx's theory of the labor process (Marx, 1975:357–514) through the era of monopoly capitalism. Second, Richard Edwards undertakes in *Contested Terrain* (1979) a historical and sociological analysis of the changing organization of work in twentieth-century United States with an eye to revealing shifts in the foundation of managerial authority. Piecing together industrial data against a backdrop of developments in the general political economy of U.S. industry, Edwards concludes that the segmentation of economic organizations (core and peripheral) has transformed managerial mechanisms of control from personal to bureaucratic authority. Third, Michael Burawoy's *Manufacturing Consent* (1979) challenges many of the assumptions of prior work in industrial sociology, as well as some of Braverman's, through an analysis of how labor's willingness to participate in its own exploitation is "manufactured" through the organization of production. By asking "why do people work as hard as they do?" Burawoy avoids the traditional assumptions of harmony or conflict between managers and workers prevalent in earlier researches and constructs a theory that argues for the analysis of how force and consent are combined in the labor process.

Each of these writers has attempted to make explicit connections between changes in the structure of the capitalist economy and strategies of control in the workplace. All three argue that the development of large-scale, highly capitalized, monopoly-sector firms has made it possible for some capitalists to pay higher wages, offer more extensive benefits, and thus secure higher levels of stability and commitment from their workforce.

There is, however, a catch to contemporary labor process research and theory. While analysts such as Braverman, Edwards, and Burawoy have been quick to point out that the labor process in late twentieth-century capitalism differs significantly from Marx's nineteenth-century observations, their theories have by and large sought to squeeze twentieth-century observations into a nineteenth-century model. To be more precise, Braverman, Edwards, and Burawoy focus on the transformation of the labor process coincident with the transformation of the capitalist economy and enterprise. Each offers a distinct approach to the context and consequences of the rise of large-scale, monopolistic organizations. Yet all three largely adhere to a model of society which places primary emphasis on class as the fundamental category of social life and social action and which locates the origin of inequality in the labor process. To substantiate this argument, let me consider each one in turn.

Though Braverman's argument seems to capture the historical sweep of capitalist development, a major theoretical problem remains: he fails to provide an adequate explanation for the continuing division of the population along the lines of race, gender, and, increasingly, citizenship status. Race and gender inequality is subsumed under the more general, but less useful, rubric of the industrial reserve army of labor (pp. 377–401). For Braverman, the industrial reserve army of labor is a segment of the working class created and sustained as a buffer for the oscillating and uneven development of capitalism. This "relative surplus population" (p. 386) is composed, in part, of those people unemployed as a result of business cycles, technological change, and regional or sectoral uneven development. However, a significant segment of that labor pool is accounted for by those for whom steady employment is rare or unattainable or those who are crowded into relatively limited niches in the economy (e.g., service, agricultural, or domestic employment). It is in this portion of the industrial reserve army that one finds a disproportionate share of blacks, Hispanics, women, and immigrant workers.

It is, however, precisely this coincidence between nonmarket status and real or potential market position which constitutes the major problem for the reserve army formulation. Why should blacks, women, or other groups be concentrated in the industrial reserve army? Moreover, how do we account for this historical persistence of that concentration? Braverman provides few clues to these questions. In large part, his conceptualization of capitalism as a system of inequality presumes that the categories of actors in that system are determined entirely by their positions in the labor process. Thus, all other categories and organizations are determined entirely by, or are a function of, that fundamental relationship. Yet what is often critical in the case of the industrial reserve army composed of blacks and women is that they are full- or part-time participants in something other than a capitalist labor process: for example, housework or welfare transfer programs. In other words, participation in those other organizations provides the means for material existence when an individual is *not* engaged in value-producing activities; and, at the same time, participation in those organizations confers a status separate from class position.

Unfortunately, Braverman's use of the industrial reserve army concept does not provide sufficient clarity as to how or why certain groups should show up in its ranks consistently or what distinct status is attached as a result. Thus the reserve army comes to represent a residual category. I would argue, by contrast, that it is necessary to develop a better understanding of the distinctive processes responsible for constructing the category and for maintaining its important social and political consequences.

Edwards (1979), in contrast to Braverman, recognizes that race and gender are important considerations in the analysis of work organization and stratification. For example, he writes: "For members of both groups (blacks and women), their daily existence as workers is always conditioned by their special status" (p. 197). Yet Edwards is only slightly more helpful when it comes to identifying the basis of that special status or demonstrating how it is reproduced over time. With the exception of passing reference to the "special dialectics of race and gender" (pp. 194, 196) and to a cultural legacy of slavery and women's subordination to patriarchal authority (p. 197), the analysis focuses instead on the labor market positions of blacks, women, and, to some extent, alien workers.

While it might be unfair to criticize Edwards for not having broadened his analysis to account for parallel systems of inequality, the "special status" of blacks, women, and other identifiable groups plays an important role in his research on the labor process. In particular, his concept of "simple control" (pp. 34–36) in peripheral enterprises is built around the additional (nonmarket) leverage exercised by employers over workers. Simple control infers paternalistic authority, lack of formal job rights, and arbitrary employment practices. This form of control, according to Edwards, is rooted in both the personal qualities of the employer and in the vulnerable position of employees. What accounts for their vulnerability?

The only answer provided by Edwards is a partial one: vulnerability derives from the concentration of workers into specific (segmented) labor markets. That is, when there exists an overabundance of people to fill a limited number of positions and when those positions require little personal or organizational investment in training, then the specter of replacement by a labor market competitor creates vulnerability among employees and, therefore, leverage for employers. However, that explanation is incomplete in two senses: (1) it fails to account for the mechanisms that produce the vulnerability of secondary workers *external* to the labor process; and (2) it displaces to the level of the labor market the explanation for why some markets are crowded (and competitive) and others are not.

Again, let me suggest that for Edwards, as for Braverman, the inability or unwillingness to allow for the existence of a system of inequality not directly determined by the structure of the labor process leads to a rather incomplete explanation. Although Edwards concludes that racism and sexism have "become real material forces in society" (p. 195), we are neither directed to a material base nor to a set of organizational practices that might serve as their foundation.

Finally, there is the recent work by Michael Burawoy (1979). While Burawoy offers an important theoretical contribution to labor process research, he also creates an obstacle to explaining the relationship between race, gender, and citizenship and the organization of work. In the introduction to his case study of a modern machine shop, Burawoy warns (p. 25):

> The political, legal and ideological institutions of capitalism guarantee the external conditions of production. Under capitalism, these institutions mystify the productive status of work-

ers, capitalists, managers, etc. Thus, the political, legal and ideological apparatuses of the capitalist state transform relations among agents of production into relations among citizens, sexes, races and so on.

In other words, the explanation for the continued participation of workers in the capitalist inequality relationship lies squarely in the labor process. For Burawoy, the organization of the labor process simultaneously obscures the capitalists' appropriation of surplus and secures workers' participation in the wage labor contract (pp. 23–30). Therefore, workers' interests cannot simply be taken as given, nor can opposition (or cooperation) between workers and managers be assumed as invariant characteristics of industrial organization. Rather, interests, opposition, and consent are manufactured through the activities of the labor process.

Although Burawoy's argument presents a formidable challenge to underlying (but generally unsubstantiated) assumptions about conflict or harmony, his theory of the structural determination of interests and attitudes tends to overlook the ways in which the status of workers external to work organizations can be manipulated internally. This is evident in two ways. First, the theory is heavily weighted in the direction of work structures and practices found in monopoly or core industries. This insulation of the machine shop he studied from the vagaries of market fluctuations made possible the development of bureaucratically administered job structures and increased the importance of seniority and job rights over and against other worker characteristics, such as race and gender. However, outside of such enterprises, Burawoy's theory lends little insight. How, for example, do we account for the manipulation of women or minorities in settings that do not provide job rights equivalent to internal labor markets?

Second, even in those enterprises or industries ostensibly employing internal labor markets, job segregation by race and gender have not been eliminated. As Doeringer and Piore (1975) point out, internal labor markets can operate quite effectively to produce segregated job ladders in which the recruitment of women and minorities facilitates the separa-

tion of labor processes. Equally important, supposedly objective testing criteria within internal labor markets are often
suborned by subjective assessments made about workers by
supervisory personnel.

In this light, Burawoy's assertions about the primacy of
activities in the labor process must be questioned. If statuses
created external to the organization do indeed have consequences internally, then how are those statuses produced and
what impact do they have on work organization? Similarly, if
those statuses are manipulated to the advantage of employers,
ought we not expect them to have a direct bearing on relationships between workers as well?

CITIZENSHIP, GENDER, AND THE
ORGANIZATION OF WORK

In this study I will address those questions initially through
a detailed analysis of citizenship, gender, and the labor process in capitalist agriculture and then in connection with a
broader consideration of citizenship, gender, and race as systems of inequality *parallel* to class. Using the case study of the
lettuce industry as the starting point, the analysis will progress
in three steps. First, chapter 2 will examine how highly sophisticated economic organizations, such as are found in the lettuce industry, have been able to develop within what has
traditionally been referred to as a competitive sector of the
economy while employing what others have termed "primi-
tive" labor relations (Gordon, Edwards, and Reich, 1982:13–
14). In the early stages, I will argue, economic prosperity and
control over work was facilitated by the direct manipulation
of labor supply, most especially through political intervention
in labor market processes, for example, the direct importation
of alien workers. In the later stages, by contrast, direct manipulation of the supply of labor has been replaced by more
general political and economic processes which have created
a labor market distinguished by *citizenship status* (citizens,
documented aliens, and undocumented aliens) and *gender*
(men and women).

But, in contrast to most segmented labor market models, I will argue that segmentation in the labor market is as much a product of processes *external* to the workplace as it is a result of the way workers are used internal to capitalist enterprises. More specifically, I will argue that agribusiness firms, as well as their counterparts in other sectors of the economy, do not create the distinguishing statuses of citizenship, gender, or race, but rather seize upon them and transform those characteristics to the organization's advantage. In this sense, I will argue that it is crucial that we move beyond notions of the simple exploitation of disadvantaged workers to analyze how the use of those workers may further the employer's purpose. This focus is particularly important in developing less mechanical schemes for explaining different systems of control over labor and the labor process.

The second step, beginning in chapter 3, will involve a closer examination of how externally created statuses—citizenship and gender—are related to organizational advantage and control. Through an analysis of income determination among lettuce workers in chapter 4, I will demonstrate that citizenship status and gender have a tangible effect on earnings, that being an undocumented worker or a woman not only distinguishes you from other labor market participants but also materially affects how much you will earn, though not necessarily in the direction one might expect. Thus it will be argued that differences in citizenship status and gender do not necessarily reflect market-based characteristics (e.g., skill, education, experience, or seniority) but do reflect statuses produced external to participation in economic organizations. This part of the analysis will be linked back to an examination of the type of labor relations system found in the lettuce industry. In chapter 5 I will argue that, though they may lack the outward manifestations of internal labor markets and bureaucratic controls found in other settings, labor relations and methods of managerial control are no less complex. Specifically, chapters 5 and 6 will show that citizenship and gender affect not only the distribution of individuals into the labor process but that they also provide distinct advantages to employers in the creation and maintenance of different labor processes. Through a comparison of two separate harvest processes—ground-pack and wrap-pack—I will demonstrate how citizenship and gender are manipulated to enhance managerial control over the organization and the pace of work. In considering the way in which these statuses augment managerial control, I will also argue how those statuses affect relations *among* workers.

The third and final part of the study involves a broader analysis of the relation among nonmarket statuses, labor market structure, and organizational control. In this section (principally chapter 7), I will argue that citizenship and gender have a material basis external to the labor process, that is, that they are not simply labels attached to workers. But to understand the origin of those statuses, it is necessary to step outside the confines of the labor process. In this regard, I will suggest that it is necessary to conceive of systems of inequality that are related to but not directly determined by the class structure of capitalist society. Political inequality, as it pertains to citizenship in capitalist society, will be offered as an example of one such system. Citizenship, I will argue, must be more broadly conceived—to include its political *and* economic dimensions. Thus, citizenship will be used as a key mechanism for reconsidering the processes of labor force segmentation, particularly in terms of differential claims against political institutions and economic organizations.

DESIGN OF THE RESEARCH: THE CASE STUDY AND MULTIMETHOD APPROACH

As argued earlier, this investigation is not intended solely to explore the interstices of the lettuce production system, nor, for that matter, does it restrict its sights to capitalist agriculture, though only a small number of systematic analyses have yet appeared. Rather, the intent is to utilize the analysis of a specific production setting as a means to address much more general problems in the sociological study of work organization, labor market structure, and political inequality, both separately and in terms of their interaction. The fact that a case study design is employed reflects two considerations: first, as mentioned earlier and discussed at greater length in Thomas (1980) and Friedland, Barton, and Thomas (1981), the availability of good, systematic research on the political and economic structure of agricultural production in the United States has been extremely limited until recent years. As Friedland (1979) and Buttel and Newby (1980) have argued, organizational constraints and ideological blinders in the discipline of rural sociology and a predominantly urban/industrial focus in general sociology have combined to virtually exclude agriculture from sociological investigation. While rural sociology contented itself with questions of "who will adopt new techniques?" and "why farm children leave the farm?" and general sociology pondered the "big" questions about the future of urban-industrial society, little of the data necessary for cross-sectional analyses has been generated. Thus, this case study benefits from comparative data drawn from a limited number of cases but lacks the desired breadth of an exhaustive political economy of agriculture.

Beyond the dearth of comparative data, however, the southwestern lettuce industry is representative of a much more distinctively capitalist agriculture than other segments of agricultural production in the United States. Using the analytic distinction between capitalist agriculture and "simple commodity production" outlined by Friedmann (1981), firms in the lettuce industry are profit-maximizing enterprises whose primary source of labor is satisfied through hired workers and whose economic livelihood is dependent upon direct interaction with product markets. Thus, in contrast to simple commodity producers whose primary source of surplus is a combination of land rent and nonmarket exploitation of family labor, capitalist agricultural enterprises operate in much the same environment and under generally similar circumstances as other recognizably capitalist organizations, such as auto companies, textile manufacturers, and so on. Though as I have suggested, the lettuce industry poses distinctive problems for recently developed schemes for analyzing types of capitalist enterprises (e.g., the monopoly-competitive analysis of economic segmentation suggested by

O'Connor, 1973, and others), the value of an in-depth case study in the lettuce *industry* (as opposed to attempting to characterize agriculture apart from manufacturing or construction) is that it allows for comparison *across* agriculture/ industry boundaries. Indeed, given the diminution of "pure" agriculture with the rise of an integrated food industry (Friedland et al, 1981: chap. 2; Frundt, 1981; and Hightower, 1972), one is virtually compelled to drop traditional but outworn distinctions between agriculture and industry in an effort to analyze the course of structural change in both. Hence, the questions posed in the introduction to this chapter must necessarily be answered in terms of the forces and relations of production characterizing capitalist production in general.

The design of the study was also directly affected by a strong desire to develop some means by which to link macro and micro processes. The questions posed at the outset suggested that data had to be collected from a variety of sources at different levels. Thus the analysis of historical records had to be supplemented by interviews with key figures in the setting. The goal of connecting structural arrangements with day-to-day practice demanded that other forms of data collection had to be employed. Fieldwork in the lettuce harvest therefore became part of the research design.

However, the elaboration of a multimethod research design was important not only because it could potentially cover "all sides of the question" but also because it seemed the *only* available means by which to attempt to measure the interaction of macroprocesses with people's lived experience. In reaction to many macrostructural analyses that, by their very nature, are compelled to ascribe meaning to the experience of people "on the line" or in the fields, I felt (and still do feel) it necessary to put myself in a position to ask people meaningful questions about their experiences and about their theories of how and why things work the way they do. Rather than assume that people are unconscious of the world around them (and that, by inference, only sociologists are), or assume that their consciousness is false and thus be forced to ascribe true consciousness to a few remotely observed acts, I undertook intensive interviews and field work to try to get a clearer sense of the meanings people attach to their actions and those of people and groups around them.

A further predisposition stimulated my use of a combination of approaches to data collection: a healthy distrust of a priori theory. Though I find it absolutely essential to use theory as a guide to sociological investigation (and thus would not argue that this study began without a fairly elaborate set of hypotheses), I also began with the working hypothesis that many of my ideas were probably wrong. For some, this approach may not appear all that extraordinary; indeed it seems directly in line with accepted canons of scientific method. But my own observations of sociological research had given me the (perhaps unfounded) impression that too often concern for the integrity of a priori theory leads to a rather restrictive approach to data collection—that which fits the model is data and everything else is noise. In an effort to maximize the chances that I could be wrong and therefore to be compelled to alter my assessments, I consciously exposed my ideas to those people with whom I came into contact via interviews and field work. Thus the methodology of the research attempted, within the limits imposed by my role as researcher, to make possible both theory testing and, as Glaser and Strauss (1967) so aptly put it, "the discovery of grounded theory."[2]

Data collection for this study took place over the period of a year and centered on three main activities: in-depth, open-ended interviews; fieldwork in the lettuce harvest; and survey interviews with a sample of harvest workers.

The in-depth interviews were designed to be both exploratory and focused. Involved were an initial set of interviews with representatives of the major actors in the industry: (1) growers, managers, and industry representatives; (2) organizers and staff from the leading unions involved in the lettuce industry (i.e., the United Farm Workers and the International Brotherhood of Teamsters); and (3) active and retired lettuce workers. The latter interviews as well as the survey interviews were conducted primarily in Spanish. These interviews sought to establish basic characteristics of work organization, labor-management relations, and labor market

structure. The first round of interviews were followed at intervals during the study period both by further interviews with
original respondents and more focused interviews with a
larger group of new respondents. In all, sixty-two such interviews (averaging 60 minutes in length) were completed.

Between the first and second round of in-depth interviews,
over four months were devoted to participant observation
research in the lettuce harvest. During that period I worked
with two different harvest crews and kept daily field notes for
later reference. Both crews in which I worked (i.e., one
ground crew and one wrap crew) were employed by one of
the largest firms in the industry: Miracle Vegetable Company.[3] The fieldwork provided two important inputs to the
research. First, the work experience and informal contact
with lettuce workers on a day-to-day basis enabled me to
identify major aspects of the labor process which might have
gone unnoticed. For example, the role of individual and collective work experience emerged as a central feature of the
ground crew. Beyond specific features of individual and crew
experience, the field work helped me formulate pertinent
questions for the survey instrument and, perhaps more importantly, it aided me in figuring out how to ask them. Second,
contacts with work mates in the fields provided the basis for
carrying out interviews with undocumented lettuce workers.
These interviews (both in-depth and survey) added a very
important comparative perspective for the analysis of work
organization and income determination.

Finally, a quota sample of 152 lettuce workers was selected
for the survey interviews. The sample was drawn from men
and women working as lettuce harvesters during the summer
of 1979 in the Salinas Valley of California. The sample was
split 3:2 to reflect the approximate ratio of men to women in
the labor force. The choice to sample in this fashion was based
on a desire to compare work histories and earnings of men
and women. As it turned out, this procedure resulted in an
oversampling from the wrap crews. However, this facilitated
a stronger comparison of ground and wrap crews than would
have been possible with a more accurate representation of the
proportion of workers in each organizational situs.

The survey included 188 items focusing on three major areas: work history by crop, company, and crew; patterns of migration, residence, and family organization; and items concerning earnings and citizenship status. Although the majority of questions were closed-ended, a number of open-ended questions were included to allow respondents to elaborate on important items, for example, views of work organization, unions, specific management practices, and alternative careers.

The lengthy and, at times, tedious nature of the survey instrument was necessitated by the lack of data about farm workers. Though some researchers have called for the establishment of a more detailed reporting system on the characteristics of farm labor (Barton, 1978), data drawn from specific labor markets and/or industries remain unavailable. The reports filed by the Department of Employment in the state of California (Report 881-A) only provide an employer's estimations of demand for labor in particular areas, crops, and activities. To overcome this obstacle and to avoid the assumption that harvest labor is undifferentiated, I sought to include a range of survey items which would prove useful in this study and, perhaps, in other more systematic researches at a later date.

This combination of methods permitted a much more holistic approach to the empirical subject. Of particular importance, observation, participation, and structured interviewing helped inform one another so that insights or issues raised through one approach could also be explored through another. For example, without the fieldwork it would have been impossible to include the undocumented workers. Likewise, the initial round of in-depth interviews facilitated access to the field and helped shape both the content and conduct of the survey interviews.

Beyond the informational interplay, the melding of methods provided insights into issues and problems which could not be gathered through more formal data sources. In particular, as will be seen in chapter 4, the fieldwork revealed organizational dimensions to citizenship inequality which were not accessible by way of the survey instrument. That is, while data could be collected on earnings and work tenure in the survey, the effect of differences in citizenship status on crew organization and control over productivity were beyond the reach of even the most incisive formal questions.

Finally, it should be noted that equal weight and emphasis were given to each of the elements of the research design. Though at times certain parts of the argument in this study will rely heavily on one or another method, the belief was held throughout the research that the individual elements would provide equally important and rigorous contributions to the overall work.

2

Politics of Labor Supply

The numerical dominance of alien, noncitizen labor constitutes a distinctive feature of labor markets in southwestern agriculture. Despite the periodic influx of citizen workers, with the Dust Bowl in the Plains states, for example, the past 150 years have been marked by the continuous employment of foreign workers in the fields. Chinese, Filipino, Japanese, and Mexican workers have, over the years, harvested the crops of the fertile western valleys. Mexico has been the major source of farm workers (compesinos) for the past four decades. Why have foreign workers been such an important factor in agricultural production? How has their numerical dominance in farm work been maintained? What has been the impact of a noncitizen labor force on the organization of work? These are the central questions to be addressed throughout this study of the social organization of lettuce production. To lay the groundwork for the study, I will begin in this chapter with an examination of the relationship between labor demand and labor supply in agriculture.

CONTINUITY AND CHANGE IN
SOUTHWESTERN AGRICULTURE

The traditional praise of the agricultural employer as a "last frontiersman" and guardian of rural values is nowhere more incongruous than in the agricultural economy of the Southwest. While a few descendants of the original pioneers and homesteaders continue to farm the fields in California and Arizona, most have forsaken the farm for more lucrative employment in other, urban locales. Many were driven out of business by larger corporate competitors. Some traded their farms for managerial positions in giant agribusiness enterprises.

Yet, despite the growth of vertically integrated firms, the specialization of input industries, and the concentration of production into fewer and fewer firms, employers and their political representatives paint a picture of agriculture remarkably similar in its detail to that of a century ago. An editorial in a leading agribusiness journal proclaimed in 1979:

> At no other point in time has the farmer been in graver danger than now. Without the assistance of the state and federal governments in helping farmers cope with the special conditions of agricultural production, this nation will waste its greatest economic strength. . . .The vulnerability of the farming enterprise to the unpredictability of weather, natural disaster and labor shortage makes it unlike any other industry in our economy. (*Western Grower and Shipper,* November 1979)

It has been precisely this kind of platform—which Friedland and Thomas (1974) dub "agricultural exceptionalism"—that has served as the basis of employer demands for special treatment in relation to economic policy and, more importantly here, in terms of labor supply. Lloyd Fisher (1953:94) described this paradox succinctly:

> The California farmer, like other American farmers, is one of the principal audiences for the physiocratic legend. No matter whether he travels by private plane, employs a chauffeur, ships by air express and owns a produce market or two in Baltimore and New York, he is insistently a farmer engaged in society's most useful and necessary enterprise, and entitled to the special consideration which the dignity of his occupation commands. He regards himself as a natural agent of the forces of freedom, which he is more likely to define as freedom to raise, harvest and market his crop than as freedom of speech and assembly for those whose stake in society is less than his own. He believes that he has a right as a farmer to an adequate supply of labor.

Historical consistency in the ideology of exceptionalism should not, however, obscure the fact that considerable change has taken place in the organization of southwestern agriculture and agricultural enterprises. The average production unit has more than doubled in size since the 1920s (Census of Agriculture, 1954, 1978). The value of investments in machinery, including harvesting equipment, in the fruit and vegetable industries has increased by more than 250 percent since 1940 (Census of Agriculture, 1954, 1978). A secular decline in the number of unincorporated enterprises has been charted since the early 1960s (Census of Agriculture, 1954–1978; Villarejo, 1980) and the well-publicized incursion of nonagricultural corporations into agribusiness has significantly changed the capital and product markets of a number of major commodity groups (see Villarejo, 1980; Fellmeth, 1973; Friedland and Barton, 1975; Zwerdling, 1980).

Moreover, seasonal producers remain but many industries are now dominated by enterprises that are no longer dependent on the profits of a single season or commodity to remain viable. Many of the new agribusiness giants (e.g., Tenneco, United Brands, Castle and Cooke) have freed themselves from restraints of seasonality by expanding production between geographic areas (Villarejo, 1980; Fredricks, 1979; Hightower, 1972). In many of these cases production is spread across disparate regions, allowing planting and harvesting to be carried out on a multiseason or year-round basis.

Changes in organizational structure have also coincided with changes in employment and work organization. Although the precise relationship between these factors will be a central question to be considered in this analysis, it is important to briefly note some effects here. In some cases, employment has been converted from highly seasonal to more permanent (see Friedland and Barton's 1975 study of the processing tomato industry). In other cases, seasonal hiring remains but has been accompanied by employer efforts to stabilize employment relations in order to ensure themselves of experienced labor (e.g., in the citrus and fresh-market grape industries). And, in other instances, more traditional casual employment has persisted. The increased diversity of employment patterns is the important point here. Changes in work organization are equally significant. The introduction of mechanical harvesting devices (e.g., in processing tomatoes and grapes) has added greater differentiation in the occupational structure of some industries (see Friedland and Nelkin, 1972, for a study of similar effects in northeastern agriculture). In others, such as the lettuce industry, two work processes—one a craftlike division of labor built around stable teams of workers and the other a machine-paced "assembly" (wrap) division of labor—have been developed. In still others, highly labor-intensive work processes founded on the coordination of very simple tasks continue to exist, unchanged for over half a century.

More accurately, then, it should be understood that the economic organization of southwestern agriculture is far more diverse and complex than the ideology of exceptionalism tends to portray. Though all firms have a vested interest in acquiring inputs (including labor) at the lowest possible price, not all firms are structured the same, or have the same demands for land, capital, and labor, or organize production in similar fashion. Indeed, some of the largest and most prosperous firms have much more in common with nonagricultural firms than they do with the stereotypical family farm.

What has appeared constant or stable, in contrast to changes in the organization of agriculture and agricultural enterprises, has been the supply and the structure of agricultural labor markets. Viewed broadly, agricultural enterprises—large and small, well-heeled and struggling—have had in common access to a distinctive supply of labor: a supply distinguished historically by its mobility, its elasticity, its responsiveness to fluctuating economic conditions, and perhaps most important, its lower price relative to other segments of the national labor force. As the figures below indicate (table 1), wages in southwestern agriculture have historically lagged well behind those received by workers in the manufacturing sector.

What has been described to this point as diversification in the organizational structure, employment conditions, and

Table 1. Average Hourly Earnings for Farm Labor
as Percent of Hourly Earnings in Manufacturing, 1948–1975

Year	California farm labor (%)	U.S. farm labor (%)
1948	65	58
1949	57	53
1950	54	51
1951	55	53
1952	55	53
1953	55	51
1954	52	49
1955	51	47
1956	51	47
1957	49	45
1958	47	45
1959	45	46
1960	47	45
1961	46	45
1962	46	44
1963	46	45
1964	46	45
1965	46	45
1966	49	48
1967	50	48
1968	49	50
1969	50	49
1970	50	49
1971	49	49
1972	48	49
1973	51	45
1974	55	45
1975	50	57

Source: U.S. Department of Agriculture, Statistical Research Service, *Farm Labor*, 1948–1977. State of California, Office of the Governor, *Economic Report of the Governor*, 1964 and 1977, Sacramento.

labor process in agriculture should lead one to expect substantial change in the structure of the labor market. How, then, do we account for the capacity of complex and highly profitable firms to acquire labor so cheaply? Do agricultural firms have unchallenged access to that labor? If so, why? And, perhaps more to the point, has the agricultural labor market changed? If so, how have changes in the supply of labor affected the organization of production and the organization of agricultural firms?

The questions raised here pose thorny problems for both radical and mainstream theories of labor markets and work organization. Though I will argue later (chapter 7) that these problems are not unique to the lettuce industry or to agriculture, starting from an empirically grounded set of questions offers the opportunity to assess the robustness (or flexibility) of more general theoretical approaches that have been constructed on the basis of rather broad assumptions about "what's going on in the factory or the field." In this section I will consider the appropriateness of sectoral explanations for the organization of labor markets and work in agriculture. The general model, borrowing from more conventional theories, will be shown to provide a useful but partial approach to understanding the dynamics of industrial structure, labor market operation, and work organization. The limitations in the model derive in part from an incorrect assessment of change in industrial structure and, more broadly, from insufficient attention to the interactive character of demand and supply in the labor market. This latter point will be used as the starting point for a reanalysis of the relationship among industrial structure, labor markets, and work organization in southwestern agriculture.

SECTORS, SEGMENTS, AND THE "STRUCTURELESS LABOR MARKET"

Research on the relationship between labor market organization and economic sectors (i.e., the sectoral approach described by Kalleberg and Sorensen, 1979) has tended to locate the whole of agriculture in the "competitive" or peripheral sector. In other words, agricultural firms are conceived of as falling into that segment of the economy characterized by small-scale, labor-intensive production and low levels of capitalization (Averitt, 1968; O'Connor, 1973; Edwards, 1975; Beck et al., 1978). Likewise, agricultural labor markets are seen as consisting of low skilled, unstable, low status workers, that is, members of competitive or secondary labor markets (Piore, 1975). Following the general identification of sectoral organization and labor market structure suggested by Edwards (1975) and others, the undifferentiated demand for labor within small-scale firms results in the creation of a comparably undifferentiated labor market.

While monopoly/competitive and primary/secondary distinctions may serve as useful analytic devices in comparing forms of organization, the application of the schema to the lettuce industry presents a peculiar result: the conjunction of "monopoly" type firms with "secondary" labor. That is, the extant characteristics of the dominant economic organizations in the lettuce industry (called "grower-shippers") resemble most closely the category of monopoly firms described by sectoral analysts (as will be outlined in chapter 3). The two largest firms, Miracle Vegetable and Verde Lettuce, are subsidiaries of corporations ranked in the top two-thirds of the Forbes 500 (*Forbes* magazine, 1982). While other firms in the industry do not have such illustrious parentage, neither are they peripheral economic organizations. Firms like Miracle Vegetable and Verde Lettuce are large, vertically integrated, and diversified agribusiness giants. These two firms rank in the top 2 percent of agricultural firms in California, including cotton and livestock producers, in terms of acreage and sales (Villarejo, 1980). In a state in which large corporate organizations dominate most agricultural production, these firms can hardly be equated with the small, localized, and marginal position accorded competitive/peripheral firms. Finally, within the lettuce industry alone, the top four firms (including Miracle and Verde) account for 50 percent of the half a billion dollar annual sales of head lettuce (see table 3, chap. 3).

Since many agricultural firms have been mislabeled as competitive or peripheral, agricultural labor has tended to be incorrectly characterized as uniformly belonging to a secondary labor market. As Piore (1975:126) describes the secondary labor market: "Jobs in the secondary sector . . . tend to be low-paying, with poorer working conditions, little chance of advancement . . . and tend to be characterized by considerable instability in jobs and a high turnover in the labor force." Yet, as I have suggested (and will demonstrate in chap. 3), the harvest labor force in the lettuce industry appears much more stable and more skilled than would be expected within a secondary labor market. The use of the term "secondary labor market," at least as defined by Piore and others (e.g., Edwards et al., 1975; Edwards, 1975), is further confounded when the labor market in lettuce exhibits certain characteristics consistent with the definition—low wages, poor working conditions, limited advancement—and others that are inconsistent—high stability and low turnover.

If sectoral approaches to the study of southwestern labor markets are problematic, so are the mainstream analyses. Like the sectoral theories, neoclassical explanations tend to focus on the undifferentiated character of firm and labor market organization in agriculture. Indeed, harvest labor markets in California and the Southwest have been pointed to by both groups as the closest available approximation of the orthodox economic conception of the competitive labor market (Cain, 1976; O'Connor, 1973:21; Doeringer and Piore, 1975:1–2). In the competitive labor market

> The actors, workers and firms, have perfect information, maximize utilities in particular earnings, and are unable to influence prices given by the market. Furthermore, wages respond to changes in supply and demand, and workers can move freely in response to changes in supply and demand in different parts of the market. (Kalleberg and Sorenson, 1979:354)

The high degree of seasonality in production, the variability in demand for labor, the low level of skills, and the competitiveness of firms with respect to the market, according to this characterization, make agriculture the paradigm of the competitive labor market.

Two major problems, however, confront competitive labor market theory when applied to agriculture. The first concerns the relative political and organizational strength of firms and workers historically. The second concerns the process of wage determination. The most efficient manner in which to examine these problems is to focus on what has come to be considered the classic study in this field, Lloyd Fisher's (1953) *Harvest Labor Markets in California.*

Fisher characterized the harvest labor market in California as "structureless" (1953:7). By that he meant to specify a form of labor market in which:

1. there were no unions, seniority hiring, or other limitations on access to the labor market;
2. there developed no personal relationships or obligations between employer and employees, that is, employment was mediated by a third party, such as a labor contractor;
3. employment was uniformly unskilled and therefore accessible to a large, unspecialized labor force;
4. piece-rate payment schemes predominated;
5. production employed little or no capital in machinery (1953:7–11).

The structureless labor market, he argued, was ideally suited to the needs of agricultural firms. Without restrictions on access to work or differentiation in the skills required for harvesting, workers could be drawn from various sources to meet the highly seasonal and variable needs of agricultural employers.

Fisher, however, went well beyond simple description to question why such a labor market existed and how it was maintained. Taking as his starting point the physical and temporal isolation of preharvest and harvest activities, he argued that for the majority of firms the harvest represented the single most important part of the production cycle: "The agricultural employer approaches the harvest as though it were a separate enterprise. The necessary costs antecedent to the harvest are costs which have been irrevocably incurred" (1953:96). Under conditions in which (1) the demand for harvest labor was undifferentiated by skill or experience; (2) individual piece-rate payment tended to level any qualitative differences among workers; and (3) the size of a given crop determined the volume of labor for the harvest, the profitability of the harvest enterprise rested almost entirely on the market price for the commodity and the labor cost per unit of the commodity (1953:95).

Like any other category of entrepreneur, Fisher suggested, agricultural employers sought to reduce costs and increase prices where possible. Given the fact that few firms (if any) were capable of influencing market prices, on the one hand, and that the amount of product marketed was limited by the size of land holdings, on the other, labor cost became the main target of strategies to increase profits. However, the organization of production around individual piece-rates and unskilled labor also made the demand for labor fixed in the aggregate. In other words, with a fixed volume of output and an immutable division of labor (or a division of labor that could only be replicated across a larger volume of product), reductions in labor cost could only come about through reductions in the wage rates for a fixed volume of output, that is, what Marx referred to as an increase in absolute surplus value.

The most common strategy pursued by agricultural employers, which Fisher documents thoroughly, was wage-fixing:

> The profitability of the harvest enterprise, in large measure of the total enterprise, depends upon the relative bargaining position of employer and worker. . . . The agricultural employer in California takes every precaution to see to it that there is no doubt or uncertainty as to where the bargaining power resides. (1953:96)

Through the creation of durable political and business organizations, agricultural employers succeeded in gaining substantive control over wage rates offered to farm laborers. A variety of weapons were held in the employers' arsenal, including labor importation, vigilante tactics, stimulation of ethnic rivalries among workers, and red-baiting. Thus, while the market prices for agricultural commodities varied, the price of labor was held at a consistently low level. According to Fisher, therefore, the functioning of the structureless labor market depended on the political intervention of employers in the process of labor recruitment and organization.

The importance of political intervention in the labor market extends into control over the production process as well. However, the point to be made here is precisely that the "perfect" or near perfect competition commonly attributed to harvest labor markets in California is itself the product of a rather severe structuring of the labor market. That is, the situation in which a model of perfect labor market competition appears is not one characterized by political equality between labor and capital, but one characterized by the most severe inequality. Clark Kerr, in addressing this issue with regard to industrial relations in large-scale cotton farming, understates this critical conclusion:

> *Except for this organization of buyers, there would be a substantially perfect market for labor.* There exist many buyers and sellers, homogeneity of units of labor, mobility of workers, relatively full knowledge of the market on both sides, constant bargains, and free entry into the market, among other characteristics. (Cited in Fisher, 1953:97, emphasis added)

This point is emphasized for a very important reason: it makes the analysis of the relative political and organizational strength of employers and workers an integral part of the study of the labor process and wage determination. Rather than beginning the analysis of wages and employment with a presumption of pure competition (as is commonly done with most agricultural/neoclassical economics), the focus on political intervention in the labor market questions the conditions under which competition is produced. Though this will be explored more fully later in the study, the implications for other, nonagricultural settings are important: how are we to conceptualize "competition" in other labor markets, for example, especially those in which women, blacks, Latinos, and young people tend to show up most often?

The connection of a political dimension to the economic process, however, necessarily raises the question of how employer monopsony over labor is perpetuated or reproduced over time. Here Fisher is less helpful. Though he points to three principal causes for the peculiar organization of agricultural labor markets—segregation, accessibility of work in the fields, and employer noncompetition for labor (1953:13–16)—only the last speaks directly to the political construction of the labor market. Even then, the fact of employer cooperation in wage-fixing does not explain (1) how political control is created and maintained as a continuous feature of labor market organization, or (2) what effects changes in the organization of production or in agricultural enterprises have on the system of control.

Recent work by Burawoy (1976) expands on Fisher to conceptualize political intervention in the labor market as part of the organization of a labor system. In comparing research on migrant labor in California and South Africa, he concludes that the enforced circulation of workers between politically and economically distinct units enables employers to perpetuate the political vulnerability of labor and to lower the costs of reproducing labor. That is, the circulation of labor between two separate political units serves to make inequalities in political status (especially citizenship) part of the structure of the labor system. Thus, Burawoy argues, the denial of employment rights and protections associated with citizenship in the United States serves to impose a distinctive, nonmarket status on Mexican workers; likewise for black mine workers from the reserves who are denied full citizenship in South Africa. The physical separation of predominantly male workers from their families (what Burawoy terms the separation of the "productive" worker from the "reproductive" worker) further stimulates the circulation of labor across political boundaries and thus serves to reproduce the distinctive status of workers (1976:1052).

According to both Fisher and Burawoy, then, the employer monopsony over labor ensures firms of an abundant supply of seasonal, temporary labor which can be engaged when needed and jettisoned to an alternative polity and economy when not needed. Labor's disadvantaged political status precludes the creation of large-scale worker organization against employers and, at the same time, restricts workers' mobility between agricultural and nonagricultural employment.

Fisher's analysis provides considerable insight into the persistent disparity between agricultural and nonagricultural wage levels. However, the applicability of the "structureless labor market" is limited by the fact that it is not so much a theory of labor market organization as it is a model that operates under certain specific conditions. The key element in the model is the structure of labor demand, that is, holding constant the capacity of employers to exercise political leverage in the labor market, the organization of production into small-scale, unsophisticated, and largely undifferentiated firms serves as the single most important precondition for the development of Fisher's structureless labor market. The undifferentiated structure of demand, and therefore of the enterprises themselves, creates the need for seasonal, unskilled, and undifferentiated labor. Any substantive violation of that particular condition would presumably sunder not only the homogeneity of labor demand but, following the conditions Fisher lays out (1953:3–11), it would also likely dissipate the cooperation between employers which provides the organizational basis for political control over labor supply. Put more concretely, were any agricultural industries to undertake change in the way they produce or the way they are organized, the assumptions of Fisher's model would be violated.

To summarize, two problems emerge directly from an examination of sectoral and labor market approaches to the situation of southwestern agriculture. First, the assumption of homogeneity in demand for labor and/or homogeneity in the environment faced by firms leads to faulty conclusions about the dynamics of industrial structure and labor market organization. While it is clear that there are still many small firms in agriculture which "fit" the competitive market model, changes in the political economy of agriculture suggest much greater diversity in organizational form and, implicitly, demand for labor than the sectoral model gives credit for. Moreover, even in those theories (such as Burawoy's) which seek to provide an explanation for the common interest in vulnerable labor, the assumption of homogeneity of demand among firms leads one to question if it is possible for such diverse organizations to consistently produce unified action. And, second, Fisher's model of the structureless market and, by extension, much of the sectoral literature which builds off it, assumes a crucial feature which it needs, in fact, to explain: the continuous availability of a category of people that can be acted upon in such a fashion as to suit the demands of agriculture. The appearance, historically, of a succession of alien and/or low status workers has been used to a large extent as its own explanation when, I will argue, the production and reproduction of those groups and their distinctive political statuses have to be explained.

More broadly, I suggest, these problems derive from three general difficulties: (1) mistaken or historically partial assumptions about the manner in which demand for labor is structured; (2) partial explanations about the organization of labor supply; and (3) a relative insensitivity to the interaction between demand and supply. With regard to the first issue, it is conceivable that agricultural capital acting as a unified force has, for at least part of its history, succeeded in translating its demands for labor into an appropriate supply. But the capacity to act in a unified fashion depended on a relative homogeneity in demand, as reflected by employment of quite similar labor processes in production. To the extent that agricultural capital or agricultural labor processes have diversified, then the capacity of agricultural capital to act in a unified fashion should be undermined. One indicator of this should be the removal from agricultural capital's direct control influence over the structuring of labor supply.

As for the second issue, explanation for the organization of labor supply, it is necessary to think more broadly about how labor is *made* vulnerable. It is one thing to argue that agricultural firms demanded politically vulnerable (or unprotected) labor; it is quite another, however, to explain how that vulnerability is produced and reproduced over time. The direct importation and confinement of alien workers may provide an adequate explanation for the ability of agricultural employers to fix wages or unilaterally determine working conditions for a time; it does not account for why alien workers and not some other disadvantaged groups. Nor does it explain why the composition and the structure of that supply should change.

Finally, with regard to the interaction of demand and supply, it is necessary to consider how each may structure the other. That is, while both the sectoral and structureless labor market approaches orient one to looking at how industrial structure shapes the system of labor supply, it is also necessary to analyze how a system of supply may shape industrial structure. I will argue that a labor supply system which effectively serves the needs of a relatively homogeneous industry may prove an impediment to the diversifying industry it helped make possible (e.g., through its inability to provide a source of stable, experienced labor). Such a situation attempts to alter the system of labor supply. Alternatively, changes in a system of labor supply may occur beyond the reach or against the wishes of any industry or group of employers. Thus, exogenous factors or relations can have an impact on the structure of supply and, by extension, the organization of production.

POLITICS AND
LABOR SUPPLY

The demand for an adequate and consistent supply of labor has long been a rallying cry among agricultural employers. As a precondition for economic survival, that position is not, of course, unique to agriculture. The means by which demands for labor have been met, however, constitute a factor separating agriculture from other sectors of the economy. In particular, the overtly political character of labor market construction involving direct intervention by the state in issues of labor supply has served to distinguish the industry (see Majka and Majka, 1982; Weiner, 1978; Galarza, 1964; Burawoy, 1976; and Sosnick, 1978, among others). Specifically, the importation of alien workers, the creation of contract labor programs, the dual standards of protective labor legislation (exclusion of farm labor from coverage under the National Labor Relations Act) have directly and indirectly set agricultural labor markets and employment conditions apart from other basic industries.

The argument that agricultural labor markets have been affected by political forces is not unique to this study. This analysis departs from previous work, however, in its emphasis on the interaction of industry structure, labor market operation, and work organization. There are three parts to the analysis. First, I will argue that while the relative homogeneity of agricultural enterprises prompted early efforts to construct a separate but internally undifferentiated agricultural labor market, the increasing diversity in organizational structure and demand of agricultural enterprises resulted in a differentiation in demand which could not be satisfied by traditional means.

Second, the extension of the trade union movement and pressures for broader social welfare legislation in the post-World War period affected the structure and operation of the agricultural labor market in several ways. Most important, efforts to break down the political barriers separating agricultural and nonagricultural employment coincided with the expansion of social welfare and political entitlements, making both employers' political power over labor and farm laborers' alien status appear antithetical to the gains sought by citizens. Thus, I will argue, efforts to alter the system of labor supply from outside agriculture help explain changes in the structure of agricultural labor markets.

Third, strategies pursued by nonagricultural business in the post-World War period had further impact on the structure of agricultural labor markets and, by extension, on the organization of agricultural production. Of greatest consequence, rising union wages and social welfare costs prompted some employers to seek reliable sources of less expensive labor. For some firms, this took the form of expansion into the Southwest where such labor was easily within reach. More generally, however, many employers began to recruit unprotected, noncitizen labor for work in the United States. But, by contrast to agricultural employers who had exercised direct control over the system of labor supply, these firms (many of which were urban and spread across numerous industries) sought an unregulated supply of labor, that is, one which capitalized on the growing differences in legal protection and entitlement between citizens and noncitizens but which did not directly challenge (through overt action) the trade union or civil rights movements.

To understand how employer demands for labor have been transformed into political policy and what impact that intervention has had on the organization of production, it is first necessary to analyze briefly the structure and development of agriculture in the Southwest.

The development of agriculture in the American Southwest (especially in California and Arizona) can be broken into two broad and roughly overlapping historical periods. The first period (from 1800 to 1890) was characterized by extensive dry-farming (i.e., grains and feed). The second period (from 1870 onward) is characterized by the increasingly irrigated production of fruits and vegetables (McWilliams, 1971:59–60). With the annexation of the territory of California, Arizona, and New Mexico in the mid-1800s, the large Mexican land grants were converted from production for the consumption of wealthy aristocrats to production for national and international markets. As the benefits of climate, irrigation, and soil fertility came to be realized, large tracts of land were turned over to more lucrative fruit and vegetable production. Some of these tracts remained under the tillage of large entrepreneurs; others were broken into smaller acreages that were then leased or sold to small farmers.

Three factors in the development of agricultural production in the Southwest combined to create a highly uneven demand for labor. First, the environmental and physical characteristics of crop production (particularly fruit and vegetable production) created a pattern of labor use quite different from that found in other production systems. Most important is the temporal separation of the activities of planting and harvesting. The resulting process of production is characterized by periods of considerable activity (planting and harvesting) separated by periods of slack while plants mature or seasons change. This pattern of labor use is not peculiar to the Southwest, but it is especially important when the commodity under production is highly perishable and must be harvested within specific time limits.

Second, the intense market orientation of production made labor availability crucial to the success of the agricultural enterprise. The high value of farm production for rapidly expanding urban markets and for export (stimulated by the growth of rail transport in the late 1800s and by the expanded use of refrigerated rail cars at the turn of the century) undercut subsistence production and intensified cash-farming. Large farmers sought to capitalize on the production of lucrative fruits and vegetables. Smaller farmers, many of whom were tenants, were forced to produce cash crops in order to make payments on highly valuable land (McWilliams, 60–65).

Finally, the geographic separation of farming areas and the variety of property forms in the Southwest led to the creation of seasonally and geographically disjointed production. Though large landholdings were (and are) far more common in the Southwest than elsewhere in the United States, few individual firms bridged production areas and seasons. For example, large enterprises developed in the Central Valley of California, but until the 1940s only a handful produced crops in any other production areas in the state. Thus, geographic regions were characterized internally by diversity in sizes and types of production units, and production across regions was organizationally and seasonally discontinuous.

These three factors—the environmental effects of weather and crop perishability, intense market orientation, and geographically and organizationally discontinuous production—combined to create a highly seasonal and variable demand for labor (see fig. 1). This interaction of environment, market, and property form produced a demand for labor which could be available in steady supply despite the fact that employment

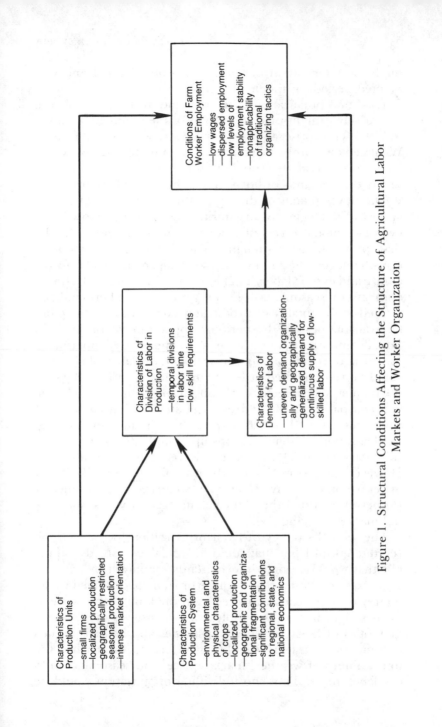

Figure 1. Structural Conditions Affecting the Structure of Agricultural Labor Markets and Worker Organization

might be intermittent (or intense for only limited and segmented periods of time).

This conceptualization of the demand for labor flows from
a relatively straightforward analysis of the interaction among
industry, enterprise, and labor process as determinant factors.
What remains problematic is labor supply: to wit, how was a
labor force created? And how was it constructed so as to
satisfy the demands of burgeoning agricultural enterprises?

The development of this agricultural economy fostered a
variety of strategies for organizing and utilizing labor. However, two modal forms of labor organization emerged. The
first, prevalent among tenant farms and small family operations, engaged the family itself as a means by which to organize and extract labor. That is, within the context of a heavy
emphasis on seasonal cash-farming, family members could be
trained in the totality of production skills and maintained to
be available despite the periodic application of those skills.
Equally important, if one leaves aside the issue of inheritance
as a form of return on labor investment, the labor of children
could be remunerated at less than its market value. That is,
the nonmarket character of the social and economic exchange
between parents and children facilitated the employment of
children's skilled labor at a fraction of its market value. A
marketization of that relationship would have altered considerably the social and economic relations of production.
However, the normative bonds of family and the likelihood
of return on labor investment (i.e., in terms of inheritance of
property) provided the inducements necessary to sustain the
nonmarket exchange.

The second strategy of labor organization focused on the
recruitment of labor that could be available in steady supply
but that would be only intermittently employed by any one
organization. Rather than acquire or train labor skilled in the
totality of production activities, as in the family labor system,
firms sought instead to simply avail themselves of sufficient
quantities of labor for specific activities and limited periods
of time. The strategy sought, in effect, to externalize the
uncertainties of weather, market price, and seasonality onto
the labor force. Thus, no individual organization would be

saddled with the responsibility of supporting skilled labor for which there was no productive employment. The problem of steady employment would have to be solved by the workers themselves. Such a strategy was employed by larger firms and by those which had grown beyond the capacity of family labor. It is this latter strategy for meeting labor demand which is critical to the understanding of the organization of work and labor markets in southwestern agriculture.

A seasonal or periodic demand for labor is not peculiar to the history of agricultural production. Indeed, many industries have been characterized by regular periods of high and low labor demand. The construction industry, as Stinchcombe (1959) has pointed out, is marked by both fluctuations in market demand and seasonality in production. However, organizational response, and the response of the workers themselves, to fluctuations in the construction industry differ markedly from that found in agriculture. Stinchcombe, in comparing the administration of construction and manufacturing industries, argues that the reliance on teams of highly skilled workers to both interpret and execute complicated demands in construction represents a rational form of administering production (1959:168–187). While Stinchcombe underemphasized the importance of workers' organization in protection of their market position, the pattern of "craft" administration in construction enables firms to avail themselves of highly valuable labor when it is needed—at wage levels sufficiently high to sustain workers during periods of low employment—and to disemploy it when unneeded.

A different practice emerged in agriculture. In place of highly skilled labor, firms sought to acquire labor skilled in very limited aspects of the production process. Instead of paying a high price for labor skilled external to the organization or investing in the training of workers in the totality of production tasks, agricultural firms sought instead to minimize costs of training labor by reducing or limiting the skills required in production. This approach combined a relatively unsophisticated division of labor, that is, a division of labor based on the temporal isolation of activities and the performance of unskilled chores during periods of peak labor demand (e.g., planting, weeding and harvesting), with a demand for undifferentiated gangs of workers to carry out those simple tasks. Workers would be hired for the duration of planting or harvesting (which could last a few days or several weeks) and then would be sent on their way.

The Politically Mediated Labor Market

The demand for labor in the mid-1800s was satisfied in a variety of ways. Family farms carried out most chores themselves, hiring labor on occasion from other farm families when harvests did not overlap. Other, larger enterprises sought out Native Americans from the abandoned missions and Chinese workers who had left railroad construction projects in Nevada, Utah, and Arizona (McWilliams, 1971:58–67).

As farmlands were improved and market possibilities expanded with better transport facilities and urbanization, the demand for labor increased. Indeed, as viewed in the late 1860s, the only real obstacle to further growth in the agricultural economy was labor (McWilliams, 1976:152). The extreme importance of adequate and timely supplies of labor was accentuated by the sensitivity of crops to temperature variations (which could hasten or delay a harvest by several weeks) and by the economic vulnerability of many firms to the loss of all or a portion of their seasonal output. The uncertainties of weather and market price argued against the creation of stable and permanent employment of the labor necessary to work only two to five months out of the year. Equally important, the investment in sufficient numbers of skilled or, at least, permanent employees would make employers vulnerable to wage negotiation or strikes at harvest time.

While regional demands for labor were satisfied by using local labor pools through the 1860s, a regularized labor system began to take shape in the latter part of the decade. At root was the disemployment of large numbers of Chinese immigrant workers following the completion of the transcontinental railroad in 1860 (London and Anderson, 1970:7–8). Though state and federal legislators helped to stimulate the movement of the Chinese into agricultural labor markets

through direct importation, another issue was also important
in the creation of that labor pool: opposition among domestic
white workers and unions to the potential use of the Chinese
as replacement labor in the expanding factories and mines
(McWilliams, 1971:67–109). The militance of both organized
labor and urban merchants (who feared competition from
Chinese entrepreneurs) helped close off alternative employment to fieldwork. Furthermore, the lack of political rights
and the generally low status of the Chinese made them virtually incapable of mounting a sustained battle against either
labor or agricultural capital. As early as 1854, the California
Supreme Court ruled that Chinese immigrants would be
restricted in their legal and political rights along with blacks
and Indians (McWilliams, 1971:68). Thus, the Chinese
formed the core of the first regularized supply of labor for
agriculture.

The history of the Chinese labor force is important at several levels. First, the availability of Chinese labor facilitated
the expansion of agricultural production. The large and
relatively stable labor pool spurred investments in land im-
provement and increased plantings. As McWilliams notes,
"The value of California farm land came to be capitalized,
ultimately, upon the basis of actual and anticipated profits
accruing from the extensive use of cheap labor." The amount
of acreage under irrigation climbed steadily in the 1870s and
1880s as did the volume of fruits and vegetables marketed
and sold to the canneries (Taylor and Vasey, 1936a, 1936b).
The expanding agricultural economy of the Southwest therefore came to bank heavily on the availability of Chinese labor.

Second, the vulnerable political and economic position of
the Chinese workers served not only to limit their alternatives
in employment but also to undermine their capacity to bargain over wages and working conditions. Backed by local
police and merchants dependent on farm business, employers
dictated the terms of employment to Chinese gangs and
enforced the movement of workers from one production area
to the next. Formal and informal committees of ranchers
organized to formulate "acceptable" wage scales in order to
prevent price competition in their own ranks (Fisher,

1953:chap. 5; McWilliams, 1971:74). These committees, in turn, became the foundation for later cooperative labor supply and union-busting efforts.

Third, low wages, unsanitary conditions, and migrancy combined with the already disadvantaged position of the Chinese to attach a low status to farm work in general. Farm work (particularly that of hired labor) had historically been viewed two ways in the United States: as a temporary station occupied by younger men trying to make a stake in order to purchase their own land, or a condition of servitude characterized by indentured labor and slavery. The Chinese farm worker was mired between the two statuses: never openly referred to as a slave but never as highly valued socially as a hired hand on his way to becoming a farmer. Differences in language and custom further isolated the Chinese. Because the immigrants accepted the brutal conditions of employment out of need and powerlessness, growers and rural populations came to view their (i.e., the Chinese) migrancy and low living standards as a group trait rather than a condition of employment. Adaptive behavior became a symbol of the inner character of the workers themselves. Equally important, that negative connotation (along with the undesirable conditions of employment) served to discourage the influx of domestic workers who might have been able to demand an upgrading of conditions (McWilliams, 1971:76; London and Anderson, 1970:chap.1).

The Southwest's growing agricultural economy thus was fueled by the creation of an abundant and politically ostracized supply of low-status labor. However, the actual construction of a labor system, that is, an organized system of labor recruitment and allocation, did not develop until the supply of Chinese workers became problematic.

The opening rounds in the battle over Chinese labor were fired as the giant railroad projects declined in the 1870s and Chinese workers began to spill into urban centers, especially San Francisco, and into the mining districts. Organized Anglo workers in the cities and mining districts confronted the dilemma of wage competition and undertook a campaign of harassment against the Chinese. The entrapment of citizen workers in a contest with Chinese immigrants fueled union opposition to legal protections for aliens and contributed to the xenophobia and anti-black bias that characterized segments of the labor movement in other regions of the country (see Bonacich, 1976, analysis of the role of white labor unions in the curtailment of employment of black workers during the same period). In an effort to shore up their endangered labor market position, Anglo unions terrorized Chinese workers, struck businesses and mines employing the Chinese, and boycotted goods produced by the immigrants.

Unions were not alone in their opposition. Small manufacturers who were incapable of withstanding strikes and boycotts and who could not use Chinese labor as efficiently as larger firms joined the fight against the importation of Chinese immigrants (McWilliams, 1971:72–74; Majka and Majka, 1982:21–36). Employers in the service sector who found themselves in competition with Chinese entrepreneurs pressed for restrictions on the immigrants' entry into business. Urban politicians, in the name of civic betterment and labor peace, sought to appease unions and employers by removing Chinese settlers and prohibiting farm workers from "wintering" in the cities. Finally, small farmers who relied on little or no hired labor suffered from the deflated market prices for their crops resulting from the low cost of Chinese labor. The campaign of political pressure and harassment culminated with congressional action in 1882 to suspend Chinese immigration. It was followed by the Immigration Act of 1885, which prohibited the use of foreign contract labor (London and Anderson, 1970:8).

Though the tumult over Chinese labor created significant economic and political headaches for agriculture, the large employers and processors of agricultural goods were not bereft of resources or political support. Furthermore, while the Chinese experience demonstrated the vulnerability of agricultural enterprises to fluctuations in labor supply, it did not prompt a decrease in the scale of production units or in the intensity of production. Rather, the exclusion of the Chinese accentuated the importance of the large producers to the regional and national economies. Uncertainties in the market for fruits and vegetables resulted in higher prices for consumers in the expanding urban markets. The sugar beet industry in the Southwest, which had already come to prominence for the national economy, appeared directly threatened by the collapse of the Chinese labor supply. The railroads, which had expanded broadly into the rural areas of California, banked heavily on the commissions they charged for transportation and crop brokering and on the inflated value of land they had acquired as right-of-way.

Faced with the potential for considerable growth in an expanding economy yet limited by the curbs of Chinese immigration, large employers, processors, and their financial backers sought to replace the laissez-faire politics of labor supply with a more systematic approach to creating and maintaining adequate sources of labor. Labor recruitment organizations, which had previously been regional in character, began to make linkages across production areas and crops (Chambers, 1952). Statewide conventions of growers met to discuss state and federal legislative strategies (Fisher, 1953:103–105). State and local political action committees were formed and funded by membership dues and contributions from the financially powerful canneries, refineries, railroads, and banks (Chamber, 1952).

While the Chinese experience demonstrated the vulnerability of agricultural enterprises to fluctuations in labor supply, it did not promote a decrease in the scale of production units or in the intensity of production. As suggested above, the exclusion of the Chinese instead accentuated the importance of the large producers to the economy of the Southwest. As the furor over Chinese labor slowly subsided, consortia of large farmers, canners, and refiners (particularly in the rapidly expanding sugar beet industry) sought successfully to open up other labor pools (McWilliams, 1971:105–110). Capitalizing on the economic potential of the domestic sugar market (protected by high tariffs) and the already high level of concentration in the industry, refiners and growers persuaded Congress to sanction the importation of Japanese and Mexican workers (McWilliams, 1971:105–110). By 1910, over 70,000 Japanese and nearly 100,000 Mexican workers were weeding and harvesting southwestern crops (McWilliams, 1971:106).

With frequently successful efforts on the part of Japanese workers to bargain over wages and to acquire their own land, employers focused their energies on establishing a more durable labor system built around Mexican nationals (McWilliams, 1971:110–116). Acquiring Mexican labor had never been a problem for growers: poorly fed peasants and refugees from the battles of the Mexican Revolution streamed across the border in large numbers (see Gamio, 1930). But to simultaneously insulate the labor supply (i.e., restrict its employment to agriculture) and prevent it from becoming a political and economic burden on local communities, external supervision of the labor force was needed. Thus, in 1926 a grower spokesman in Washington, D.C., urged Congress to "get us Mexicans and keep them out of our schools and out of our social problems" (cited in McWilliams, 125). Congress responded by lifting sanctions on the influx of Mexican workers and gave local communities the right to refuse relief to unemployed Mexican migrants (London and Anderson, 1970:28).

At the same time that lobbying efforts at the federal level were bearing fruit, employers expanded and intensified their organization at the state and local levels. In the period of the 1920s and 1930s, powerful employer associations emerged in the Southwest. Among the most influential were the Agricultural Producers Labor Committee, the Western Growers Protective Association (of which most lettuce firms were members), the San Joaquin Valley Labor Bureau, and the Associated Farmers (McWilliams, 1971:188–95; Fisher, 1953:103–118; and Glass, 1966). With overlapping memberships, these organizations enrolled the majority of large agricultural producers in the Southwest.

Though some of these organizations, like the Western Growers, ostensibly sought to regulate marketing procedures, their primary focus was on regulating labor. For example, the Associated Farmers grew out of a collaborative effort of the California Farm Bureau Federation and the state Chamber of Commerce to deal specifically with labor issues

(McWilliams, 1971:231). In that regard, they served two major purposes: controlling the supply of labor and prohibiting the entry of unions. Labor supply functions were handled through regional employment centers that generated employer estimates of demand, recruited labor from Mexico, and distributed the workers among firms. Employer organizations also provided staunch and unified opposition to the encroachment of trade unions in the fields. By decrying the "red menace" of communist and socialist unions (e.g., the United Cannery, Agricultural, Packinghouse and Allied Workers, and the Industrial Workers of the World) and declaring their defense of the free farming enterprise, the Associated Farmers, Western Growers, and others marshaled support for continued labor importation and opposition to unionization. Though farm worker organizations occasionally succeeded in winning wage increases, most of their gains were temporary (Jamieson, 1945; Galarza, 1964, 1971; Weiner, 1978; Jenkins and Perrow, 1977; Majka and Majka, 1982).

THE BRACERO PROGRAM:
MANAGED MIGRATION

Two factors contributed significantly to the success of southwestern employers in insulating and protecting their labor supply from Mexico. The first, as suggested previously, was the importance of food production to the regional and national economy. While the methods with which employers quelled worker insurrections were considered crude, farm output was critical. This was even more the case with the onset of World War II. As domestic labor deserted their strongholds in the canneries and packing sheds for duty in the armed forces and more lucrative employment in the war industries, employers pressed harder their demands for federally supervised labor supply programs (Galarza, 1964: 46–71). The necessity of food for the armed forces enabled growers and their political representatives to put the slogan "national defense" alongside "defense of free enterprise" in their lobbying campaigns.

The second factor contributing to employer control over

labor supply resided in the considerable political strength of the American Farm Bureau Federation. Though, as McConnell points out, the Farm Bureau never developed a coherent set of programs reflecting the varied concerns of farmers, it did serve as a powerful lobbying force in the matters of labor supply (McConnell, 1977:chap. 8). The Farm Bureau became both a clearinghouse for information on legislative action and the prime spokesman for southwestern agribusiness. The concentration of financial support in the political muscle and acumen of the Farm Bureau paid off handsomely: administration of relief programs for unemployed agricultural workers was transferred from federal to state and local control in 1933; fieldworkers were excluded from coverage by the National Labor Relations Act in 1936 (an exclusion that remains in effect); and, in 1942, the first long-term arrangement for contract labor from Mexico was established. The latter, generally referred to as the bracero program (formalized as Public Law 78 in 1951), was the crowning achievement.

The bracero program, described initially as an emergency measure designed to meet the World War II labor shortage, remained in effect for twenty-three years (1942–1965). During that time, nearly 5 million braceros were imported for seasonal work (Kiser and Kiser, 1979:67) and, in 1959 alone, nearly one-half million Mexican workers were admitted (Sosnick, 1978:378). The overwhelming majority were put to work in Texas, Arizona, and California.

The terms of the bracero program ceded to employers and their labor recruitment organizations direct control over the volume of workers, the level of wages, and the conditions and duration of employment (Galarza, 1964; Scruggs, 1960; Craig, 1971). Braceros were bound to a labor contract elaborated and enforced external to any labor market process. Work certifications, generally good for six weeks to three months, were subject to manipulation by employers. As Galarza documents in his study of the program, threats of decertification and deportation were used to squelch independent efforts at wage negotiation (1964:183–198). Though wage rates were supposed to be set by the Department of

Labor (to prevent any adverse affect on the earnings and
employment of domestic workers), wages were almost unilaterally set by employers. As Fuller notes, the wage determination process reflected what employers, not workers or the
federal government, considered just earnings:

> The procedure that became typical was for an Employment
> Service agent to attend the farmers' meetings, listen to wage
> discussions and report the consensus to his administrative
> superiors as the prevailing wage. (1955:29)

Finally, the labor contract prohibited the importance of
braceros for any work other than fieldwork. When no longer
needed in a particular region, they were returned to Mexico.

This "enforced circulation" of labor (Burawoy, 1976:1051)
prevented the development of worker- or union-organized
barriers to entry into the labor market (i.e., through seniority,
job rights, or union membership). The federally approved
low "prevailing wage" levels prevented the equilibration of
wages between comparable work in agriculture and nonagricultural industries. This, in combination with virtually
unregulated working conditions, gave domestic workers the
option of competing with the braceros or seeking alternative
employment (Galarza, 1964:143–182). Farm labor organizing
efforts were severely restricted and some unions, such as the
Teamsters, sought primarily to protect the jobs of members
in the transport and canning industries which were already
covered under the NLRA (Friedland and Thomas, 1974).
Moreover, the combined state/employer regulation of labor
supply heightened the distinction between the rights accorded
to citizens (as formally free labor market participants) and the
noncitizen braceros (who were accorded neither equal protection before law nor market freedom).

The Bases of Discord

Despite its outward appearance as the perfect solution to the
question of labor supply for agriculture, the bracero program
created new conflicts while solving old problems. One set
of conflicts that, for analytic purposes, can be considered

internal to agriculture arose from the changing organizational structure of agricultural firms and the differentiation in demand for labor. The other set of conflicts involved the support of a growing civil rights movement and elements of organized labor for increased social welfare entitlements, a movement in direct opposition to state intervention on behalf of employers. Examination of each of these factors will provide important background to consideration of the present situation.

Internal Conflicts

Despite the broad support for a program of contract labor voiced by political representatives such as the Farm Bureau Federation, the benefits of the bracero program were unevenly distributed among categories of agricultural enterprise. The major labor supply organizations, such as the Western Growers Association and the San Joaquin Valley Labor Association, were heavily dependent on the financing and support of the largest and most prosperous agribusiness firms. During the period from 1942 to 1951, when these associations directly supervised the recruitment and distribution of Mexican workers, they sought first to meet the needs of their most powerful members and, in the process, often left smaller firms waiting for labor while their crops baked in the sun (interviews with retired vegetable grower, 1979). In some cases, large growers abandoned the labor supply associations when the latter could no longer respond quickly enough to fluctuating demands for labor. Furthermore, during this period employers were expected to advance expense money to cover the recruitment, allocation, and transportation costs of braceros (Majka and Majka, 1982:143–145). For many smaller employers, cash was a scarce commodity and the additional debt burden ate into profit margins.

When the federal government took over the role of principal administrator of the bracero program in 1951, problems in the distribution of labor were reduced (Galarza, 1964:156–171) but the cost-effectiveness of bracero labor remained tilted in favor of larger employers. Since the market price of fruits and vegetables reflected both the low cost of Mexican labor and the economies of scale accruing to large producers, small enterprises found themselves in a bitter struggle for survival. As Mandel (1968:chap. 5) points out in his analysis of profit margins in agriculture, the returns to investment in the least productive unit are forced to a minimum and the returns for more efficient units are thus inflated. More concretely, as in the earlier case of farmers faced with market prices reflecting the cost of Chinese labor, the income of the small producer barely exceeded that of the labor force. Given that the larger firms also exercised greater leverage in determining the prevailing wage (Fuller, 1955), the bracero program amounted to an even larger subsidy for agribusiness.

In addition to the disparities in benefit accruing to sheer size, the competition among firms in the same industries continued. That is, despite the appearance of harmony among employers when it came to issues of labor supply, the construction of the bracero program did little to enhance cooperation among firms in the marketplace. In most industries, particularly those engaged in the production of "fresh-market" or "consumer-market" commodities, the cutthroat character of competition hardly abated. While industry representatives and employers interviewed during the course of this study alluded occasionally to efforts by some companies to disrupt or misdirect orders for braceros from their competitors (as a way to foul up their harvesting schedules), much more common were efforts to succeed through effective price competition. Thus, even with fairly regularized supplies of labor at predictable wage rates, market competition between and among large and small producers expanded.

In an effort to compete successfully in the marketplace and thereby increase their share of sales, many of the larger firms undertook aggressive marketing strategies. One particularly significant approach undertaken by a number of producers of fruits and vegetables was forward integration to the market. This strategy was often accompanied by a move to diversify production—both to provide a broader range of fruits and vegetables to buyers in terminal markets and to balance overall profits to the firm (see Fredricks, 1979, for a case history of one successful diversified producer who followed this strategy).

Forward integration and diversification offered opportunities for growth, but even the largest firms were incapable of affecting prices or, for that matter, withstanding the impacts of highly volatile markets. Hence, the profitability of agricultural production and survival in the market for even the largest firms could not leave untouched the problem of increasing the productivity of labor. But here the advantages of the bracero program began to break down. Most important, as these larger firms sought to diversify and extend their production over time and space, the bracero program became more of a constraint than an advantage: (1) the limited work certifications of braceros meant they had to be replaced at intervals, necessitating the retraining of workers and the added expenses of transportation; (2) the uniformity and level of product quality—a factor of great importance to firms seeking to establish a reputation in the market—fluctuated as workers were cycled through their tenure in the fields; and (3) the potential for increased productivity of field labor was thwarted both by the nature of the system itself (i.e., the provision of undifferentiated and largely inexperienced labor) and by the lower levels of commitment to be expected from coerced or semicoerced laborers.

The degree of constraint felt by different enterprises undoubtedly varied and, without detailed analyses of work organization during this period, it is quite difficult to assess how a cross section of firms responded. However, interviews with several lettuce growers (to be discussed in greater detail in chapter 4) indicated that it was recognized that an alternative source of labor was necessary. Specifically, employers seeking to contravene the legal limitations on braceros turned to an equally accessible, if virtually unregulated, labor pool: undocumented workers. In contrast to braceros, undocumented workers had no legal protections and were subject to harassment by police and border authorities. They were, paradoxically, a more flexible labor supply than braceros: undocumented aliens were not limited by work certifications and could be trained in a broader range of activities (or, at least, made to achieve consistency in product quality).

Additional evidence about the role of undocumented workers which is provided by Galarza indicates that indocumentados were not only an important alternative source of labor but that they were often used to fill positions requiring greater skill than braceros (1964:30, 57–62, 69–71). Before and during the life of the bracero program,

> Braceros found the Wetbacks as anxious to please as they were willing to endure. From among them the employer selected the more able workers for tasks requiring skill, such as irrigating and truck driving. They became differentiated from the common run of illegals, serving in specialized operations and becoming stable, regular employees. The employer would make unusual efforts to keep them and to arrange for their return if by chance they were picked up by the Border Patrol. (1964:30)

These workers, often referred to as "specials," acquired a status above that of the bracero or "stoop laborer" in large part because they were multifunctional:

> As the Wetbacks spread from crop to crop and area to area, they proved adept and useful in many farming operations besides stoop labor. They became handy men, irrigators, pruners, tractor drivers, sorters and pickers. In these and other tasks the lower wages they accepted made them a favored lot. Employers chose experienced illegals and sought to prolong their employment by more than customary precautions against arrest. (Galarza, 1964:59)

The attraction between specials and large employers was mutual: (1) the bigger firms offered greater anonymity as well as implicit protection from deportation—they were rarely raided by the Border Patrol; (2) large employers offered longer-term employment, thereby reducing the amount of exposure (which accompanied the job search) undocumented workers experienced, and allowing greater potential earnings for individual workers; (3) those firms more often required a substantial number of relatively skilled workers (e.g., for pruning vines, irrigating, and spraying fields); and (4) many of those firms were the ones engaged in efforts to integrate forward to the market, placed greater emphasis on high levels of consistent product quality, and, therefore, placed a premium on a stable and experienced labor force.

While reliable data on the composition of the harvest labor force are not available, it is clear that even during the height of bracero importation—roughly 1955–1959 (Galarza, 1964:79)—undocumented workers constituted a sizable fraction. Besides their utility as a source of labor to fill the gaps created by the inefficiencies of the bracero program (Majka and Majka, 1982:142–146), however, indocumentados (and specials, in particular) filled an important need that braceros could not: they could be hired, trained, and used to fill important positions for which braceros, by virtue of the program itself, were unsuited. Thus, as I argued at the outset of this chapter, changes in the structure of agricultural enterprises were initially fueled by the availability of low-cost, managed labor; with efforts in increase market share leading to concerns with product quality and productivity, however, the bracero program came to represent a limiting factor. The search for an alternative to the highly regulated bracero led to the undocumented special.

External Conflicts

Far more visible than conflicts arising from the relative inflexibility of the program was the opposition among liberal, labor, and religious groups to the exploitative conditions of farm work. For many of the groups allied with the civil rights movement in the late 1950s and early 1960s, the bracero program (P.L. 78) and its abuse at the hands of agribusiness came to symbolize another side to poverty and discrimination in America (Jenkins and Perrow, 1977). As such, attacks on P.L. 78 increased in intensity at the federal level from 1959 onward as a coalition of forces sought to dismantle agribusiness' "ideal" labor system (Pfeffer, 1980:34). These attacks, coupled with renewed efforts on the part of local worker organizations to demonstrate the adverse effects of bracero labor (Majka and Majka, 1982:158–160), began to eat away at the political fortress protecting the program. Finally, in 1964, the anti-bracero forces and Kennedy administration appointees forced the expiration of the last bracero agreement.

Why did the bracero program finally succumb to its opponents' blows? This question has attracted a great deal of attention from social scientists and journalists (Bach, 1978; Craig, 1971; Galarza, 1977; Hawley, 1966; Jenkins and Perrow, 1977; Majka and Majka, 1982; Pfeffer, 1980; and Scruggs, 1960, among others) and, while their accounts vary, most, like Jenkins and Perrow (1977), peg the changing mood in national politics as the principal explanation. According to Jenkins and Perrow, the combination of efforts to eradicate the vestiges of legal discrimination in the South and the mass media coverage of poverty and exploitation in the Southwest (e.g., through such vehicles as Edward R. Murrow's "Harvest of Shame" in 1960) made it possible for financial and organizational resources to be mobilized in opposition to the bracero program (1977:252–258). Majka and Majka (1982:160), arguing that national elites were not solely responsible for the demise of P.L. 78, point to the long-standing efforts of poorly staffed and underfunded farm worker unions to create a local infrastructure of opposition as equally important factors in the victory. While the Majkas' analysis offers a better picture of the combined local and national efforts, it is clear from the historical information that both levels of action were important in stripping away at least the surface layer of agriculture's ideology of exceptionalism.

Missing in the detailed analyses presented by Jenkins and Perrow and the Majkas', however, is a more general consideration of the factors that guided efforts to terminate the bracero program and that, I will argue, had a significant impact on the post-bracero labor system. Two factors are important here and both are linked to the ideology and the practice of citizenship. First, the civil rights movement, which provided both a backdrop and a vanguard to the anti-bracero campaign, formulated two broad objectives: (1) the formal, legal guarantee of citizenship rights and entitlements to black Americans and other minorities; and (2) the extension of the practice of citizenship beyond the traditional boundaries of voting and legal equality to include new categories of claims against the collectivity (or national community) to ameliorate poverty and underemployment. These objectives called upon the state to mitigate the negative effects of the prejudicial attitudes and structural barriers which denied formal market freedom to blacks and other minorities and, where necessary, to extend collective resources to those who suffered from ideological and structural discrimination. The objectives were constructed with the language of communal equality—citizenship—and directed both to the state apparatus as a collection of visible institutions and to the society as a whole. They called upon "Americans" and America's "heritage of freedom and equality" to guarantee equal treatment to all citizens.

Demands for citizenship rights provided a powerful linkage to anti-bracero sentiments in all but one crucial respect. They made the bracero program and *all other* forms of alien labor inimical to the guarantees of citizenship. By positing a program by which the rights and entitlements associated with membership in the community were strengthened, the civil rights movement accentuated the significance of differences between members and nonmembers of the national community and, as I will later argue, helped increase the vulnerability (and, therefore the attractiveness to all employers) of those who were least members of the community: undocumented workers.

The second factor that needs to be considered is the role of organized labor, both with respect to the bracero program and, more importantly, with respect to citizenship. As the Majkas (1982:158–166) and Galarza (1964, 1971, 1977) describe in fascinating detail, organized labor on a national scale demonstrated a profound ambivalence with regard to the bracero program and its predecessors. The American Federation of Labor (AFL, and later the AFL-CIO) occasionally sponsored forays into the fields but provided only minimal financial support to domestic workers attempting to organize. The Teamsters and various AFL affiliates made progress in some of the more stable and skilled occupations (e.g., in canneries, packing sheds, and trucking) but all but threw in the towel when it came to farm work. Even the Teamsters, who acquired the first major contract covering field labor in 1961, ventured forth only when it was financially productive and the employer in question offered a contract in exchange for a loan from the union's pension fund (Friedland and Thomas, 1974). When organized labor finally stepped into the fray, it did so as much out of pressure from its progressive elements—particularly its more militant union affiliates like the United Auto Workers and the Longshoremen's Union— and general sympathy for the civil rights movement as out of concern for farm workers.

Here again, the broader linkages to the ideology and practice of citizenship are important. For organized labor, the formal guarantees of market freedom—the freedom to enter into the wage contract—had been cemented through state intervention to facilitate unionization. Moreover, trade unions, as Marshall (1977:121–126) argued, had come to represent collective citizens in the economy, negotiating the terms and rewards of the labor contract within the broad mandates of a system of industrial justice/collective bargaining (Selznick, 1969). At the most general level, an affinity between organized labor and the civil rights movement grew out of a common interest in the political enforcement of citizenship guarantees in the face of an unequal distribution of economic resources. More specifically, protections from the discriminatory practices of employers reduced (though it by no means eliminated) the potential for blacks and other minorities to be treated as second-class citizens and to be used to undercut the position of organized labor. Moreover, the extension of political intervention in the economy (e.g., through a strengthened minimum wage) and the broadening of entitlements for those who are disemployed (e.g., aid to children, medical care for the elderly and poor) served both to buttress the position of unionized workers and to provide greater protection for workers dislocated as a result of business cycles. The net effect of organized labor's focus on citizenship, however, was a strengthening of the distinction between citizens and noncitizens. Where blacks or other minorities suffered from discrimination by employers, American workers (black, white, and Hispanic) suffered at the hands of both agricultural employers *and* braceros, argued leaders of the AFL (Fuller, 1955; Majka and Majka, 1982:164). Braceros and other aliens, it was contended, should be replaced by Americans.

A significant paradox was created through the victory over the bracero program: gains for citizens had been won and the guarantees of citizenship extended, but the political and economic vulnerability of noncitizens was increased. Without a frontal assault by labor on the conditions and the structure of agricultural employment and a demonstration that sufficient supplies of citizen labor were available, the bracero pipeline would be closed but the indocumentado floodgate would be opened.

EXIT BRACERO, ENTER GREEN-CARD AND INDOCUMENTADO

On the surface, the cancellation of P.L. 78 signaled the arrival of optimal conditions for the entry of domestic workers and unions into the fields. The legislative victory of the anti-bracero forces was, however, soon muted by the tactical successes of agricultural employers. Though employers had lost direct administrative control over the supply of labor, the gap left by the cutoff of the bracero pipeline portended serious consequences for the southwestern regional economy. Some industries immediately sought to replace braceros with mechanical harvesting devices (Friedland and Barton, 1975) and others raised wages slightly in a feeble effort to attract domestic labor. But domestic workers did not rush into the fields. Since the termination of the bracero program did not mandate change in the conditions of the status of agricultural employment, workers with potential alternatives in urban labor markets or more extensive entitlements from the welfare system (which had been expanding rapidly during the period of the Great Society, see Piven and Cloward, 1971) chose not to pursue low-status, low-paying jobs in the fields.

In response, employers sought once more to parlay their economic strength in the region into political support for labor importation. That support appeared in two forms: "green-cards" and undocumented workers. Green-cards (named after the color of the identification card formerly given to permanent resident immigrants), certified under provisions of the McCarran-Walter Act of 1952, began to be admitted as early as 1965. With the grower's written promise of employment in hand, thousands of former braceros flocked across the border to reclaim their jobs. In addition to these seasonal workers, many more daily commuters were given passes to shuttle back and forth across the border to work in California, Arizona, and Texas. Current estimates show that at the peak of production, more than 40,000 commuters cross the border into these states on a daily basis (Kiser and Kiser, 1979:215).

By far the largest group to enter southwestern agricultural labor markets with the end of the bracero program, however, have been the undocumented immigrants. Although accurate figures on the number of undocumented workers in the United States are impossible to develop, estimates based on apprehension of illegal immigrants show clearly that they constitute a sizable segment of the agricultural labor force (see table 2). Failing sufficient *mordida* (bribe money) or time to obtain one of the limited number of legal passes, Mexican workers have been drawn across the border to work "illegally" in the fields (Portes, 1977; Jenkins, 1978).

The Broader Functions of Unprotected Labor

Until recent years, a common misconception was that undocumented immigration was a phenomenon restricted largely to the rural Southwest. Now, however, it is generally recognized that undocumented workers have come to play an important role in a number of urban labor markets for a distinctive category of employer (North and Houstoun, 1976). Moreover, as data presented by Portes (1978) and Jenkins (1978) suggest, undocumented immigration has persisted even in the face of increased unemployment.

Table 2. Undocumented Immigrants Apprehended by
Type of Employment in the U.S., 1970–1981

Fiscal year	Agricultural workers	Total workers	Agricultural as % of all workers
1970	55,909	129,681	43
1971	78,713	154,782	50
1972	85,795	184,003	46
1973	105,726	231,646	45
1974	117,071	241,376	48
1975	114,926	250,388	45
1976	122,820	259,085	47
1977	109,046	248,337	43
1978	107,572	233,403	46
1979	113,495	233,746	48
1980	58,205	142,031	40
1981	82,314	168,369	48

Source: United States Immigration and Naturalization Service, Form G-
23.18, for the years cited.

The broader distribution of undocumented immigrants
represents an effort on the part of nonagricultural and non-
rural employers to avail themselves of the advantages of
vulnerable labor. Undocumented workers have come to serve
a broader set of functions than before and those functions
are directly related to the achievements of the civil rights
movement and the post-World War II wage gains of organized labor. Indocumentados serve to replace a segment of
the urban labor force protected by expanded citizenship entitlements in the form of welfare; these aliens must remain
economically active in order to survive because they have no
other viable alternatives. Eschewing simple models of "push-
pull" in elaborating a similar argument, Portes (1978:37)
contends:

Reasons why massive illegal immigration is permitted in the
United States must be sought in the interface between the needs

of the competitive capital sector and the nature of illegal labor. Relative to other countries, especially those of the periphery, the American economy is one of high labor costs. This occurs less because of the exhaustion of the domestic labor supply than because of its organization and power. A series of labor-promoted legislative measures have, in turn, resulted in a welfare system that supports the unemployed and maintains a "floor" under the salaries of domestic workers. Other things being equal, higher labor costs tend to decrease the rate of profit. This is especially true of small competitive firms which, unlike those in the monopolistic sector, find it difficult to pass on labor costs.

Thus, employers in quite different sectors and regions find a common use for undocumented labor.

Though the termination of the bracero program greatly diminished growers' direct control over the supply of labor, a new and far broader system of labor supply has replaced it. This new system of labor supply is not only broader and more flexible in its use but it is much less susceptible to challenge as the property of one or another industry, unlike the bracero program.

Despite recurrent protests from organized labor and urban politicians concerned about employment and the cost of social services for undocumented workers, efforts to deal with the issue have been focused on the near impossible task of policing the 1,000-mile border between Mexico and the United States. Legislative attempts to affix penalties on employers for hiring the undocumented workers have been consistently blocked. As a result, employers in the Southwest have retained access to Mexican labor and farm worker unions, as I will show in chapter 5, have been stymied in their efforts to regulate the supply of labor.

I have attempted to show in this chapter that the construction of agricultural labor markets in the Southwest has been and remains an overtly political process. Political intervention in matters of labor supply and control has been manifested through the ability of agricultural interests to transform their economic power into governmental policy and administrative apparatus. The politically mediated labor market, in turn, has served to perpetuate low wages, low levels of unionization, and highly labor-intensive production.

This discussion, however, really only provides the framework for understanding how nonmarket statuses are manipulated to the advantage of employers. What must be considered next is how those statuses, such as citizenship and gender, directly and indirectly affect wage determination and work organization. In particular, how have changes in the structure and organization of firms interacted with labor market processes? How have firms, such as those found in the lettuce industry, created skilled work teams without ceding control over production to them? What role do citizenship and gender play in the maintenance of stability and regularity in labor supply?

To begin to answer these questions, a more focused analysis of the social organization of production in the lettuce industry follows.

3

ECONOMIC ORGANIZATION, LABOR FORCE, AND LABOR PROCESS IN THE LETTUCE INDUSTRY

The public already knows all it needs to
know about the lettuce industry.

—California lettuce grower

While the growth of "agribusiness" and the large-scale vertically integrated agricultural enterprise have received great
attention in the media, few attempts have been made to analyze how the structure of the enterprise, the labor system and
the labor process interact with one another. For the most part,
studies in the tradition of rural sociology have avoided such
topics (Friedland, 1979). Other works have focused on elements of the production system, such as farm labor (Weiner,
1978; London and Anderson, 1970), farm worker unions

78

(Taylor, 1975; Levy, 1975; Jenkins and Perrow, 1977) and corporate agriculture in general (Fellmeth, 1973; Hightower, 1972; Perelman, 1976). Though of considerable value to understanding change in the agricultural sector, these studies fail to provide a cogent analysis of how agricultural enterprises go about organizing and utilizing labor or what impact or advantage noncitizen labor has for particular labor processes.

A recent work by Friedland et al. (1981) makes some headway in broaching these issues with its emphasis on the potential social consequences of technological change in agriculture. However, even this work (which focuses on the lettuce industry) leaves aside the critical dimensions of labor force organization, controls over production, and political intervention in the labor market. Thus, for a study concerned with projecting the conditions under which technological change will take place, the labor system and the labor process variables are largely absent.

Here I will focus on elucidating the structure and characteristics of the economic organization, labor force composition, and labor process in the lettuce industry. While part of the purpose of the chapter is description, three central features of the production system will be emphasized. The first section will show that the dominant firms in the industry are quite sophisticated and complex organizations that exert considerable influence on the functioning of the system. In the second section, it is argued that, despite the increasing concentration and stabilization of production in large firms, the labor force continues to be overwhelmingly noncitizen. Equally important, I will show that labor regularly circulates between the United States and Mexico. The third and final section turns to an examination of the harvest labor process. I will argue that the two predominant forms of harvest organization—the skilled ground crew and the unskilled wrap machine crew—represent two fundamentally distinct labor processes. The examination of these two organizations will subsequently inform the analysis of citizenship and gender and their effects on income determination and control over the labor process.

ECONOMIC ORGANIZATION OF THE INDUSTRY

The lettuce industry is a thriving one. National production of "Nature's Concentrated Sunshine," as it was described in a 1930s advertisement, amounts to some 6 billion pounds annually. The most common variety, "iceberg" or head lettuce, is grown commercially in fifteen states, but lettuce acreages are concentrated largely in California and Arizona. Close to 80 percent of the lettuce consumed yearly comes from a handful of production areas in one of the two states (Federal-State Market News Service, 1980).

Growing lettuce is big business. In 1981 gross returns to the industry in California and Arizona surpassed $500 million, accounting for nearly 25 percent of total fresh vegetable sales in the two-state area (Salinas *Californian,* Jan. 23, 1982). Ninety-five percent of the lettuce was consumed in the United States, with the remainder exported to Canada and Western Europe, along with regular airlifts of lettuce to McDonald's franchises in Tokyo and Hong Kong (Boas and Chain, 1976: 149–158).

As table 3 shows, the lettuce business is big in another way. The three largest firms (or 3.2 percent of all firms) account for nearly 35 percent of lettuce production. The top seven are estimated to control over 53 percent of the crop. I have segmented firms in the industry into three tiers: bottom, middle, and top. This analytic division is based on two factors: (1) market position, that is, the share of total production and sales accounted for by individual firms; and (2) production activities, that is, the range of activities carried out by the firm in the production-to-market process, including growing, harvesting, shipping, and/or sales.

Two notes should be made with regard to production activities. First, the classification of firms refers primarily to those enterprises that organize and supervise the actual production of lettuce. Though there are separate firms that specialize in the transport, sales, and final marketing of lettuce (and other commodities), the principal concern here is with the organization of production from the standpoint of the manufacturer and the labor force. Thus, shippers, brokers,

Table 3. Concentration of Production in California/Arizona
Lettuce Industry (1978)

Tier	Number of harvest workers[a]	Number of firms[b]	Percent of firms[c]	Percent of volume[d]	Cumulative percent volume
Top	1,000 or more	3	3.2	35.0	35.0
	500–999	4	4.3	18.0	53.0
Middle	300–499	7	7.6	14.0	67.0
	200–299	5	5.4	9.0	76.0
Bottom	199 or less	73	79.5	24.0	100.0
Total		91	100.0	100.0	

[a]Data obtained through interviews with and mailed questionnaires to growers and interviews with industry representatives and union officials.

[b]The number of firms involved in producing lettuce during any season or year will fluctuate according to projected prices. For example, in 1978–79 industry sources reported that many firms "rushed into" lettuce production in anticipation of a shortfall in supply due to the United Farm Workers Union strike (Salinas *Californian*, May 1, 1980).

[c]This includes all firms known to produce lettuce. Harvesting, shipping, and/or sales may be handled by another firm or cooperative under prior agreement (see Moore and Snyder, 1969).

[d]These figures are based on data supplied by the *Redbook* for 1978 (an industry financial rating guide), the *Packer Produce and Merchandising Availability Guide*, and Drossler (1976). All production figures are approximations provided by the companies themselves. Figures for the larger companies (500 employees or more) have been corroborated by industry representatives in confidential interviews and by the FTC (1976:1671–1676).

and retailers will be left aside except where they directly affect the organization of production (for a further discussion, see Friedland, Barton, and Thomas, 1981:chap. 3).

Second, the two main types of firms engaged in lettuce production are "growers" and "grower-shippers." Growers are those firms that deal primarily with the growing and harvesting of the lettuce crop. Grower-shippers will generally grow, harvest, ship, and market a crop, that is, they will control the crop from "seed to supermarket" (Segur, 1973). Both growers and grower-shippers may also produce a variety of other agricultural commodities and, in doing so, assume different roles in those crop-industries. Finally, while the amount of land owned by a firm generally serves as a good indicator of its size, many of the largest firms (particularly those in the top tier) actually own less land than they lease. Therefore, land ownership does not necessarily provide an accurate indicator of the size or scale of an organization (Villarejo, 1980).

Bottom tier firms are largely small farming operations whose production is dwarfed by that of the Goliath firms which dominate the lettuce industry.[1] Such operations are commonly family owned and operated and hire relatively small numbers of field laborers (generally 50 workers or less). Few, if any, have the necessary capital supplies or sales apparatus to finance the harvesting, transport, or distribution of a lettuce crop. Many are heavily mortgaged in their land and grow lettuce as a means by which to increase the cash-flow for their small enterprises. In many cases, they produce lettuce under contract with a larger firm (either another grower or a shipper from the middle or top tier). The small grower contracts to grow lettuce under the supervision of the larger firm. The larger firm will generally supply the major means of production (capital, machinery, labor, and seed) and the landowner provides the land and a certain amount of his/her labor and expertise in return for a predetermined price (per unit of output, e.g., cartons of lettuce), a fixed rate per acre, or a percentage of the profits from sale of the crop. This arrangement allows the contract grower a reasonably certain source of income (from all or part of his/her land) while at the same time it provides the larger firm with the capacity to expand or contract production without bearing the burden of maintaining unproductive or unused land.

The middle tier largely consists of smaller grower-shippers. There are basically two types of firms in this category: (1) large firms rooted in one production area and (2) partnerships of firms operating in disparate production areas. In the first instance, a company may own and/or lease considerable acreage in a single production area (e.g., the Salinas or Imperial valleys of California) and thus produce and market a high volume of lettuce during only a portion of the year.

Many of these firms are closely held, family-based corporations. In the second instance, individual firms rooted in different production areas will form limited partnerships for the purposes of establishing year-round production and marketing. The express intent of these alliances is to establish regular marketing channels for their product. Some small marketing cooperatives operate in similar fashion—bringing together smaller producers for joint sales—though they are usually limited to less than twenty members.

The top tier lettuce firms (the top seven) are the most powerful and organizationally sophisticated companies. Of the three largest firms, two are wholly owned subsidiaries of multinational corporations that have extensive holdings in agricultural, fast food, luggage, banking, and other industries domestically and internationally. One entered lettuce production in true conglomerate fashion in the 1960s with the purchase and consolidation of six lettuce firms into one large firm, Verde Lettuce, Inc.

The other multinational firm acquired the second largest lettuce producer, Miracle Vegetable, in the late 1970s after the latter had already established itself as the leading lettuce manufacturer in terms of volume and innovation (Fredricks, 1979). With earlier aid from a major chemical company's financial subsidiary, Miracle Vegetable had pioneered the field-wrapping of lettuce in plastic film, as well as having established inroads in international agricultural production and sales. Stock in the third firm, Salad Giant, Inc., is divided among members of the founding family, managers, and a major insurance company. As part of a larger holding company, Salad Giant grows, ships, and markets lettuce, produces and distributes lettuce seed, and manages vast tracts of grape vineyards and cattle range. Verde Lettuce and Miracle Vegetable will be discussed in greater detail in chapter 5.

Together, these three firms market over 30 million cartons (¾ of a billion heads) of lettuce each year. Estimated total sales for the three (in lettuce) in 1978 came to nearly $275 million. Most of the top tier firms own or lease acreages (up to 23,000 acres annually) in several production areas in the states of California and Arizona. Figure 2, below, shows the

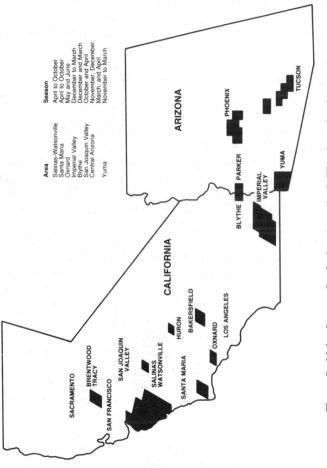

Area	Season
Salinas-Watsonville	April to October
Santa Maria	April to October
Oxnard	May and June
Imperial Valley	December to March
Blythe	December and March
San Joaquin Valley	October and April
Central Arizona	November, December,
	March, and April
Yuma	November to March

Figure 2. Major Lettuce-Producing Areas in California and Arizona

major production areas in the two states. Verde Lettuce, for example, grows and harvests lettuce in the following areas: Salinas-Watsonville, San Joaquin Valley, Imperial Valley, and Arizona. Salad Giant spreads its production across a wider terrain, including Salinas-Watsonville, San Joaquin Valley, Santa Maria, Oxnard, Imperial Valley, Arizona, and New Mexico.

The mobility of these and other grower-shipper organizations is founded on the contract and lease arrangements they make with smaller landowners throughout the Southwest. In particular, the rapidly climbing price of land has made additional acreages difficult to acquire. Urban and suburban growth has resulted in skyrocketing land prices; for example, formerly large lettuce-production areas in Los Angeles, Orange, Santa Clara, and Alameda counties in California have practically disappeared in the post-World War II era as residential and industrial uses pushed up land values and property taxes (Fellmeth, 1973). Thus, land leasing and production contracting with small firms serve two important purposes: (1) they enable lettuce firms to expand acreage without tying up large amounts of capital in fixed assets; and (2) the arrangements make it possible to harvest and market lettuce on a year-round basis. The top three firms, for example, lease over 60 percent of the land on which they produce.

Quite simply, the major lettuce companies have become as migrant as the workers they employ. Following the seasonal changes in weather, production operations—tractors, trucks, buses, equipment, phones, salesmen, managers, and workers—travel the "loop" through California and Arizona in the manner of a traveling circus. The lease/contract system thus frees large corporate agribusiness from the traditional constraints of the farming enterprise: immobility owing to landownership and vulnerability to short-run market fluctuations.

The creation of the mobile production operation has been a major advance in the rationalization of the industry; but the large firms are by no means loose assemblages of men and equipment marshaled together for the purpose of producing a crop. Rather, they are the most visible elements of organizations with sophisticated and complex managerial hierarchies, diverse staff and line activities, computer-assisted marketing staffs, and well-financed research operations. The truly remarkable accomplishments of these firms are reflected in their capacity to assemble and coordinate land, labor, and capital to market an extremely perishable commodity on a daily basis. Thus, with the exception of retail sales, the dominant firms have the industry covered from seed to supermarket.[2]

THE LABOR FORCE

As was demonstrated in the previous chapter, noncitizen (alien) labor has historically played a major role in southwestern agriculture. Though the lettuce industry only began to emerge as a significant segment of southwestern agricultural production in the late 1920s (with the advent of refrigerated rail and long-distance transport), lettuce firms have actively engaged in the recruitment and use of alien workers (see Lamb, 1942). With the increased production in California and Arizona, individual firms and industrywide labor supply organizations were thoroughly enmeshed in the politics of labor supply. In the 1920s and 1930s, Depression and Dust Bowl refugees, and Japanese, Filipino, and Mexican immigrants harvested the crop and lived on ditchbanks and in shanty towns surrounding Salinas, Watsonville, and El Centro. When Mexican nationals were brought in under the bracero program, the industry switched heavily to that supply (Smith, 1961; Glass, 1966). Within a year Mexican workers dominated the harvest in California (Galarza, 1964:119).

The use of bracero labor was intensified in the early 1950s with the introduction of a new cooling technology. The new process, vacuum-cooling, eliminated the need to ice lettuce crates before they were shipped. Instead, a vacuum-cooling process could be established separately near the fields but without requiring the availability of ice or ice storage facilities. The new technology enabled growers to shift trimming, packing, and refrigerating operations from centralized packing sheds to integration with cutting operations in the fields (Glass, 1966). Packing shed activities had been dominated by Anglo (citizen) "fruit tramps" and their unions (United Packinghouse Workers of the AFL-CIO, and the Teamsters). Application of the new technology resulted in the dismantling of the sheds and the dispersal of the shed unions (Watson, 1977). The shift to field-packing integrated the harvest and simultaneously made the labor force overwhelmingly alien.

The termination of the bracero program in 1964–65 precipitated a shift from a bracero-based labor supply to one based on a mixture of citizens and documented and undocumented immigrants. Interviews with lettuce workers carried out in this study revealed that many who had been braceros received, purchased, counterfeited, or ignored legal documentation in order to come back to work in the fields.

Data on the composition and characteristics of the contemporary force in lettuce (summarized in table 4) were collected

Table 4. Selected Characteristics of Lettuce Worker Sample by Citizenship Status (N = 152)

	U.S. citizen	Documented immigrant	Undocumented immigrant	Percent of sample
Percent of sample	12.5	63.8	23.7	100.0 (152)
Percent male	10.5	55.7	100.0	60.5
Permanent resident in Mexico	0.0	69.0	100.0	67.7
Family in Mexico	58.0	93.8	100.0	91.0
Projected place of retirement				
U.S.	73.7	1.0	0.0	9.9
Mexico	0.0	64.9	77.8	59.9
Don't know	26.3	34.1	22.2	30.2
Intend to become U.S. citizen	- -	3.0	0.0	2.0

through interviews with a sample of 152 harvest workers. Those interviewed were workers contacted through a residential sampling in the communities of Salinas, Greenfield, Gonzales, and Chualar in Monterey County, California. The state of California does not regularly report on the characteristics of the agricultural labor force; rather, in an illustration of the politics of labor supply, the only data collected by the state refers to the general estimates of *labor demand* (reported by employers) for particular crops and production activities. Census efforts often fail to enumerate farm workers because they are migrant, temporarily residing in the United States, and/or Spanish-speaking.

The labor force in the lettuce industry remains overwhelmingly noncitizen, as table 4 demonstrates: 87.5 percent of the workers in the sample were Mexican nationals. The three major legal statuses in the sample are citizens, documented immigrants, and undocumented immigrants. Each of these will be considered in turn.

Citizens

The relatively small percentage of citizens found working in the lettuce harvest coincides with estimates made by other researchers. For example, Zahara et al. (1974) suggest that less than 20 percent of the lettuce labor force are citizens of the United States. Of the citizens I interviewed, all but one were Mexican-Americans born either in the United States or Mexico. The majority were children of immigrants who had settled in the lower Rio Grande Valley of Texas or in the border areas of Arizona and California. Though most of the citizens considered the United States their home, over half had family still in Mexico and nearly a quarter were undecided as to whether they intended to live in the United States when they or their spouse retired.

Table 4 also shows that citizenship status is strongly related to sex. All but two (i.e., 17 of 19) of the citizens in the sample were women. Among the women, 70 percent were married to men who worked in the fields or related agricultural employment; the remaining 30 percent were single or divorced with at least one member of their immediate family working in agriculture.

Documented Immigrants

Documented workers, frequently referred to as "green-cards," constitute nearly 65 percent of the sample. This category includes only permanent immigrants.[3] Interviews with industry representatives and researchers suggest that 80 percent of the labor force in lettuce comes under this classification. Such conjectures, however, fail to take into account the presence of undocumented workers; thus, the actual percentage of the labor force which is documented is likely to be less.

The permanent immigrant classification has several stipulations attached to it: first, workers are only allowed into the country under this classification when the Department of Labor has declared a "labor shortage" with respect to either a particular industry or profession. Thus, lettuce workers may be admitted into the United States in much the same fashion as foreign doctors, actors, or athletes. Second, applicants for a green card must have an offer of employment in writing before entering the country. Legally, green-cards may be deported if they cannot find employment or have been disemployed for a long period. Third, green-cards must establish a permanent residence within the United States. Aliens admitted under this classification are not, however, expected or obligated to seek citizenship. Finally, permanent immigrants are not eligible for state or federal welfare assistance before five years of continuous residence in the United States. They may, however, receive job-related benefits such as unemployment and workmen's compensation (Sosnick, 1978:402–420). Thus, though green-cards may enjoy some of the benefits associated with citizenship, their status is clearly contingent on active participation in the economy. Green-cards may legally join and participate in unions, but their inability to make full claims on the state for nonwork support means they are only minimally better protected than the braceros.

Since 1965, the Immigration and Naturalization Service (INS) has restricted the allocation of new green cards in accordance with new immigration quotas established for many countries, including Mexico. This move has increased the value of valid documentation—such that workers interviewed in the course of this study revealed that substantial bribes and lengthy waiting periods must precede acquisition of immigration papers. Not surprisingly, immigration restrictions have created a thriving industry in counterfeit documents (e.g., drivers' licenses, green cards, social security cards, among others). The price for counterfeit documents varies with the quality of the forgery: from less than $100 for drivers' licenses to over $500 for professional counterfeits of green cards and forgeries made on stolen, but valid, green card blanks (Portes, 1977).

In the subsample of permanent immigrants shown in table 4, nearly 70 percent reported that their permanent residence was in Mexico—despite the visa stipulation that they establish a permanent residence in the United States. Those who would comment on this inconsistency said they (a) alternated in residence between the United States and Mexico, that is renting in the States for the period of their employment and then returning "home" to Mexico; (b) worked alone in the United States (without family) for a specified period while their family remained in Mexico; or (c) maintained only a mailing address in the United States to meet legal requirements but did not establish a permanent residence.

In-depth interviews with other workers confirmed that these three practices were common among green-cards. Furthermore, returning to table 4, 94 percent of the green-cards reported having close family (i.e., brothers or sisters, wife, husband, children, and/or parents) still living in Mexico. Of the men, nearly 60 percent were married and worked alone in the United States while their wives remained in Mexico. Of the women, over three-fourths were married and working in the United States with their husbands. The majority of that group worked for the same company as their husbands (though often in different capacities). Only a very small percentage of the women green-cards (2.2 percent) worked and traveled by themselves.

Undocumented Immigrants

Commonly referred to as "illegal aliens" by press and politicians, undocumented workers are an important but shadowy presence in the fields. No one quite knows how many are working in agriculture (or other sectors of the economy) or what percentage of the lettuce labor force they account for. Actual interviews with undocumented workers (called *indocumentados* or *sindocumentos* in Spanish) have been few and largely limited to samplings of apprehended workers (e.g., North and Houstoun, 1976). Industry representatives and union officials in the lettuce industry generally refuse to guess about numbers since they are wary of the public's reaction. Workers interviewed in this study estimated that between 10 percent and 50 percent of the labor force lacked papers, but those conjectures reflected the number of friends or acquaintances workers knew to be undocumented. Since more reliable figures are unavailable, I will suggest on the basis of my own observations and counts that between 25 percent and 50 percent of the labor force in lettuce is undocumented. This range is sufficiently large to include that portion of the work force which claims to have legal documentation but, in fact, does not.

For this study, a total of thirty-six (self-identified) undocumented workers were included in the survey group; with an additional fifteen interviewed in-depth separately. Access to this "invisible" sample was developed through contacts made in the field during the participant-observation stage of the research. The importance of the undocumented worker group for the analysis of earnings and work organization will be demonstrated in chapters 4 and 5. Here, however, it is sufficient to point out the utility of the participant-observation methodology in making those interviews possible.

Undocumented workers differed from the others in the sample in two important repects. First, indocumentados are more closely tied to Mexico than either the documented immigrants or citizens. None has established a permanent residence in the United States, nor has any concrete plans to settle there. Second, the undocumented workers are exclusively male. That is, in contrast to legal immigrants and citizens, indocumentados work across the border without wife or family—though over half these men reported that they were married. These two factors, in particular, lend credence to the argument that undocumented Mexicans, in contrast to earlier waves of immigrants, view their participation in the U.S. economy as a temporary venture (Piore, 1979).

This brief examination of the lettuce labor force has highlighted two important factors. First, the harvest labor force in the lettuce industry remains overwhelmingly noncitizen. Despite the end of managed migration with the bracero program, noncitizens carry out the majority of harvest work. When citizens do show up, they are primarily women of Mexican descent. Second, the harvest labor force tends to circulate between the United States and Mexico on a fairly regular, if not seasonal, basis. Furthermore, the larger part of the labor force maintains strong social and economic ties to Mexico. In particular, undocumented workers (and male workers generally) manifest the least attachment to permanent settlement in the United States.

THE HARVEST LABOR PROCESS

Lettuce production is highly labor-intensive. Despite the increasingly intensive use of chemical fertilizers, pesticides, herbicides, and energy-intensive machinery, hand labor remains the overwhelming force in cultivation and harvest operations. Approximately 12,000 to 15,000 workers weed and harvest the crop each year. Of that number, 7,000 to 8,000 are employed annually in the California and Arizona harvest.

Harvesting is carried out in two organizational forms: the ground or piece-rate crew and the wrap machine crew. Close to 80 percent of the lettuce shipped from California and

Arizona is harvested by ground crews; the remainder is wrapped in the field (Drossler, 1976). I will briefly describe the labor process in each.

Ground Crews

The average-size ground or piece-rate crew (the names are used interchangeably) consists of a total of thirty-six workers (table 5). The major subunit of the overall crew is the three-man team or *trio;* an average crew will contain nine trios and nine auxiliary workers. Each trio is a team of two lettuce cutters and one packer. The auxiliary workers assemble and distribute cartons for the packers, seal the filled cartons, and load them onto trucks for transport out of the field. Top tier companies (the large grower-shippers) often have in excess of twenty crews working during the peak harvest.

The cutters lead off the crew and walk stooped through

Table 5. Comparison of Average Crew Size and Activity: Ground Crew Harvest and Wrap Crew Harvest

Activity	Ground crew	Wrap crew
Select-cut-trim	18	14
Wrap	–	9
Pack	9	4
Spray	1	0
Close	2	2
Load	4	3
Carton assembly/distribution	2	
Machine operator	–	1
Total crew	36	33
Ground crew equivalent (in terms of output)		66

Source: Johnson and Zahara (1976:380).

the rows of mature lettuce cutting and trimming the heads. Packers follow behind squeezing the heads into empty cartons (24 heads per carton). The cartons are then glued, stapled shut, and loaded for transport to the cooling facilities where they will be stacked on pallets and forklifted onto trucks or railroad cars headed for market.

In the field, all the work is done by hand. With the exception of a stitching machine for constructing cartons, no other form of machine—pneumatic, hydraulic, or electric—is used in the harvest process. Cutters wield razor-sharp knives for cutting and trimming heads. Packers use crude wheelbarrows to hold cartons while they fill them. Closers carry spring-action staple guns to seal the cartons. Loaders lift the fifty-pound cartons over their heads and toss them to the back of trucks for stacking.

Although the length of the workday may vary according to weather, field, or market conditions, the physical exertion required in the work is tremendous. One need only imagine walking stooped for eight to ten hours a day or completing 2,500 toe-touches to get a sense of the endurance required in the cutting and packing of lettuce. The demanding character of the work is only heightened when the fields are muddy from late irrigation or recent rains and workers must slog through claylike soil. The speed and endurance required in harvesting takes its toll on workers. "Careers" in the industry are short: older and retired workers interviewed reported that a worker's career is generally limited to between ten and eighteen years. Most common among the physical complaints (and reasons cited for quitting the harvest) are back injuries, arthritis, hernias, and slipped discs. The age-earnings profile of workers in the survey (fig. 3) shows that earnings peak around age thirty-one and steadily decline thereafter.

The harvest labor process of the ground crew may be quite demanding and destructive, but it is also incredibly productive, efficient, and adaptive. The division of labor among crew members is quite precise and controlled: workers interact with one another in such a fashion as to minimize extraneous movement and establish a routine. A crew of thirty-six workers can, under normal conditions, cut, pack, and load between

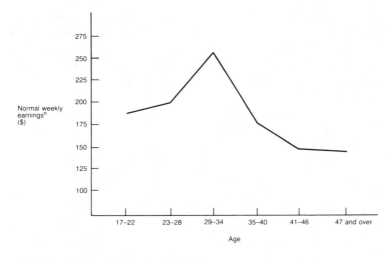

^aEarnings figures plotted represent the average for each age group.
^bAmount reported for an average week during the harvest.

Figure 3. Age-Earnings Profile for Male Lettuce
Workers[a] (N = 90)

3,000 and 3,500 cartons of lettuce per day—enough to fill
three to three-and-a-half railroad cars. To be more specific,
an efficient, experienced crew can produce a completed carton of lettuce every 15 seconds.

In most cases, the trios are paid on a per-carton, piece-rate
basis. This means that cutters and packers divide among
themselves the total earnings of the trio for production during
a given period, usually a week. The auxiliary workers, with
the exception of the loaders, are most often paid on an hourly
basis. When pairs of loaders are teamed with a set of trios, a
joint piece-rate may be established for the trios and loaders.
In most cases, however, the loaders will be assigned a piece-
rate separate from the rest of the crew. However, efficiency
and productivity are based much more on crew coordination
than on individual or trio ability. While individuals and trios
may be particularly adept at the activities they perform (e.g.,
cutting and packing), wages are ultimately determined by the
overall speed and, therefore, coordination of activities within
the crew. Individual workers reported that the time required

for acquiring particular skills is relatively short: as little as a day or two. Crew coordination and articulation, however, is much more difficult to obtain. From my own field experience, the crew in which I worked only began to operate with a high degree of teamwork (and therefore earn near-normal pay) after the fifth week of being together.

The coordination of all crew members is quite important in determining the pace of work and, therefore, the crew's earnings. Because the auxiliary workers (closers, carton assemblers and distributors, loaders) carry out services for groups of trios, the timely performance of their jobs can affect the work of the cutters and packers. If, for example, the carton distributors (often called windrowers) fail to evenly or adequately distribute empty cartons, they slow the packers down. If the packers are slowed, the lettuce heads sit too long in the sun and begin to wilt. In the case where cutters must wait for packers to catch up, the output of the crew diminishes. Thus, in order for the crew to work at or near maximum capacity, the coordination between trios and auxiliary workers must be precise. In similar fashion, if the cutters work at an uneven pace (with respect to one another), they will throw off the efficiency of the packers who must pack for two cutters; the windrowers, who must unevenly distribute cartons; and the loaders, who must load for several trios at once. Cutters, in particular, push fellow members to coordinate their activities and to maintain a pace in the crew. For example, cutters may give pep talks to the rest of the crew during the infrequent breaks for rest or food. During one such break, the fastest cutter in the crew to which I belonged berated both the less experienced cutters and the auxiliary workers:

> You guys aren't making our job easy. You have to keep up or you mess up the rhythm. My money depends on you getting the boxes closed good. And your money depends on me cutting a lot of these heads. If you [younger packers] start falling behind, then you screw everything up—because Cruz [one of the closers] has to walk back and close your cartons and then run up to close mine.

The collective dimension of skill in the harvest crew is, therefore, embodied in the high degree of mutual coordination and experience which shows up among crew members.

In this regard, the ground crews bear remarkable similarities to other work groups that rely on the immediate and mutual coordination of group members in the labor process. Gouldner's description of the contrast in interaction between surface (factory) workers and miners highlights the common features of mining and harvesting crews:

> Unlike most workers in the board plant, members of the mining teams worked together in closest association. The size of their work group was larger, their rate of interaction more intensive, and their expectations of informal work reciprocities were more pronounced. . . . The nature of their work permitted them a greater degree of discretion. Since they themselves determined the speed at which they worked, the rest pauses they would take, and the strategy of digging the gyp[sum] out and propping the roof, the miners were in constant communication with each other. (1954:133)

Whyte's study of glass workers also stresses the individual and collective elements of skill in the performance and administration of glassblowing (1961:220). In his analysis of longshoring gangs, Finlay concludes, "The gang is an amalgamation of different activities, and the element of skill derives from the coordination of these activities—it has no single occupational base" (1980:7). For harvest crews, like the miners, glassblowers, and longshoring gangs, the administration and performance of the activities of production are united.

In addition, most harvest crews are characterized by social interaction beyond the workplace itself. That is, they also exist as relatively cohesive units external to the labor process. This shows up in two ways: in recruitment of new members and in the ways in which they deal with the exigencies of migration. In the first instance, many crews recruit and help train their own members. Though the process of labor recruitment will be discussed in greater detail in chapter 5, kinship serves as an important avenue of entry into a crew and usually involves some real or fictive attachment to one or more of its members. Sons, brothers, cousins, or brothers-in-law may be brought in when a vacancy occurs (either at the level of cutter/packer or auxiliary worker). Alternatively, people who are in auxiliary positions may exert a claim to try out for a job. In the crew in which I worked, half the workers were or claimed to be related to at least one other member of the crew. In addition, overlapping ties, such as distant family relations or common village origin in Mexico, served to bind the crew socially and facilitate entry.

The other form of social cohesion involves the migrancy of the crew. For the duration of the harvest, the crew represents a fairly closely knit collection of married and single bachelors. Most, if not all, crew members are away from home for the majority of the season. All retain close family ties in Mexico. Crews often break down into smaller groups (usually two or three close friends) for the purposes of lodging, travel, food buying and preparation, and laundry. These small groups help make life a little more bearable during the monotonous days of the harvest.

Finally, the adaptability of the group crew is an important aspect of work organization in the lettuce harvest. Weather conditions and market prices are the major determinants of the availability of work. Even in the largest firms, where stable marketing and sales arrangements have been negotiated with large buyers, fluctuation still exists in the amount of work available in any given period. Skilled harvest crews, in contrast to capital-intensive machinery, can be activated for varying periods of time, adapted to a wide range of field conditions, and easily transported between production areas or fields at literally a moment's notice.

Taken in combination, these attributes—productivity, efficiency, and adaptability—underscore the critical role played by the ground crews in the harvest labor process. As suggested earlier, these lettuce crews constitute formidable *social* harvesting machines.

Wrap Crew Production

Approximately one-fifth of the lettuce shipped from California and Arizona is sent out enveloped in plastic film (Drossler,

1976). Known as "wrapped" or "source-wrapped" lettuce, it is the product of a labor process that differs in several respects from the ground crew organization. Two of the most important differences are: (1) the capital intensification of production, and (2) the restructuring of the harvest labor process.

The wrap machine (fig. 4) and its auxiliary equipment mark a significant increase in the capital intensity of lettuce harvesting. The machine itself consists of a steel frame with hinged wings capable of being folded back for highway transport. The entire device is powered by a large diesel (tractor-type) engine with auxiliary motors for generating electricity. Electrically powered conveyor belts are mounted on the wings and the center section of the machine for moving lettuce between work stations. Hydraulic lifters and steering mechanisms enable the wheels of the machine to be driven

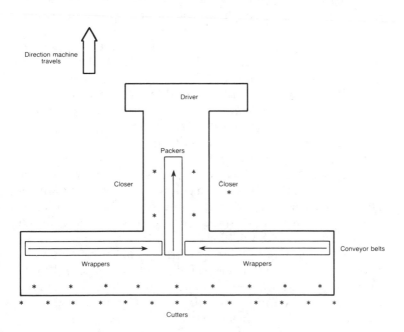

Figure 4. Diagram of General Wrap Machine
Design (Top View)

independently, thus allowing the contraption to move through damp fields and make turns in a short radius.

Individual machines cost in the neighborhood of $75,000 to $100,000 each—approximately the price of the largest and most powerful generation of tractors. Variations in price are largely due to differences in design. Some companies purchase their frames from machine manufacturers and then make modifications in their own engineering shops. Besides the machine itself, auxiliary equipment in the form of special trailers for transporting machines between production areas, forklifts for handling palletized cartons, and spare parts boosts the investment necessary to transform production from naked to wrapped lettuce. Given the fact that *two* machines (Zahara et al., 1974) are necessary to replace the output of one ground crew, investments approach nearly a quarter of a million dollars per ground crew equivalent. Thus, in contrast to the minimal hand tools necessary to outfit the ground crews, wrap machines constitute a sizable increase in fixed costs.

Altogether, only nine firms produce source-wrapped lettuce. Of those nine, the top three, which are also the three largest firms in the industry, account for somewhat between one-half and two-thirds of wrapped lettuce.[4] Miracle Vegetable Co., the industry leader, wraps roughly half of its lettuce; Salad Giant wraps nearly 40 percent; and Verde wraps between 30 percent and 40 percent (interviews with company representatives). In those firms committed to production of wrapped lettuce, therefore, the increase in fixed costs associated with the machine is a major investment. For Miracle alone, the investment in equipment, not including increased investments in maintenance and repair facilities or design shops, approaches $2 million.[5]

The second major element of change in the labor process is the elimination of the critical element of skill found in the ground crew: mutual coordination. In effect, the machine appropriates the mutual coordination of ground crew members while leaving in place many of the activities they previously performed. Workers still cut, pack, and load lettuce but now a machine regulates the pace and coordinates the performance of those activities. Therefore, the mutual co-ordination and experience of the ground crew has been reproduced mechanically as a set of motor-driven conveyor belts.

Like the industrialization of automobile production some sixty years earlier, wrap machine technology has had important consequences for the social organization of production (Chinoy, 1955; Braverman, 1975; Marx, 1975:375–409). First, the elimination of the coordination and skill of the ground crew cutter has transformed the cutter on a wrap crew into a sort of detail worker. Cutters are trained to perform a single, repetitive task. Individual workers in a wrap crew, like the individual workers on the line in an auto assembly plant, need not even have a passing acquaintance with fellow crew members or their work in order to perform adequately. The orientation to the parts but not the whole of the labor process, though not produced by a subdivision of work activities, contrasts sharply with the social cohesiveness and the orientation to the whole of the ground crew. Second, the pace of work has been subordinated to mechanical control, like an assembly line. The volume of lettuce arriving at any one of the work stations is manipulated externally by supervisory personnel. Thus the pace of work is less affected by the actions of any particular category of workers than by the speed of the machine and its conveyor belts. Finally, the pay rate for wrap machine workers has been converted from a piece-rate to an hourly basis. Thus, the variability and the high level of wages which had characterized different crew positions and different crews in the ground pack has been replaced by a flat, hourly wage structure.

These changes, in turn, have important implications for the social organization of the harvest crews. First, while the wrap machine process does not eliminate any of the individual activities carried out by ground crew workers it does, however, *increase* the demand for labor. Since two crews of thirty-three workers (and two machines) are necessary to replace one ground crew, the volume of labor needed is nearly double (table 5). However, the wage of the average worker is reduced to *less than half* what workers can make on the piece-rate.

When the premium paid to growers for wrapped lettuce is added to the total, the wrap-pack method proves quite competitive with the ground-pack method. Second, the elimination of crew-based coordination and the reduction in wages have also undercut the basis for worker commitment to crew and company. Although wrap machines are deployed on a continuous basis, the reward from commitment has been reduced in two important aspects: (1) the connection between crew experience and earnings has been replaced by an hourly wage that is largely unaffected by experience; and (2) the low level of wages discourages migration with crew and company. In other words, in addition to deskilling the *crew* and enhancing mechanical control of work pace, the transformation of the labor process has actually increased the seasonal demand for labor.

This chapter has made several important distinctions with respect to the social and economic organization of production in the lettuce industry. First, the industry has been transformed from a collection of economically vulnerable enterprises into a system dominated by a small set of highly complex and sophisticated organizations. Second, these organizations continue to employ a largely noncitizen labor force; despite the process of rationalization that has taken place at higher levels within those firms, the bulk of production is carried out by low status, unprotected labor. Finally, production is carried out in highly labor-intensive harvest teams. Even more important than the volume of labor required, production is characterized by both highly skilled and self-regulating production teams and lesser-skilled, mechanically paced crews.

With this examination as background, the organizing questions seem all the more important. How do these firms get such valuable labor at so low a cost? How is the stability and regularity of labor supply maintained?

4

CITIZENSHIP, EARNINGS, AND WORK ORGANIZATION

The analysis of southwestern agricultural production presented in chapter 2 argued that political intervention in labor market processes historically abridged both labor market competition and market determination of wages. In other words, the political construction of the agricultural labor market enabled employers to (1) avail themselves of a steady supply of low status, politically vulnerable labor, and (2) exercise arbitrary authority over the wages received by those workers. Yet, as was noted in the preceding chapter, two sets of circumstances now need to be considered.

First, the end of the bracero program took away from employers administrative control over the labor supply. Presumably, therefore, employers can no longer directly control the volume of labor available for employment nor act in bureaucratic fashion to determine wage levels. Has this meant that labor market processes have been freed from political controls? Have nonmarket statuses, particularly citizenship status, lost their salience as far as occupational attainment and earnings are concerned? The second set of circumstances bears more directly on the empirical case of the lettuce indus-try. As described in chapter 3, lettuce production is divided into two different organizational situses: the skilled ground crew and the unskilled wrap crew. Yet, the wages received by both ground and wrap crew members are very low (see table 6), especially when one considers the seasonality of production and the costs associated with migrancy. In particu-lar, the ground crews do not seem to be able to transform their collective skill and organizational potential into higher wages, higher status, more secure employment, or less de-structive working conditions. Why do wages remain so low? Why does labor supply and control over production seem so nonproblematic?

In this and the following two chapters, I will focus directly on the issues of earnings and work organization in the lettuce industry. In doing so, I will make two related arguments. First, I will argue that citizenship status continues to be a central variable in labor market and wage determination processes. Using data collected from the lettuce worker survey and interviews, I will demonstrate that citizenship and, to a somewhat lesser extent, gender act to specify the relationship between skill and income. While an individual's earnings are most strongly related to his or her position in the labor process and the skills required for work, citizenship status and gender strongly affect the allocation of individuals into crews. Thus,

Table 6. Mean Annual Income From Lettuce Employment
and All Sources from Sample and Crew Types
(Jan.-Dec., 1978)

	Income source	
Group	Lettuce	All sources[a]
All workers	$5,810	$7,550
Ground crew only	$7,600	$7,860
Wrap crew only	$5,500	$6,410

[a]Includes income from other employment during period, spouse's income, welfare, and unemployment compensation.

I will argue, market variables reflecting individual characteristics—age, experience, job tenure—are of secondary importance to citizenship status and gender in terms of their ability
to explain the distribution of income.

Second, I will argue that the relationship between citizenship status and crew organization can be explained in terms
of the relative advantages to employers of distributing workers with varying degrees of political vulnerability to different
positions in the labor process. I will show that the concentration of undocumented workers into the ground crew has two
important effects: (a) the subjection of productivity levels
to political manipulation, and (b) the denial to both undocumented *and* documented workers of the capacity to claim
higher status or reward for their skills. However, the concentration of documented and citizen workers, especially women,
in the wrap crews has the effect of ensuring the availability
of low-skilled workers, and using the social and economic
restrictions associated with gender roles and alien status to
ensure work force stability. I will suggest, therefore, that
citizenship status and gender—variables that are politically
and socially constructed—are economic *and* organizational in
their consequences.

These arguments will be elaborated and supporting data
presented in the next three chapters. Survey and qualitative
data will be combined to illuminate the arguments made at
the level of the labor market and at the level of the labor
process.

CITIZENSHIP, WORK SITUS, AND EARNINGS

Citizenship is a key variable in the allocation of individuals to
the positions in the labor process and, subsequently, in the
allocation of rewards associated with those positions. The
critical dimension informing the citizenship variable is political vulnerability. Each category of citizenship—citizen,
documented, and undocumented—represents a different
level of vulnerability or susceptibility to external influence
based on the formal legal mechanisms for controlling and
legitimating claims on the polity. Thus if citizenship were to

be redefined in terms of the level of political vulnerability, the categories would be ranked in the following fashion: citizen = low; documented immigrant = medium; undocumented immigrant = high.

In the analysis of the politics of labor supply presented in chapter 2 it was argued that the bracero program (1942–1965) introduced a new category of citizenship status. This program was developed in a period in which both the political and the economic rights of citizenship were being extended. In the case of political rights, increased claims on the polity for nonwork support were being institutionalized in the "welfare state," for example, increased federal allocations for welfare and general assistance medical care programs for the unemployed and underemployed and federally financed public housing programs (Piven and Cloward, 1971; Marshall, 1977). Eligibility for these programs depended on nonparticipation in the economic sphere. At the same time, the economic rights of citizenship were being extended. Guarantees of "market freedom" and rewards for participation were bolstered in such measures as the extension of New Deal legislation regarding the right to join unions and to bargain collectively over wages and working conditions; the growth of job-related rewards such as private pension and medical plans; and the establishment of federally mediated low-interest loans for home ownership.

The bracero program, by contrast, made an entire group's right to be in the country entirely dependent on participation in economic organizations. In other words, where citizens had the option (both voluntary and involuntary) to withdraw from economic organizations and exercise their political rights of citizenship or remain employed and enjoy the benefits associated with it, braceros had neither.

The termination of the bracero program in 1965 meant, in effect, the generalization and intensification of that status. As table 2 suggests, the closing of the bracero pipeline coincided with the opening of the undocumented floodgate. More important than the question of the volume of that flow is the status of its members: where the bracero had some minimal degree of protection from employer abuse, the indocumentado had (and has) none. Less dramatic, but equally important, the undocumented worker does not have the rights with which to make claims for higher status or reward for skills acquired through participation in economic organizations or independent of them. This is not to suggest, as for example Burawoy (1976:1051) does, that these workers can somehow be paid less than the value of their labor. Rather, it is to argue that they are severely hampered in their ability to make and enforce claims for higher status and reward based on their labor market position.

Concretely, an examination of income determination processes in the lettuce industry should likely reveal the strong interrelationship of level of political vulnerability (represented by citizenship status), skill, and earnings. There are three arguments here. First, skill levels should be positively related to earnings. Second, degree of political vulnerability should be positively related to both skill levels and earnings. And third, degree of political vulnerability should be more strongly related to skill and earnings than any market-based or individual characteristics of the labor force.

Sampling Procedures and Issues

Data collected from a sample of 152 lettuce harvest workers will be employed in the testing of these hypotheses. The data collection process involved a sampling of residences in the Salinas Valley area during the summer of 1979. Residential locations included private homes and apartments, labor camps (employer, public, and privately owned and administered), and transient hotels. The survey was administered by the author both in English and in Spanish.

Two aspects of the sample and sampling procedure require comment. First, the sample can be considered only partially random since the social situation in which farm workers exist precludes simple identification of areas in which they are to be found. The exigencies of travel, employment, social status, and housing discrimination result in workers being scattered across a wide variety of locations. Therefore, the criteria for inclusion in the sample was more often based on whether a person simply worked in the lettuce harvest than on a randomized identification and sampling of the universe of lettuce workers. Second, the declarations of citizenship status made by respondents were impossible to verify, even in the case of those who admitted to being undocumented. Because insistence on proof would undoubtedly have precluded the completion of most interviews, no effort was made to verify citizenship status. The analysis of the effects of the citizenship variable therefore may be somewhat compromised. However, as will be demonstrated below, the inclusion of respondents who identified themselves freely as undocumented workers helped enormously in overcoming that obstacle. The undocumented workers were included in the sample as a result of contacts made during the field research but were intially identified solely through their citizenship status. Thus, their occupational situs was unknown prior to interview and their similarity in position to other indocumentados was later corroborated by in-depth interviews.

Precisely because the above factors limit the generalizability of the survey data, the survey results by themselves are not considered conclusive. But the research was designed to take these limitations into account and survey data were supplemented by interviews and participant-observation. Thus, the analysis of survey results in this section is accompanied by the analysis of qualitative data. This form of methodological triangulation, I argue, adds measurably to the confidence with which conclusions can and will be made.

Analysis of Survey Data

The strong positive relationship between weekly earnings and work situs is demonstrated in table 7. As expected, the higher skill levels required in the ground crew form of production result in higher levels of payment than the lower-skilled, mechanically paced wrap machine production.

The central issue to be addressed, however, is the factors that influence distribution of workers into different work situses and income categories. Table 8 summarizes the zero-order correlations between market and individual charac-

Table 7. Average Weekly Earnings by Type of
Crew Organization (N = 152)

Average weekly earnings	Crew type (%)		Total (%)
	Wrap crew	Ground crew	
$101 – 150	37.0	0.0	37.0
$151 – 200	17.5	6.0	23.5
$201 – 250	2.7	24.8	48.3
$251 and over	1.4	10.7	12.1
Total	58.6	41.5	100.0

Gamma = .74

Table 8. Zero-Order Correlations Between Human Capital
Variables and Earnings, Type of Crew Organization

Independent variable	Dependent variable	
	Average weekly earnings	Type of crew organization
Age	–.08	.03
Years of experience as farm worker	–.09	–.07
Years of experience as lettuce worker	.02	–.13
Years of experience in present job	.11	.01

teristics of respondents in the sample of the work situs and earnings variables. From conventional models of income determination (e.g., Becker, 1964) one would expect that variables measuring labor market and job experience would be positively related to earnings, particularly in a labor market featuring a hierarchy of skilled occupations. The general and specific skills acquired through time in the labor market and job should represent investments that will bear an appreciable return; alternatively viewed, they would represent increments in the marginal productivity of labor which would generate higher income. However, table 8 shows that for lettuce harvesters *none* of the characteristics associated with human capital investments is strongly related to either work situs or earnings. Age, general work experience, industry experience, and job experience yield no measurable benefit for lettuce workers.

By contrast tables 9 and 10 demonstrate the role of citizenship status in occupational attainment and earnings. Both the strength and the direction of the relationships between citizenship status and the two dependent variables are as predicted. Undocumented aliens, the most politically vulnerable workers, tend to show up in the most skilled jobs. Citizens, the most politically protected labor, tend to show up in the least skilled, mechanically controlled work. Documented aliens are distributed between the work situses. The distribution of workers into income categories in turn reflects the occupational distribution. In other words, the termination of the bracero program, that is, of employer administration of

Table 9. Percentage Distribution of Harvest Occupations
by Citizenship Status

Harvest occupation	Citizenship status (%)			
	U.S. citizen	Documented immigrant	Undocumented immigrant	Total (%)
Ground crew (skilled)	5.3	34.1	83.4	42.1
Wrap crew (unskilled)	94.7	65.9	16.6	57.9
Total	100.0	100.0	100.0	100.0
	(19)	(97)	(36)	(152)

Gamma = .77

Table 10. Percentage Distribution of Average Weekly Earnings
by Citizenship Status of Respondent

Average weekly income	Citizenship status (%)			Total (%)
	U.S. citizen	Documented immigrant	Undocumented immigrant	
$101 – 150	47.4	48.9	0.0	36.9
$151 – 200	47.4	22.3	13.9	23.5
$201 – 250	0.0	21.3	58.3	27.5
$251 – 300	5.3	8.5	25.0	11.4
$301 – 350	0.0	0.0	2.8	0.7
Total	100.0	100.0	100.0	100.0
	(19)	(94)	(36)	(149)

Missing = 3; Gamma = .65

labor supply, has not introduced market principles of occupational attainment or income.

CITIZENSHIP AND GENDER

The relationship among citizenship status, skill levels, and earnings is clearly documented. However, the impact of gender must also be taken into account. As is shown in tables 11 through 13, gender is strongly related to all three variables: citizens tend to be women; women tend to be found exclusively in the wrap crews; and women tend to be among the lowest paid harvest workers (which follows from the preceding table).

Are the observed correlations between citizenship, skill, and earnings really masking the effects of sex segregation in the labor market? The situation is too complex to respond simply "Yes" or "No." Though chapter 6 is devoted to an examination of the role of gender in work organization, it is possible to assess here the *independent and combined effects* of citizenship and gender. This argument is supported in two principal ways. First, when one looks at the distribution of workers into work situses and earnings levels by citizenship status, it is clear that even when women are removed from the sample the effects of citizenship are visible (tables 14 and 15).

Table 11. Percentage Distribution of Citizenship
Status by Gender

Citizenship status	Gender (%)		Percent difference
	Men	Women	
U.S. citizen	2.2	28.4	−26.2
Documented immigrant	58.7	71.6	−12.9
Undocumented immigrant	39.1	0.0	39.1
Total	100.0	100.0	
	(92)	(60)	(152)

Table 12. Percentage Distribution of Crew Type by Gender

Crew type	Gender (%)		Percent difference
	Men	Women	
Ground	69.6	0.0	69.6
Wrap	30.3	100.0	
Cutter	(17.4)	(1.7)	(15.7)
Packer	(13.0)	(25.0)	(12.0)
Wrapper	(0.0)	(73.3)	(73.3)
Total	100.0	100.0	
	(92)	(60)	(152)

Second, briefly summarizing material to be presented later, the role of workers' citizenship and political vulnerability both with regard to general labor market functioning and the operation of the skilled crews is separable from the effects of

Table 13. Percentage Distribution of
Weekly Earnings by Gender

Average weekly earnings	Gender (%)		Percent difference
	Male	Female	
$101 – 150	22.2	59.3	–37.1
$151 – 200	12.2	40.7	–28.5
$201 – 250	45.6	0.0	45.6
$251 and over	20.0	0.0	20.0
Total	100.0	100.0	
	(90)	(59)	(149)

Missing = 3

Table 14. Percentage Distribution of Male Workers by
Crew Type and Citizenship Status

Crew type	Citizenship status (%)		Percent difference
	Documented immigrant	Undocumented immigrant	
Ground crew			
Cutter/packer	52.9	75.0	–22.1
Auxiliary	11.8	8.3	3.5
Subtotal	64.7	83.3	–18.6
Wrap crew	35.3	16.7	18.6
Total	100.0	100.0	
	(51)	(36)	(87)

Table 15. Percentage Distribution of Weekly Earnings by
Citizenship Status of Male Workers

Average weekly earnings	Citizenship status (%)		Percent difference
	Documented immigrant	Undocumented immigrant	
$101 – 150	37.7	0.0	37.7
$151 – 200	11.3	13.9	−2.6
$201 – 250	37.7	58.3	−20.6
$251 – 300	13.2	25.0	−11.8
$301 and above	0.0	2.8	−2.8
Total	100.0	100.0	
	(53)	(36)	(89)

gender. As will be shown with regard to the ground crews, in particular, the capacity of employers to affect productivity and enhance managerial control on the basis of political vulnerability cannot be explained by gender differences.

The importance of gender in terms of labor market and work organization, however, shows up in the creation and perpetuation of a large and stable supply of workers in the wrap crew situs. It is in that locale, I argue, that the combined effects of citizenship *and* gender must be considered. The effects of citizenship and gender overlap and act to create, through different circumstances, a set of consequences similar to that found in the ground crews (chap. 6). In essence, citizenship and gender inequalities are used to construct an abundant supply of labor, to increase the stability of the work force, and to enhance managerial control over work organization and wages.

In summary, data collected from the farm worker survey strongly support the hypothesis that citizenship status acts to specify the relationship between skill and income. Citizenship status, beyond all other variables (including gender), influences how individuals are allocated into positions and, furthermore, what the level of rewards is for those positions. The combined effects of citizenship and gender, in turn, even more strongly influence occupational location and earnings.

Three additional points should be made in this connection. First, to argue that human capital variables seem of secondary importance in explaining variations in earnings is not the same as denying their importance. Indeed, among male lettuce workers differences between the skilled ground crew workers and the unskilled wrap crew workers are substantial. The greater experience of the former group is reflected in their earnings. Yet, the clear correlation of citizenship status and earnings cannot simply be explained by the kind of work background these people bring to the job. Close to 80 percent of undocumented *and* documented workers had worked in agriculture before taking their present jobs in the lettuce industry and, while undocumented workers tended to have spent more of their working lives in agricultural employment, a roughly equal share of documented and undocumented workers (35% vs. 28%) had worked at one time in a nonfarm job. Thus, as Bustamante (1977) has demonstrated, immigrants with a rural background tend to find employment in agriculture. *But* work backgrounds in this case do not explain why undocumented workers should be more likely to work in the ground crews than documented workers.

Second, it might be possible to argue that undocumented workers are somehow better suited to the physically arduous work of the ground-pack if there were some indication that they possessed special characteristics other than their political vulnerability. However, the survey data revealed no such special characteristics. As mentioned earlier, undocumented workers had the same general backgrounds as other male workers. Both documented and undocumented workers were attracted to work in the lettuce harvest by the expectation of higher earnings than those available in other pursuits, but motivations cannot explain why the sorting process implied by the distribution of workers into jobs operates the way it does. If, as I argue in the next section, undocumented workers push themselves harder than others, that is a product of their inability to effectively protect themselves from external pressures.

Third, and finally, the preceding analysis of earnings data underscores a major contention in this study: there is no reason why immigrants should be better suited to do this kind of work than any other workers. The growth of large-scale agribusiness firms has dramatically altered the economic structure of the industry. Employment opportunities, for ground crew workers in particular, are no longer highly unstable. Minimum wage laws have been applied to agricultural labor. The work, though arduous, can be compared to many factory jobs and is probably less physically impairing than other livelihoods, such as mining or foundry work. Moreover, during the time of this study and afterward, domestic unemployment was climbing to record levels. What accounts for the predominance of immigrant workers and women in the harvest labor market is the construction of an enclave wherein the vulnerability of these workers is employed as a device for pushing wage levels down below a level acceptable to domestic workers, and a means by which to attach the lower status of aliens and women to the work itself—making it appear as a livelihood beneath that which other, higher status workers should accept.

CITIZENSHIP AND THE RELATIONS
OF PRODUCTION

As was suggested at the beginning of the chapter, citizenship can also be considered an organizational variable. Previously the labor market effects of political vulnerability were emphasized. Here I will turn to the consequences of citizenship for the relations of production in the ground crew situs. In this analysis I will make three major points: first, that the political vulnerability of undocumented workers enables employers to train and/or employ them as skilled workers without ceding control over the labor process; second, that competition between undocumented and documented workers for higher paid work (in the ground crews) acts to diffuse their common organization against employers; and third, that undocumented workers are used as a category of "rate-busters" to increase the productivity of all ground crew workers. Each of these arguments will be dealt with in turn.

Undocumented Aliens as "Special Workers"

Even during the period of the bracero program, the stream of labor from Mexico consisted of both certified contract workers and indocumentados. The resulting pool of undocumented labor was also fed by braceros who overstayed their temporary work certifications. The majority were, however, workers who bypassed the bureaucratic red tape and bribes (mordida) necessary to obtain their certification as braceros (Galarza, 1964:119).

While there are no reliable estimates as to the relative size of these two groups—braceros and undocumented aliens—certain advantages were associated with the use of undocumented workers. They could be used in occupations from which braceros were restricted, for example, tractor and bus driving, packing shed work, and landscaping. Often these were occupations that required more skill or that necessitated longer periods of employment than were allowed under the time limits imposed on bracero work certifications (e.g., irrigation work, seeding, and even maintenance). According to Galarza, undocumented workers even showed up as low-level management in the fields, such as row bosses or foremen's assistants (Galarza, 1964:169). Many were used to form a stratum of "special workers" in relatively permanent positions within agribusiness firms. This stratum of undocumented workers was especially significant within the lettuce industry, particularly in the creation of stable, experienced harvest crews. Crews of undocumented workers existed during the period of the 1950s and 1960s in two forms: those organized by labor contractors and those organized by individual firms.

Crews organized by labor contractors operated in much the same fashion as custom harvesters in other crops, such as custom harvesting teams found in the grain industry. The labor contractor, an individual entrepreneur who traded in the labor of undocumented workers, would recruit and supervise the production operations of the harvest. For a contract fee negotiated with the grower, the contractor would provide sufficient labor to harvest the crop and would, in turn, organize housing, food, and transportation for the crew.

Hiring a labor contractor and a professional crew enabled smaller firms to externalize the recruitment and supervision of production to another agent. While direct labor costs were higher for the employer, the system as a whole offered an efficient and less complicated alternative to the use of braceros. A retired lettuce grower from the Imperial Valley in California, whom I will call Burt Tuller, described the situation thus:

> Using a labor contractor and his crews wasn't strictly legal, of course, but as far as I was concerned, it saved me a lot of headaches. . . . I hired braceros out of the Labor Supply Association like everybody else did for thinning and lighter chores. Those were chores that didn't need a lot of supervision and all I really needed was bodies.

But, when it came time to harvest the crop, Tuller and other growers turned to labor contractors:

> There were two big advantages to hiring a labor contractor. One, he handled all the dealings with the workers. I was out there just to make sure they gave me a good pack. The contractor, though, he brought them together. He was to see to it they got fed and all. The second thing was that those guys were fast. They'd go through a field like a buzzsaw. Real teamwork. See, the difference was that the braceros we got worked pretty hard, but they didn't have that teamwork. A lot of them were just interested in drawing their pay and that's it. . . . They weren't getting rich, not at 86 cents an hour. On the other hand, they had no incentive.

Problems associated with training workers to perform the individual tasks and, subsequently, keeping them together long enough to acquire "teamwork" derived from the bracero program itself. According to Tuller and other employers I interviewed, undocumented workers alleviated the problem of trying to contract the same group of workers year after year through the bracero apparatus. According to Tuller:

> In the first place, it cost you money to train them (braceros). That meant you had to be out in the fields all the time. By the time they were working good together, the season was practically over. Then where were you? . . . The other problem was that it got damned expensive when you tried to get the same guys back the next year. Either you had to spend a lot of time down at the border when they came in [when braceros were processed through the certification stations] or you had to pay a lot of bribe money—they called it mordida—to this and that guy to make sure they got funneled to you. I figured it cost me $20 in bribes per guy! That was just too much. In the end, using a labor contractor cost me maybe a few pennies more a carton.

Taking into consideration the combined costs of training, supervision, and recruitment, Tuller (and other employers he named) opted for a system that existed alongside the bracero program but was far more productive and efficient. The use of a labor contractor and undocumented workers precluded the organizational task of constructing a training program within the firm and provided a regular supply of skilled labor.

A parallel system developed within a number of large grower-shipper firms as well. Unlike the seasonal hiring of labor contractors and crews, however, some larger firms sought to incorporate the system. That is, foremen (some of whom were former labor contractors) were used to create crews of undocumented workers to accomplish the same ends desired by employers like Tuller. Low-level managers and functionaries assembled the crew and then ensconced them physically within the organization. Interviews with Tuller (who revealed the process while arguing that the use of un-documented workers was widespread even during the bracero program) and retired lechugeros elucidated the operations of this system.

Crews were assembled from two major sources: from work-ers in Mexico who were unable to get certification as braceros and from the ranks of braceros who overstayed their certification once in California. As one retired worker who joined such a crew in 1961 explained:

> The *mayordomo* [foreman] came up to a bunch of us one day and wanted to know if we wanted to keep our jobs. We knew he meant to stay around after we were supposed to go back home (to Mexico). It was so hard to get work as a bracero that most of us decided to stay.

Once in the job as an indocumentado, work was more permanent but gone were the meager legal protections afforded braceros. As the same worker remembered,

> We got paid better than we had before as braceros, but it was like we were in prison. They kept us out of sight, away from the other workers. We couldn't leave the camp except to work. Any time we complained the foreman would just say, "You want to work someplace else? Go ahead and try."

Physical isolation was only part of a strategy used by employers to construct and control their teams of skilled harvesters. Threats of deportation were alternated with reminders of the worker's superior earnings to keep undocumented workers in line.

Undocumented workers played a specific role once they were internalized or made a more permanent part of the labor force: they were the special workers, the firstline crews in the harvest labor process. According to interviews with retired workers, undocumented crews worked apart from the braceros, harvesting the first-grade or top quality lettuce.[1] Skilled and stable teams of undocumented workers, according to Tuller, were more efficient and produced a more uniform quality pack compared with the uneven, heavily supervised bracero crews.

The construction and internalization of crews of undocumented workers provided the efficiency of skilled production teams. At the same time, however, it virtually ensured the attachment of that labor to the firm while denying workers the means by which to claim greater status based on skill or organization position. It is not clear how generalized a practice this was across the industry since employers interviewed in the course of the study, with the exception of Tuller, denied having done so. Most suggested that such a practice would have been illegal. Interviews with workers who had participated, however, indicate that the practice was not uncommon.

This form of labor organization, as I noted earlier, was constructed *alongside* a labor program that had already proven remarkably efficient in supplying and controlling large numbers of agricultural workers. The bracero program, however, proved inefficient as a means by which to establish skilled, stable production teams. For the bulk of firms (including many lettuce firms), the bracero program provided what was wanted: a stream of largely unskilled labor. As lettuce producers, particularly the larger firms, moved to increase the productivity of the labor process, the bracero program failed to fill their needs. The unregulated supply and negatively privileged status of undocumented labor became the means by which to fill those needs.

The thrust of the historical data from Tuller and other informants is that the use of indocumentados as special workers provided an important incentive to high productivity and stability at a very low cost. Employers were able to turn the investments undocumented workers had made in getting across the border (as well as their fear of apprehension) into an attachment to the firm. Considering the value of ground crew labor, the costs associated with employing a labor contractor or organizing company-specific crews were (and, as I will show in the contemporary period, are) relatively small in comparison to the incentives presently embedded in internal labor market structures. The coercive control exercised through manipulation of citizenship status allowed these firms to capitalize on both workers' independent investments in training and those of the organization without having to bargain over the price of labor. Furthermore, the ready availability of more, equally disadvantaged labor meant that even if workers sought to organize for the purpose of price bargaining their replacements could be obtained relatively easily.

RELATIONS BETWEEN WORKERS

The end of the bracero program removed the restrictions that had, at least officially, bound those workers to temporary, unskilled work. What followed, as I noted in chapter 2, was the construction of a labor market filled by documented and undocumented workers. However, differences in citizenship status produce different kinds of careers within that labor market. Documented workers tend to be distributed between work situses and undocumented workers tend to show up most often in the skilled ground crews.

In analyzing the consequences of the citizenship variable, it is important to consider its effects on the relations among workers, especially as they pertain to the organizational potential of the crews. I will begin by analyzing employment strategies from the workers' point of view, that is, how workers from different categories of citizenship status interpret their position and outlook on the work they perform. I will, subsequently, raise the analysis to the level of organizational strategy and practice to show how citizenship is used to construct the work orientations and strategies of lettuce workers.

In the survey interviews, respondents were asked why they worked in the lettuce industry (as opposed to other crops or types of employment). In fairly uniform fashion both documented and undocumented workers cited two major reasons: potential earnings and the possibility of working a greater portion of the year (see table 16).

Despite the similarities in response to the general question, however, differences in the employment strategies of documented and undocumented workers emerged from the in-depth interviews and fieldwork. Undocumented workers expressed a sense of urgency in describing their work experiences and plans. Documented workers, in contrast, focused on the monetary and organizational advantages of work in the lettuce harvest. The origin of these different orientations appears quite openly in terms of categories of citizenship status, as the comments below demonstrate. Typical of many of the undocumented workers, a young cutter summarized his position this way:

Table 16. Major Reasons for Working in the Lettuce Harvest by Citizenship Status (Male Workers)

Major reason for working in lettuce	Citizenship status (%)		Total
	Documented	Undocumented	
Higher wages	77.7	83.3	80.0
More work or steadier work	14.8	11.1	13.3
Other reason	7.5	5.6	6.7
Total	100.0	100.0	100.0
	(54)	(36)	(90)

Anywhere I work I take chances of being picked up and sent home. Sure, it's easy to get work in the strawberries or with the (lettuce) machines, but you don't make much money. . . . In the contract crews (ground crews) you work very hard, but you earn a lot more. The foremen tell you that if you get picked up they'll give you your job back, but sometimes you don't get it back. So, if you have to take so many chances, you better make as much money as you can.

Comparing his position as an undocumented worker with that of documented workers, another lechugero explained:

If I was ten years younger and I had papers, I might look at things differently. But I'm thirty years old and I've been work- ing in the lettuce for eight years. I've got six children and a wife to feed. I need the money. . . . If I could get papers, maybe I'd work as a tractor driver or something and make less money. Then I could work more years. I can't get papers because I was arrested in Salinas once and besides it takes years to get them. . . . And I can't afford to buy them either. So, I stay cutting lettuce until I can't do it anymore. Then I go home.

Documented workers tended to concentrate on achieving a balance between maximum earnings and the physical capacity to continue working. For example, in describing his annual work schedule, a green-card lettuce packer explained:

> For the first two years, I used to work for almost ten or eleven months for this company. I made good money but I was just worn out. . . . Now I work in Salinas for about seven months and then I head home to Cauchitlan and rest. This way, I figure I can work maybe six or seven years more.

A green-card who began working in the field without papers offered an insightful comparison of the differences between his past and present orientations:

> Before, I wanted to make as much money as I could when I got work. It was a struggle all the time. If I found a job, I had to lay low and keep out of trouble . . . no going to the bars, no talking back to the foreman. I worried all the time about getting picked up by *la migra*.
>   Now, it's different. I can walk the streets and not worry. That doesn't mean that the *gabachos* (Anglos) treat you much different. But for me it means that I can get a job and make money when I want. If I get tired of doing this, I can maybe try to get a job driving a truck. I won't make as much, but at least I'll be able to work.

While citizenship limits the occupational opportunities of all immigrants, the range of choices appears wider for legal immigrants than for the indocumentados. Documented workers at least can choose between higher paying, physically destructive work and lower paying, less demanding work. Undocumented workers, however, are susceptible to apprehension and deportation wherever they work, and thus many attempt to maximize earnings when and where possible. Nonetheless, as was evident in table 16, the promise of higher wages and steadier work in lettuce draws both groups to seek employment in the crews.

It is not surprising, therefore, that jobs in the lettuce industry, and the ground crews in particular, should be the object of intense and sometimes bitter competition between documented and undocumented workers. But the nature of that competition is profoundly affected by the differential statuses of the competitors. Precisely because green-cards and citizens have neither the legal nor the organizational means by which to close off the flow of undocumented aliens or to sanction employers for hiring indocumentados, they are forced to compete on the same terrain with that most vulnerable category of labor. Thus, the perpetuation of competition turns on the capacity of employers to manipulate citizenship status to their advantage, that is, to reproduce the vulnerability of undocumented workers as control over a labor process that engages both undocumented and documented workers. An important element of that control is the conflict it engenders between workers who share the same national and ethnic heritage but who have a different status in the labor market.

Competition and Control

That the vulnerability of undocumented workers affects work organization and control is quite evident in the assessments made of the "qualities" of different groups of workers. A common assessment heard in interviews with principals in the lettuce industry (managers, workers, and union officials) is that undocumented aliens "work harder" or "put out" more effort than other workers. Thus, among employers, undocumented aliens constitute an attractive labor pool. Similar assessments were heard from many employers, but one Salinas Valley vegetable grower put it most forcefully:

> In the thirty years I've been in this business, I've seen four different groups in my crews. The hardest working ones and the ones who gave you the least trouble are the illegals. They're up here because they need work. There isn't a thing for them to do in Mexico but starve. . . . So, they take the chance and come here, work hard and then live better in Mexico. The green-cards, the Mexican-Americans, and the local Chicanos are all about the same. Some of the green-cards work pretty good, but nowhere as good as the *mojados* [wetbacks]. They act like you owe them something. It's worse now because of Chavez and his union.

Filipinos were honest, hard-working people . . . but there's not many of them left nowadays.

Anglos don't last more than a day or two out in the fields. As long as there's welfare, no Anglo's going to get off his duff and do a little hard work.

For documented workers, particularly union members and supporters, indocumentados pose a significant dilemma: on the one hand, they are countrymen who share a common status as Mexicans; on the other hand, they belong to a segment of the labor force which, because of its vulnerability, has historically acted to undercut both formal and informal worker organization against management. While I examine this situation much more closely in the next chapter on relations among workers in a large unionized lettuce firm, elements of the conflict surfaced in fieldwork and interviews. For example, when looking for work in the fields, I often talked with farm workers in local gathering places such as bars, groceries, and friends' houses. In most cases I tried to tap into the grapevine by asking for an assessment of particular companies: How were they to work for? Was it a good place to learn to cut lettuce? On several occasions I was told that crews at certain companies were inordinately hardworking and that the reason for this was their high percentage of undocumented workers. On one occasion in particular I was warned:

You don't want to work at Salad Giant! They are real real fast. You wouldn't be able to keep up. They would just chew you up and spit you out.

When I asked why they were so fast, I was told by the same worker:

All those guys are illegals. Every one of them. That's all Salad Giant hires. They bring those guys up and work them till they drop. . . . They [the workers] think they are real tough, you know: real men. But they are fools and idiots. If you go there and you can't keep up? Out you go!

Efforts to more systematically sample comparisons by other workers bore similar results. Most green-cards and citizens argued that undocumented workers did indeed work harder. Those who disagreed most often argued that *all* lettuce workers worked hard, irrespective of citizenship status. As one lechugero remarked: "We all work hard. That's what this job is all about, no? We work harder than anybody else." Most telling, however, was the fact that no one I asked contradicted the general sentiment.

Most undocumented workers were hesitant to pass judgement on their output or effort in comparison to the others. The majority of those who did respond argued that they did work harder, though never were those sentiments expressed boastfully. Views on the subject ranged from righteousness to apology. One lechugero, apparently sensing that my question was intended as a criticism of undocumented workers as a group, replied:

> You are damned right we work harder. We have to. We have no protections and no laws to look out for us. If we did and if la migra would stop chasing us down, we could make a decent living without having to work so hard. . . . The growers know we have no choices so we have to work hard to keep our jobs.

Another worker, while explaining that he had gotten his first job in lettuce as a strikebreaker in 1970 (though at the time of the interview he worked for a nonunion company), remarked quietly:

> A lot of other guys think we're just *zopilotes* [buzzards]. You know, men who go around stealing other men's work. It's not that way . . . we all have to eat and we have families who need to eat. When you have no papers and you have a chance to work, you take it. It's not stealing. . . . Me and my compadres have to work harder or the ranchers take away our jobs. We all support Chavez and his union, but our stomachs and our children's stomachs are more important right now.

While comments such as these provide evidence of the effects of citizenship status, my own field experience lends further substantiation. My first attempt to gain a position in the ground crew took place in a company-organized "tryout" (*prueba*) for a new crew. The tryout began with a week of general training for all the men who showed up (70 for 30 positions). The second week constituted the trial period. Individuals chose a position for which they wanted training and stayed in it for the duration of the tryout. I chose to try out for the cutter's job, feeling that would provide the best vantage point for observation.

After a sixty-hour week of cuts, bruises, and pulled muscles from the work, and relentless cajoling from company foremen, we (15 trios and 25 auxiliary workers) were told to go all out by the field supervisor. To everyone involved, it was clear that speed and endurance were the determinants of success. The routine of amphetamine-stimulated performance was inculcated very early on, though the practice of taking drugs was neither expressly encouraged nor prohibited by foremen or supervisors.[2] Tallies of daily output (in cartons of lettuce accepted and rejected) were kept for each of the trios but were never reported. On the final day, the workers selected to make up the new crew were notified by the foreman. My trio was among the six rejected.

Sensing that my status as the only gabacho (Anglo) in the tryouts might have preordained the outcome, I offered an apology to my trio-mate, Umberto. Before I could finish delivering it, however, he interrupted:

> Your being gabacho did not help us, but what was more important was that none of us (Umberto, Pablo, or myself) was indocumentado. Most of those other guys don't have papers. . . . I know maybe twenty of those guys don't have papers. We live in the same camp. They can't hide it. That's what the mayordomo wants: guys he can step on. . . . If they know you don't have papers and if you're any good, they'll take you. I know we were just as fast as the others.

Though he did not have specific evidence that the foremen knew the chosen workers were undocumented, Umberto argued that it was common knowledge that some companies, this one included, often hired indocumentados over green-cards, especially when starting new crews. An informal survey conducted by Umberto afterward in his camp revealed that five of the nine trios hired were made up of undocumented workers. In the remaining four trios, he found that at least two workers were undocumented. Thus, parallel to the survey findings, undocumented immigrants were concentrated in the lead jobs and green-cards were spread across crew positions.

The remarks of workers both with regard to their job strategies and their assessments of performance reflect consciousness of the effects of citizenship status. For undocumented workers, vulnerability is a fact of life. Potential political sanctions get translated into strategies of work and performance which are designed to acquire and maintain employment in an unstable labor market. In other words, the accessibility of work and the ever-present threat of deportation are viewed not so much as contradictory elements of a larger labor system, but as invariant conditions of employment. For documented workers job strategies are constructed within the limits imposed by constrained job opportunities. However, the presence of undocumented workers acts to further constrain their degree of freedom both in job choice and in performance on the job. The differential effort displayed by indocumentados and the greater "desirability" of those workers in the eyes of employers are translated into competition for work and, ultimately, into competing norms of performance. These differences show up most forcefully within the context of crew organization and relations between workers and managers.

PRODUCTIVITY AND EARNINGS IN THE GROUND CREWS

Undocumented workers constituted a category of special workers during the period of the bracero program. They supplemented what was already a highly elastic and tightly controlled labor system. Unaffected by the constraints of limited work certifications and occupational restrictions, indocumentados were organized into what became the precursors of the modern harvest crews. But these workers remained largely separate from competition with the braceros—both in terms of crew composition and in terms of the distribution of occupations. In the contemporary period, however, the presence of the indocumentados has a direct effect on the organization and conditions of work for all lettuce workers, documented and undocumented.

More than simply being vulnerable labor, undocumented workers represent an identifiable and reproducible category of rate-busters within the agricultural labor market. Rather than being randomly distributed across a labor pool, these rate-busters can be identified and actively recruited by lettuce firms. Thus for industry managers they serve to maintain high levels of productivity and to undermine the organizational potential of the ground crews. Unlike the classic rate-busters depicted in the literature on output restriction (Roy, 1952; Collins, Dalton, and Roy, 1946), however, undocumented workers do not comprise one or two deviates within an informal network of workers. On the contrary, the location of undocumented workers in the most influential positions in the crews—cutting and packing—tends to shift the balance in the opposite direction: toward the imposition of sanctions against those who cannot make the rate.

Limitations on the availability of productivity data make this argument difficult to support directly. Industry representatives and employers refused to provide such information; the unions representing lettuce workers either did not have the data themselves or would not admit to having it.[3] Therefore the arguments in support of the assertion that indocumentados play a rate-busting role will have to be made indirectly through the survey and fieldwork data. The analysis of survey data, which constitutes the core of this section, will demonstrate that documented and undocumented ground crew workers achieve rough parity in earnings despite different levels of experience and patterns of employment. The analysis of data collected in the field will be approached from a slightly different angle, but with the same intent: to illustrate the consequences of the citizenship variable for productivity and control over the labor process. Because the field data is quite lengthy, it will be presented separately in chapter 5.

Although it might be inelegant to use "negative" findings to support an argument, the importance of the argument makes it necessary in this case. To be more precise, if the null hypothesis is made that the political vulnerability of undocumented workers makes them more likely to achieve higher levels of productivity than other workers, then (assuming equal piece-rates for all workers) indocumentados should earn *more* than any other workers in the same category of work. If, however, indocumentados do not show up in segregated crews (or crews are mixed by citizenship status), then both undocumented and documented workers should earn *roughly equal* wages (again, assuming equivalent piece-rates). Data presented in table 17 demonstrates that, for the workers surveyed, the latter case is more correct. In other words, citizenship status does not have an appreciable effect on earnings among workers in the same work situs.

Citizenship status, however, remains strongly correlated with the human capital variables, that is, undocumented workers in ground crews tend to be younger, less experienced in lettuce harvesting generally, and less experienced in the jobs they occupy (see table 18). Despite the fact that ground crew earnings are not directly related to citizenship status, occupa-

Table 17. Cross-tabulation of Weekly Earnings by Citizenship Status for Ground Crew Workers

Average weekly earnings	Documented immigrants (%)	Undocumented immigrants (%)	Total (%)
$151 – 200	6.0	7.5	13.4
$201 – 250	28.4	31.3	59.7
$251 – 300	11.2	14.1	25.3
$301 and over	0.0	1.5	1.5
Total	45.6	54.4	100.0
	(30)	(36)	(66)

Gamma = .10

Table 18. Zero-Order Correlations (Gammas) for Human Capital
Variables and Citizenship Status, Earnings for
Ground Crew Workers (N = 66)

Dependent variable	Independent variable			
	Citizenship status	Age	Experi-ence	Job experi-ence
Average weekly earnings	.10	−.19	.14	.12
Citizenship status (documented high)		−.42	−.63	−.59
Mean scores				
Documented		31	9.2	7.1
Undocumented		26	5.8	4.8
Standard deviation				
Documented		7.1	5.6	3.9
Undocumented		5.7	4.5	3.6

tional and general experience definitely are. This parallels
conclusions drawn in the earlier analysis.

It stands to reason, therefore, that the effects of citizenship
should again be revealed through examination of income
determination for the different categories of citizenship
status. The computations from those tables are reported in
table 19. While the small sample size tends to make gener-
alizations a bit risky, several important elements can be
suggested:

1. For green-cards, earnings tend to decline with age; for
    undocumented workers, age is unrelated to income.
    This is largely a result of the smaller variance in the
    age of indocumentados. In other words, documented
    workers tend to work longer, but suffer the effects of
    physical deterioration on earnings. Undocumented

Table 19. Subgroup Correlations (Gammas) for Human Capital
and Earnings Variables by Citizenship Status

	Zero-order coefficient	Subgroup correlation/coefficient	
		Documented (N = 30)	Undocumented (N = 36)
Earnings by age	−.19	.08	−.40
Earnings by industry experience	.14	.41	−.07
Earnings by job experience	.12	.30	.06

workers, by contrast, stay in the harvest for a shorter
period, that is, they are either burned out earlier or
rotate through the industry at a much higher rate.

2. For green-cards, earnings increase with greater experience in the harvest (up to the point where age and
physical endurance counteract). For undocumented
workers, harvest experience has no effect on earnings;
they reach a level and maintain it.

3. For documented workers, increased job experience has
a small but positive effect on earnings, suggesting that
with time in the job documented workers come to
achieve slightly better pay. Once again, undocumented
workers gain nothing from increased experience,
suggesting that levels of earnings are achieved fairly
early on and maintained irrespective of job tenure.

The survey data demonstrate that despite different levels
of experience and different patterns of employment, documented and undocumented workers achieve roughly equal
levels of earnings. Since documented and undocumented
workers reported earning equivalent piece-rates, such a
finding cannot be explained through some process of pay

discrimination, that is, a situation where undocumented workers may actually outproduce documented workers but are paid a lower piece-rate. The conclusions drawn from this analysis can only indirectly render support for the original argument—that indocumentados are used to affect productivity levels for all workers. However far from conclusive the data may be, they do illustrate that differences in work experience are related to citizenship status.

5

Comparative Case Studies: Miracle Vegetable and Verde Lettuce

Up to this point the analysis of the social organization of production in the lettuce industry has focused on the general effects of citizenship on labor market processes. I have argued that citizenship has been used both to affect the allocation of workers into different work situses and to perpetuate employer control over production. Here I will focus more directly on the ways in which the political vulnerability of labor enhances managerial control over the ground crew. I will use comparative material from fieldwork and interviews conducted at two major lettuce-producing firms to make the following arguments: first, that the recruitment of undocumented workers has the effect of increasing crew productivity and stability while decreasing worker control over production; second, that despite efforts on the part of documented workers to reproduce their skills as organization, the presence of indocumentados undercuts crew solidarity; and third, that the inability to control labor supply has resulted in major organizational problems for farm worker unions.

The rationale and the methodology behind the comparative case studies deserves brief comment before proceeding. The decision to include a comparison of the organization and managerial strategies of two lettuce firms was informed by a desire to make concrete the manner in which citizenship status surfaces in the labor process. In particular, the inability of the survey data to "get at" the organizational effects of nonmarket statuses made more detailed analysis necessary. Fieldwork in the lettuce harvest provided ample evidence that the manipulation of citizenship is not simply an idle sociological assertion. Rather, those practices and their consequences are indeed real, even if they are covered up or, as I will show in the first case, if they are officially ignored.

The choice of the two cases—Miracle Vegetable Co. and Verde Lettuce, Inc.—was made for several reasons. First, the companies offered significant differences. Though both had been acquired by multinational corporations, they had widely divergent financial histories. A comparison offered the opportunity to see whether their financial fortunes were at all related to their strategies of work organization. Miracle and Verde also had different histories and reputations in the field of labor relations. Miracle was widely regarded as a "leader" in innovative labor relations and had a long-standing relationship with labor unions. Verde, by contrast, has had a turbulent history of labor-management conflict from continuous and entrenched unionization drives. Differences in terms of management practice and union organization (since each company dealt with a different union) thus offered room for fruitful comparison.

Second, these two firms maintained sufficient similarities in organization to draw conclusions about the major arguments without too great a fear of intervening variables confounding the analysis. That is, both firms are vertically integrated and produce a variety of agricultural commodities in addition to lettuce; but, in both cases, lettuce remains the major source of revenue. Thus, Miracle and Verde could be analyzed without concern that major differences such as scale of production, breadth of activities, or market position might render the comparison groundless.

Finally, resources and time limited the inclusion of a larger number of firms in the sample. While this cannot of course serve as a scientific justification, it represented an inescapable condition of the research process. Descriptive data on the general organization of other firms were available from interviews and other sources (Friedland et al., 1981:chap. 3) but, since they did not offer any insight on the subject of this study, they were not included.

MIRACLE VEGETABLE COMPANY

The enigmatic character of Miracle Vegetable Co. is similar in many respects to that of IBM and other giant corporations which have, through one means or another, successfully avoided sustained challenges to managerial control over the work process. Long a giant in the lettuce industry, Miracle remained a place of relative calm during the highly publicized union drives among lettuce workers in the 1960s and 1970s. Miracle's reputation in the industry for technological innovations is matched by its competitors' envy for what appears to be some secret in their labor relations. As the executive vice president of a major competitor confided in an interview:

> We don't have any idea how they manage to consistently produce the highest quality pack and still have so few labor problems. Frankly, it's likely that we'll never learn. But, it would be worth a lot of money to us if we could.

The key element in Miracle's success has been its highly effective use of undocumented aliens in undercutting the organizational potential of the ground crews. The establishment and perpetuation of this form of control has been accomplished through two related tactics. First, and most important, the core organizational device in maintaining this strategy is the decentralization of recruitment and supervision to the level of the foreman, making him the functional equivalent of the labor contractor. Second, the company has effectively insulated itself from the intrusion of militant union organizers through agreements with a large rival union that has shown little interest in farm workers.

I will consider these latter issues in reverse order, since the role of the foreman is much more important to the analysis.

Low-Profile Unionism

While other companies turned to the Teamsters Union (International Brotherhood of Teamsters) for protection from the United Farm Workers (UFW) only in the early 1970s, Miracle has had a long-standing relationship with it (Friedland and Thomas, 1974; Sosnick, 1978:326–348). That relationship has been built around a series of contracts which nominally cover farm workers, but which are focused more on the protection of nonfield union members, for example, produce drivers and over-the-road truckers. The Teamster contracts have generally ceded control over work organization and technology to management in return for wage packages consistently higher than those offered by non-Teamster companies.

Union representatives keep a low profile at the company. After six weeks at Miracle, I was approached by a union representative for the first and only time. The representative came because several new workers (including me) had not yet signed dues authorization forms (allowing Miracle to subtract the union initiation fees and monthly dues). At the time of the study the union had assigned three representatives for the more than 1,000 fieldworkers employed by Miracle.

Despite a jurisdictional agreement between the Teamsters and UFW stipulating that the Teamsters will gradually remove themselves from farm worker organizing, the Teamsters have a substantial vested interest in remaining at Miracle. To be more precise, they have several million dollars in pension funds collected from fieldworkers over the period of their contracts. Although the dispensation of that money is presently being adjudicated, the Teamsters are not likely to abandon the company in the near future. As the president of Miracle concluded: "I don't think they're going to walk away from the money. Not without a fight anyway."

Most important, the Teamsters have played an insulating role for the company. While seeing to it that Miracle paid slightly better wages than its competitors, the union has acted to maintain its organizational position and has, therefore, enabled the company to carry on its activities virtually free of disturbance from outside organizers.

Decentralized Recruitment and Supervision

The most important element in Miracle's labor relations derives from its internalization of the labor contractor system, a form of labor recruitment and supervision closely tied to the use of undocumented workers. As described in the preceding chapter, the foreman operates as the functional equivalent of the old labor contractor. At Miracle, this has been carried out through the decentralization of recruitment and supervision to the level of the foreman. The approach is best summarized in the words of the director of personnel:

> When it comes to dealing with the men in the field, the lechugeros, we [personnel office] try to keep a low profile. The foremen are the most important representatives of the company. They think like the workers do and they know what it takes to make things run smooth . . . to keep the crews running and to make sure there's no problem.
>
> One of the foremen once told me, he said: "This isn't a big company. It's a lot of small companies put together." I think that's a good description of the way we like to run things.

Although the ideology of "many small companies" tends to show up in the public relations of many large corporations (particularly conglomerates fearful of being thought of as too big or powerful), the emphasis on the foreman's role in labor relations and work organization is quite concrete and purposive at Miracle. Higher level management practice is organized simultaneously to decentralize the functions of labor recruitment, supervision, and personnel relations and to tie the foreman's position and future within the organization to the performance of his crew. The result, as I will demonstrate, is a system of management that rewards foremen for effectively manipulating workers and undermining their capacity for autonomous organization. This shows up most concretely in the use of undocumented workers; however, the foreman's practice in this regard is carried out without the express consent of higher level management.

Despite the fact that Miracle maintains an office at company headquarters ostensibly for the purpose of hiring and placing workers, the bulk of hiring takes place in two locations: in the field or in the company bus yard where the crews assemble each morning. The foremen are the principal conduits into a job. Foremen use a variety of networks for recruiting workers. Interviews with foremen and workers show that there are basically four ways in which workers are recruited: through friends and family of the foreman, the foreman's own kin networks; through other workers; through walk-ons, people (such as myself) who just show up looking for work; and through coyotes (smugglers), who arrange passage and employment for undocumented workers.

Within a company like Miracle where there are no intervening layers of representation between workers and management (active union representatives or a hiring hall operated by the union), the foreman is also the prime judge of the adequacy of an individual's skills and performance. Therefore, in a situation like the lettuce industry where there is high competition for work, individual workers feel obliged to express gratitude or to offer some sort of payment to the foreman in return for being hired. Several workers told me that they had to bring other foremen a bottle of tequila, food, or a gift from Mexico in order to get work or to regain a job after some absence, after having been apprehended and deported to Mexico. As I later found out, the other half of this ritual often involves the foreman's refusal to accept a gift—therefore perpetuating the worker's debt by refusing to discharge it.

While workers are all employees of Miracle Vegetable, the foreman's capacity to hire and fire restricts the individual worker's attention to the foreman and his authority. Thus, even when I tried to initiate discussions about the company in general, my workmates tended to refer to the company in terms of crews and their respective foremen. In part this might be explained by the vague impressions workers have of conditions at other companies. But, more important, it demonstrates the central role of the foreman in the administration of production. Crews were largely defined in terms of the foreman: Don Roberto is a good foreman; Don Ignacio is a hard foreman; Don Pablo was easy to get along with, and so forth.

Upper levels of management legitimate and encourage such associations by making foremen the primary, if not the singular, contact between workers and the company. For example, all orders with respect to the amount of lettuce to be cut, the allocation of fields to crews, and the relative performance of crews, in terms of quality control and productivity reports, are communicated through the foreman. Most paperwork, such as forms for claims against the medical insurance program, the credit union, payroll advances, and even paychecks, is handled by the foreman. The foreman's role makes it possible for workers to get such things taken care of without having to travel to company headquarters, especially since company offices often close before the crews arrive back from the fields.

In a similar vein, the foreman comes to be viewed as an intermediary between the workers and the more imposing and often confusing headquarters staff. For many workers, the status differences inherent in the contrast between their soiled work clothes and limited vocabularies and the crisp white shirts and English-speaking dominance of the office staff make trips to the office trying experiences. The foreman's activities provide a means by which to avoid the embarrassment and/or humiliation created by such situations.

When it is necessary for a member of the staff, even the personnel director, to speak directly with a worker, he or she will go to the foreman to obtain his permission to pull a worker away or to otherwise disrupt crew operations. More than just a formality, such deference bolsters the foreman's respectability.

This is not to argue that workers see the foreman as invulnerable. However, the range of discretionary authority granted foremen in the area of recruitment and supervision does enable them to exercise considerable leverage over the crews.

Tying the Foreman's Position to Crew Performance

A major problem in the administration of any large-scale organization is establishing an identity of interests between lower levels of management and those of the organization as a whole. Within Miracle, upper-level management attempts to establish that commonality of purpose by tying the foreman's future to the performance of his crew. In other words, the foreman's earnings and status in the organization are linked to the performance of his crew with regard to established criteria.

In a lengthy series of interviews conducted with a former foreman for Miracle, Eliseo Mondragon, the form of this relationship was elaborated.[1] Miracle has used a variety of techniques for rewarding foremen for achieving and/or surpassing quotas in production established by higher level management. For the first year-and-a-half of his employment (he worked for Miracle a total of five years), Mondragon was paid on a piece-rate along with his crew:

> I got paid just a little more than the cutters and packers. That way, I was always a little ahead of them ... but not much. Whenever there were good fields and a lot of work, I made good money. But when it rained or when the prices [market prices] were not good I suffered too.

Like most enthusiastic new foremen, Mondragon said that he used to push his crew as much as possible. While he argued that pushing workers to put out benefited workers most, it was also clear that his position (and paycheck) depended on their performance:

> When you're just starting out, it's very important that your crew works fast and does clean work. It's what they call a "quality pack." The field supervisor lets you know all the time that your

job is to push the crew. They always say that the better your crew does, the better you do.

For the remaining three-and-one-half years of his tenure at Miracle, Mondragon was paid a salary and offered bonuses or incentives of as much as $100 a week if his crew's productivity (cartons per hour) or quality of pack surpassed specific criteria. But, longer range incentives were also offered, such as promises of promotion to assistant field supervisor or higher pay and better benefits.

These incentives meant a lot to the foremen, especially to those who aspired to a status and a position that clearly distinguished them from ordinary field hands:

> My dream was to drive around in a *carro blanco* [white company car] in a leather jacket and nice pants and to spend my day just ripping open cartons of lettuce and checking them out. You know, checking to see they're packed right and that the heads are good. I'll tell you, that's a feeling of power when you can tell some foreman that he better shape up.

Aspirations, thus fueled by incentives and promises, get translated into strategies on the part of foremen to squeeze the maximum effort out of their crews. It is in this nexus that the foreman's role as labor contractor, described earlier, comes into full play. When I questioned Mondragon about the "tricks" he might use to spur his crew on, he replied:

> There aren't any tricks. What there is are ways to do things. Lechugeros may not have much education, but they aren't dumb. So you can't trick them. What you have to have are ways to reward and to punish.

Rewards and punishments can be applied to individuals or to the crew as a unit. They become a way in which foremen can create indebtedness among individual crew members, for example, by grants of leave for trips to see family, hiring of crew members' friends, or forgiveness for unexcused absences. When I overslept on two separate occasions, the foreman of my crew, Don Pablo, chided me for missing work and threatened to have me replaced if I did not work especially hard to make up for lost time. Other incidents involved workers who left on Friday afternoon and did not return to work until the following Monday or Tuesday. In all cases, the foreman did not take formal punitive action but instead either reminded workers that they were dispensable or that they owed their jobs to the foreman himself, that is, their actions were not so much an infraction against the employment contract as an affront to the generosity of the foreman. On the crew level, foremen can occasionally secure longer hours and/or better fields for the crew, though such rewards are generally based on the past performance of the crew.

Political Manipulation of Crews

The primary strategy for control is built around the use of undocumented aliens. In an organization in which the foreman's earnings and future opportunities are determined by crew output, the most logical and rational strategy for foremen is one that maximizes the likelihood of worker cooperation. Mondragon put it quite succinctly:

> You get guys without papers and you get a crew that's going to be easy to handle. It's as simple as that. . . . They want to work and they need the money—and you're in a position to do them that favor.

Being across the border illegally creates tremendous pressures on workers, as the earlier sections of this chapter indicated. Foremen can manipulate those pressures two ways: through protection or intimidation. With regard to protection, the workplace can be made to resemble a refuge from the Border Patrol. Given that Border Patrol stations are understaffed as far north as the Salinas Valley (450 miles north of the border), raids are generally focused on sites outside of the fields—in transient hotels and bars—where the likelihood of catching undocumented workers is greater. Thus, the chances of being apprehended in the fields are reduced, though not eliminated. Many workers, both documented and undocumented, assumed that their employers were either in league with the Border Patrol or had paid them to stay away. Since no one had solid evidence of such collusion, I had to consider such remarks hearsay. However, an incident that occurred during my fieldwork suggested that there indeed existed an informal system through which foremen "protected" undocumented workers. This incident will be described in some detail because it clearly illustrates one aspect of the foreman's role.

The ground crew in which I was a cutter was working in a field bracketed on two sides by tall eucalyptus trees. These trees obscured the access road into the field. Several times during one particular day, a Border Patrol observation plane was spotted overhead. The sight of the plane sparked some concern in the crew but the foreman, Don Pablo, suggested that the Border Patrol was not interested in us. Instead, he argued, they were looking for scabs in a nearby ranch that was being picketed by the United Farm Workers. During a brief break at midday, however, one of the loaders reported a call for the foreman on the truck radio. One of the company truck drivers traveling on the freeway parallel to the field apparently had spotted two Border Patrol cars at the edge of the trees and another pair of vans approaching from the other side. The foreman jumped from the truck yelling and waving his arms. "Migra! Migra!" he yelled. Workers, cartons, and lettuce scattered in all directions as the Border Patrol vans belatedly emerged from their cover. I too ran, following a member of my trio as we scurried for the protection of a vineyard in a field adjacent to the lettuce. From our vantage point, Cipriano, a fellow cutter, and I watched as the Border Patrol agents, with visible disappointment, rooted out and took away three of our workmates. Nearly thirty minutes after the Border Patrol departed, the crew reassembled. Though shaken by the experience, workers fell back to harvesting almost immediately and the crew was adjusted to make up for the loss.

Later that evening, crew members celebrated our good fortune in losing so few to la migra, and speculated on their fate. Although there was an undertone of contempt for the

Border Patrol, Don Pablo was praised several times—even by workers who had grumbled about his methods of supervision before. "So he's a bastard," smiled Cipriano, "at least he knows he's got to take care of us." Incidents such as this help to put the foreman in good stead with the crew and further the image of the company as protector of the workers.

The other equally important side of this issue is intimidation. Foremen need never directly mention a worker's status or take action on the basis of it for the consequences of being undocumented to be understood. As Mondragon, the former Miracle foreman, advised:

> The worst thing you can do is turn a guy over to la migra. If he's been screwing up or causing you trouble, you talk to him. You remind him that he's got a family to feed. That maybe he wants to buy a car or something. . . . You maybe mention that it's tough finding work if you get fired. If he still doesn't understand, then you remind him he's got no papers. If he doesn't understand then, he won't be around long anyway.

In my own crew, it was not clear until the incident with the Border Patrol that any of my co-workers were undocumented. With the celebration that followed the aborted raid, however, Cipriano introduced me to some of the undocumented workers in the crew. As it turned out, undocumented workers outnumbered documented workers by two to one (24 to 12) and only five of the eighteen cutters carried legitimate papers.

With the exception of two of the closers, all these men had worked in the lettuce harvest before. Of the undocumented workers, the majority (15 of 24) had worked for Miracle and Don Pablo in previous seasons. The remainder had joined the crew six months before, during the harvest in the Imperial Valley. Of the documented workers, half had joined the crew in Imperial and the other half had begun work with the season in Salinas. This latter group consisted of UFW members whose companies were being struck at the time. This amalgam of workers, brought together through open hiring in Salinas as well as Don Pablo's own networks, provided an opportune unit for comparing the treatment of documented and undocumented workers.

Having observed no ostensible differences in the way in which the two groups of workers were dealt with by Don Pablo or other supervisors, I began to search out other avenues. Recruitment processes emerged as a vital link among the undocumented workers. Of the two dozen indocumentados, two-thirds had gotten their jobs at Miracle through the same network: a coyote named Dominguez who operated out of the border town of Mexicali, some fifteen miles south of the Imperial Valley town of El Centro, California. The remainder had come through other channels such as workers they knew in the crew, friends of Don Pablo, or through field-hiring, like mine. Several in the group that had come through Dominguez had similar geographic origins in Mexico (near Hermosillo), but the majority had either been told to make contact with Dominguez in Mexicali or had heard of him in a bar or a store on the border.

Dealing with Dominguez, it turned out, was no inexpensive affair: according to one worker, the trip across the border and the prearranged job with Miracle cost $500. Though it was not clear that Don Pablo was the recipient of part of that $500, Cipriano and several of the others had been placed at the same time in Don Pablo's crew. Workers in other crews, they pointed out, had also come through Dominguez.

The fact of such a sizable investment weighed heavily on the minds of the workers, even if three weeks of steady work could replenish that fund. Cipriano and another worker, Chuy, often spent time after work in hushed conversation debating alternative ways to cross the border and find work. More important, however, the time lost to repaying their loans served as a reminder of their precarious position—a position Cipriano believed they held at the pleasure of Don Pablo:

> He's a sly one. He never says anything about Dominguez, but he knows. When he gave me my paycheck last Friday, he says, "Be careful with all that money. You don't want to have to buy your way across again." He knows I have to stay in line.

Ponce, another of the undocumented workers, recounted an admonition he received from Dominguez prior to being brought to work in the Imperial Valley: "You cooperate with Don Pablo, he said, and you will make a lot of money. If you don't do what he says, you have wasted your money."

In interviews with Mondragon before I had begun my fieldwork, I had asked about the use of coyotes. Mondragon replied that he had never dealt directly with the coyotes, but knew that other foremen did. Other networks, he suggested, were equally available and occasionally provided dividends. According to him, undocumented workers were recommended by family members of friends who already worked in the crew or for Miracle. Using those channels, the foremen can get the most "cooperative" labor and, at the same time, grant favors to crew members. Those crew members, in turn, help socialize new workers to the organization of work and to the style of the foreman. Indocumentados are introduced by documented workers as well as other undocumented workers. In the former case, however, the documented worker comes to share the vulnerability of his compadre. According to Mondragon: "If his friend screws up or tries to give me a bad time, I go to the guy who brought him in and say, 'Hey, tell that guy to straighten out or you both go.'" Thus, crews stacked with a mixture of documented and undocumented workers share a community of fate determined by the status of the most vulnerable members. For the company, the investment workers make in order to get across the border acts both as a lever to compel workers to comply with the foreman's directives and as an incentive, which the company does not pay. In this sense, citizenship acts like a special human capital investment that benefits the firm, not the workers. For the foreman, the fact of illegality becomes a lever with which to move the entire crew in the direction of his (and, of course, the company's) purpose: sustaining high productivity.

The numerical dominance of undocumented workers in my own crew and their concentration in the key cutting and packing positions lent support to this argument. However, it is difficult to assess the effects comparatively; most other companies were hit by the United Farm Workers lettuce strike and data from those firms would have been biased by the presence and presumed inexperience of the strikebreaking workers.[2] The only other group available for comparison was the striking UFW members in the crew. Their observations prove enlightening.

During the time I worked in the ground crew at Miracle, the UFW members formed a close circle within the crew. They made up two trios by themselves and often isolated themselves during breaks and before and after work. As it turned out, all six had worked for Verde Lettuce prior to the strike and averaged just over three years seniority with that company. All were working at some risk to their jobs at Verde, but as Cruz (one of the workers) explained: "When you have a wife, kids, and more family to take care of, you think of them first and the union second."

Over several days of briefly asking about the progress of the strike—a subject they discussed frequently—I began to query them about working at Miracle in comparison to Verde. Their response was unanimous: things were a lot easier at Verde. The major differences centered on the pace of work and the role of the foreman. Underlying these issues, however, was a root issue: undocumented workers.

Cruz, the most open of the workers, remarked in astonishment at the pace the crew kept:

> Man, I can't believe how hard we work here. I don't even have enough time to swallow a couple of tortillas for lunch and they're already back at work. I've never worked this fast. . . . I hope they end the damned strike soon because it's nothing like this at Verde.

When I asked him to elaborate, he added:

> Here it's run, run, run. These guys all act like Don Pablo is going to give their job away if they stop to take a piss. It's crazy. . . . At Verde, we work steady, but you don't destroy yourself like this. I might make a little less money there, but at least I can sleep when I'm done. . . . I'm so sore sometimes I want to cry.

As it turned out, during the time of my fieldwork Cruz estimated that he earned $50–$75 more per week working at

Miracle. It was an insufficient bonus, he argued, to make up for the added physical punishment.

Complaints centered on Don Pablo's style of supervision as well. Unlike foremen at Verde, who cede much of the regulation of work pace to the crew itself, Don Pablo spent most of the day walking between trios, watching and commenting on our work. His comments to the Verde workers were biting at times. "Hard to keep up?" he would ask with a laugh, continuing, "They will be happy to have you guys back at Verde once you learn to work fast." As we worked side by side, Cruz once commented, "The foremen at Verde are always telling us to work more like *el estilo Milagro* (Miracle-style). Now that I know what that means, I will be sure to work *el estilo Verde*."

Gilberto, another of the Verde workers, summarized the difference in this way:

> At Verde, the union is strong. We have a lot more to say about the work. The foreman doesn't breathe on you because if he does, you slow down. You have all your friends to back you up. Here I'll bet they never even heard of a grievance.

Nevertheless, while working in Don Pablo's crew, the Verde workers and the others kept the pace set by the leading undocumented workers. This fact did not go unnoticed by the documented workers, but it was not connected to the other issues until I raised it in roundabout fashion. I asked Cruz if the UFW required identification before they gave job dispatches out of the hiring hall. "No," he replied, but went on to argue that the union served as a buffer between the workers and the company:

> There [at Verde] when you get seniority, it gives you some protection. You work with the same guys all the time and everybody backs everybody else. . . . It's not like here. Here, everybody looks out for themselves. They are always looking for la migra because they're scared if they don't work hard or keep Don Pablo happy, the pigs are going to snatch them away.

Thus, the lack of solidarity in the crew, occasioned by the vulnerability of its key members, affects the pace of all involved.

In essence, crews need not be composed entirely of undocumented workers to be manipulated by the foremen and
the company. The placement of vulnerable workers in key
positions provides the means by which crew organization is
effectively undercut. By creating conditions under which the
fate of crew members is fundamentally affected by the status
of its most vulnerable members, political control over the
labor market is reproduced as control over the labor process.

Company Policy and Foreman's Practice

Executives at Miracle Vegetable Company and other lettuce
firms expressed a fairly uniform attitude with respect to undocumented workers. First, they argued, management does
not knowingly hire undocumented workers. And second,
management should not be held legally responsible, under
any conditions, for hiring undocumented aliens. Thus, personnel staff at Miracle do not admit that undocumented workers are employed on a regular basis. Neither would they
comment on the hiring practices of competing companies.

According to Mondragon, the Miracle foreman, he was
never told or advised to hire undocumented workers. Rather,
he observed the practices of other foremen and followed suit:

> I got fired because the Border Patrol had it in for me. I gave
> them a bad time once when they stopped my bus and their boss
> told them to make life miserable for me. I guess I became a
> target and my bosses didn't like that. . . . When I started out, I
> just looked around and saw what other foremen did and I did
> the same.

"Doing the same" meant using undocumented workers as a
lever, a trump card in managing the crew and achieving the
goals established as criteria for the security and advancement
of the foreman.

Thus, at least within Miracle Vegetable Company, higher
level management, as a matter of company policy, maintains
an arm's length from the actual recruitment and hiring of
undocumented immigrants. By subcontracting these functions to the foreman/labor contractors within the organiza-

tion and establishing criteria of performance that cannot be achieved without an increment in control, the firm effectively mandates the practice of recruiting and manipulating undocumented workers in the crews. Of course this strategy of "official ignorance" has parallels in numerous other settings, especially when informal and historically accepted practices contradict the official purposes of ethics of an organization. The studies of white collar crime (Sutherland, 1977) and the Watergate experience are other examples of the same situation. It is not illegal, however, for employers to hire undocumented workers, while it is against the law for undocumented workers to seek employment.

The enigmatic character of Miracle's labor relations success therefore reduces to the institutionalization of the labor contractor system and to the development of a managerial strategy that places greatest emphasis on control through the manipulation of citizenship status.

VERDE LETTUCE, INCORPORATED

Verde Lettuce offers an important contrast to Miracle in several respects. Though, like Miracle, Verde is a subsidiary of a larger, transnational corporation, it has had a turbulent financial and organizational history. Created through the acquisition of several private firms by the parent corporation, Verde has struggled since its beginning to achieve some measure of financial stability. According to industry sources, Verde has run at a deficit for most of its existence.[3] Sources outside the company lay the blame on the inexperience of management imported from outside of the lettuce industry. Others suggest that having a "sugar daddy" parent corporation has tended to make Verde's management careless in its approach to cost and efficiency. All those interviewed, however, laid a portion (if not all) of the blame on the company's labor problems.

Labor problems take the shape of the United Farm Worker's union. Verde has been the scene of over a decade of continuous and aggresive labor organizing by the UFW, which won one of its first lettuce industry contracts at Verde and has since attempted to use the company as a model for its organizational campaigns. Union officials see Verde as both the testing ground for various innovations in work organization and union representation and as a trend-setter in contract negotiations.

In interviews prior to the 1979 lettuce strike, UFW organizers boasted of the union's influence in Verde's operations. One organizer, a former lettuce cutter who had worked for one of the companies subsumed with the creation of Verde, argued:

> We have the strongest and most militant union in the country. Here at Verde we have the foremen so scared of getting a grievance thrown at them that they just turn away when the workers refuse to do something.

While that may be something of an exaggeration, unionization does mean something different at Verde than it does at Miracle. However, what remains problematic at Verde, and throughout the industry, is the capacity of a union organization to overcome the effects of employers' nonmarket control over the labor force. Can an organization that is incapable of controlling access to the labor market or particular work situses still succeed in capitalizing on the organizational potential of the crews? Or, to turn the question around, can a union organization attempt to affect change in a system based on disadvantaged labor without simultaneously creating conflict between advantaged and disadvantaged labor?

To this point, the analysis has emphasized the effects of citizenship with regard to crew organization. Here I will turn to the argument that the political vulnerability of undocumented labor has created major organization obstacles for farm worker unionism. Despite the success of the United Farm Workers union in creating and sustaining an unprecedented level of worker organization at Verde and other companies, the inability of the union to "professionalize" the ground crews (organize and protect the labor market position) directly resulted from its inability to control labor supply. In an attempt to remove the effects of politically vulnerable labor the union has sought to replace the foreman's discretion with its own regulation of employment—the hiring hall. At the same time, however, this strategy has created cleavages in the membership along the lines of citizenship.

To illustrate these issues more clearly I will focus on two organizational factors that appear most at variance with the analysis of Miracle Vegetable Company. These two factors— the role of the foreman and the strength of crew organization—are good indicators of the degree of difference between the two companies, which may be attributed to active union organization.

The Role of the Foreman

A major UFW objective at Verde and other union companies has been the reduction of the authority of the foreman. The establishment of a union-controlled hiring hall system was intended to take away from foremen the ability to directly select crew members and thus manipulate crews on the basis of favors. Workers are now dispatched via the hiring hall to union companies for job assignments. Once in a job individuals have the opportunity to establish both seniority with a company and an occupational classification (e.g., cutter or loader). Companies like Verde are officially bound by the contract to honor seniority and to notify the union of any impending job openings. Companywide rules and regulations with regard to seniority thus reduce the foreman's discretionary authority in placing and/or promoting workers.[4]

According to the union contract, harvest crews at Verde are organized along the lines of seniority: crews are composed of workers with roughly the same amount of time in their individual occupations. For example, cutters with about seven years' occupational seniority will be located in the same crew. Thus, crews can remain intact from one season or production area to the next. The major exception occurs, however, in the low seniority crews. These crews, according to interviews with workers, experience greater turnover in personnel. Turnover is attributed to two factors: (1) workers who try harvesting lettuce and decide it's not for them, and (2) work is more intermittent and, therefore, employment (and earnings) fluctuates considerably. Because they serve as a relief valve to accommodate periods of high and low production, low seniority crews often work shorter hours.

Job security and the assurance of work are the major benefits associated with seniority. Seniority workers do not receive higher wages or piece-rates for their work but they are provided more stable work than their newer counterparts. The organizational implications of these differences are quite important.

The creation of a formal grievance procedure has also been aimed at limiting the authority of foremen. Crew representatives, the equivalent of shop stewards, have used the grievance machinery for the adjudication of complaints ranging from insufficient ice water in the fields to allegedly unjustified firings. The liberal use of grievances prompted Verde's vice president to complain:

> A grievance for them is nothing. . . . They get a day out of work maybe and we lose thousands of dollars on each one. . . . During the twenty-seven years I've been associated with agriculture, I can't remember one formal grievance being filed by any of the Teamster truck drivers . . . either against this company or any of its predecessors. During the first two years of our contract with the UFW we had no less than eighteen formal grievances filed. Those are grievances that went beyond the company to outside mediation.

While the union flexes its muscles through the grievance procedure, it further acts to undermine the traditionally paternalistic relationship between foremen and workers. Throughout its organizational campaigns, the union has constantly emphasized the formality of the relationship between workers and management. An organizer instrumental in the 1979 strike at Verde described it this way:

> One of the biggest things we have to do is break down the walls between workers. Everybody is so used to having a deal with

their foremen that they don't know that they are all working
for Mr. So-and-So and the board of directors. We just keep
saying over and over, "You're a member of the United Farm
Workers union and an employee of Verde Lettuce."

To enforce that distinction, the union seeks to remain visible in the fields. Union representatives are included in every
crew and a companywide ("ranch") committee of representatives meets regularly with management. Negotiation committees are also staffed by rank-and-file members, though like
other unions contract negotiators are primarily paid union
staff.

Although hiring halls, grievance procedures, and union
representation cannot by themselves limit the authority of the
foremen, they do act to circumscribe the foreman's discretion,
particularly when compared with the situation at Miracle. In
the ground crews particularly the union has sought to increase
the strength of the crew organization as a means by which to
ensure some protection from arbitrary managerial intervention. However, an examination of the organization of the
high and low seniority crews suggests that crew strength,
especially in terms of the crew ability to withstand management intervention in work organization, is inversely related
to crew seniority.

Crew Strength and Seniority

Interviews with a lettuce worker with eight years' seniority at
Verde and another with one year at the company provide
very different descriptions of labor-management relations in
the ground crews. Veteran workers boast of the accomplishments of the union and the strength of the crews; low seniority
workers describe the insecurity of their position and the ex-
cesses of company management. Such distinctions might be
attributable to the relative positions of older and younger
workers in an industrial plant where seniority translates into
higher skill and a more protected organizational position. At
Verde, however, there is no real skill distinction in the work
of those with more or less seniority. The workers with the

most seniority are more protected, as far as job security is concerned, but the distinctions to which low seniority workers refer are indications of something far more important. They are indications of a two-tiered system of employment and crew organization at Verde: a system consisting of stable, protected crews at the top and unstable, less protected crews at the bottom.

Interviews with union officials and senior workers give the impression that unionization has insulated harvest crews from direct managerial interference in work organization, recruitment, and work pace. Backed by the protections of a union contract and the machinery of a grievance procedure, they argue, workers have been able to fend off many of the abuses of the former labor system. Several Verde workers boasted that they were able to cut and pack *basura* (garbage or low quality lettuce) without fear of reprisal. More important, according to one union organizer, manipulation of undocumented workers has been diminished as a managerial strategy as a result of the extension of the union's organizational umbrella.

Interviews with present and former Verde workers, however, presented important departures from this overview.[5] In an effort to demonstrate how crew organization differs among high and low seniority workers, I will concentrate on three key issues in crew and work organization: demands for productivity increases; management intervention in work organization; and the role played by undocumented workers.

Increased Productivity

Work slowdowns and stoppages have been a major issue at Verde since the advent of unionization. According to the senior workers, many of these have had to do with management attempts to increase productivity. Resistance to the intensification of work is by no means unique to the lettuce fields (Roy, 1952; Collins et al., 1946; Aronowitz, 1973; Burawoy, 1979). However, the difference in the capacity of crews to present effective opposition to such moves is evident at Verde. A lechugero with nearly nine years' seniority at Verde presented this portrait of an unsuccessful speedup:

> The foreman began one week by yelling about how we were not working hard enough. He said we were going to get second-cuts if we didn't start getting over 450 cartons an hour. He complained all about quality, too. . . .
> A couple of us just told him to fuck himself . . . that we were going as fast as we could. He called up the supervisor and he came out and started yelling, too. They wouldn't listen to us, so we just stopped working until a member of the ranch commit-tee showed up. They left and we went back to work. The next day we came back and the foreman didn't say a word.

By contrast, workers in the less senior crews painted a much different picture. Said one worker,

> We're always under pressure about how we do the work and how much work there's going to be. They move the crews around all the time. The foremen and the bosses are always telling us if we don't pack fast enough that there's not going to be as much work.

Complaining of the same situation, another worker compared the situation in low and high seniority crews:

> In the seniority crews, when they don't want to work so hard, they just slow down. The foremen don't really do anything. With us, if we try that, the foremen just say, "Fine, one of the other crews needs the work." If we go to the union and com-plain, they just say we have to go along.

Following a management drive in 1978 to increase produc-tivity, the union held a number of meetings with crews. More senior workers I questioned about these meetings tended to pass off the union's pleas for increased cooperation between workers and management as a joke. Low seniority workers, however, said they felt the pressure almost immediately:

> The foreman really got down on us about quotas and quality. We went to our crew representative and he said the union told him we had to go along because the union had an agreement.

Work Organization

Conflicts over management intervention in the organization of work largely center on the issue of replacement workers. Both absenteeism and inefficiency in hiring hall procurement of new and temporary workers have been major management complaints during the life of the UFW contract. Among senior workers, the maintenance of the hiring hall and crew input on the selection of replacement workers is held as a paramount union right. In an incident described to me by a lechugero who had been with the company for seven years and with his present crew for over five years, these two points were stressed:

> Two of our cutters left to go back home because they were brothers and their father was dying. So, we were going to be short for a while. The foreman brought in two of his friends . . . and said they would work until our compadres got back. Nobody liked that. We told him that he had to get somebody through the hiring hall and that we wouldn't work with his friends. . . . He tried to put us off, but we showed him we meant business. We dropped our knives and said he had to call the hiring hall or we didn't work. He called the hiring hall.

Among low seniority crews, however, the capacity of workers to act collectively is hampered by the constraints imposed by intermittent work and lower job security. In these entry-level positions, the competition to get and keep work acts to undercut development of the solidarity exhibited in the more senior crews. Such competition gets particularly fierce as the season shifts between major production areas, such as between Arizona (in the spring) and Salinas (in the spring-summer). At Verde, operations terminate in Arizona and then shift to the San Joaquin Valley for about six weeks. Senior workers often take this break as an opportunity to return to Mexico for a brief vacation, leaving less senior crews to pick up the slack in harvesting. During those periods Verde often hires large numbers of temporary workers, many of whom seek to earn a permanent berth in the company's labor force.

Changes in the composition of low seniority crews, coupled with their shuffling between production areas, result in competition for work and divisiveness among workers. Management has interjected itself forcefully into this situation. With respect to crew control over its makeup, a green-card with six months in the company said:

> The guys in the older crews have it good. They can decide whether they want somebody to join or not to join. But, for us it's different. We can't make a choice because we have no choice. The foreman decides and we have to work with anybody who comes in.

Or, as another worker in the same crew remarked:

> If you hang around long enough, you can move up into one of the better crews. It seems like in crews like mine, if you don't say "si, patron" to everything the foreman wants, then you don't get as much work and you don't make as much money.

Undocumented Aliens

The most important difference in the organization of the high and low seniority crews is the role in each by undocumented workers. Whether out of loyalty to their workmates or true ignorance, the senior workers I interviewed reported that they knew of few cases of undocumented workers showing up in the company. One worker noted, "Hell, I wouldn't know if anybody was undocumented. I have worked with some of these guys for seven or eight years and I don't know if they have their papers." This is not to suggest that undocumented workers are not an issue in Verde or the UFW; they pose a fundamental organizational problem for the union. However, among the senior workers, the only salience the issue had pertained to the strike taking place in the fields. During the 1979 strike undocumented workers composed a significant portion of the strikebreakers imported by management at Verde and elsewhere. The union responded in the summer of 1979 by calling on the Immigration and Naturalization Service to step up raids on the fields as a means to stop production and enforce the strike.

But, in reference to normal (nonstrike) operations at Verde, senior workers refuted the notion that one's citizenship status made any difference. A common refrain from these workers was that "we are union members first."

Workers from low seniority crews relate a very different situation, which was first revealed in conversation with a lechugero picketing at fieldside during the strike:

> Those guys out there are all members of my crew. . . . We started working together last summer. In the winter, when the union decided to strike, I figured they would stay home like the rest of us. But they didn't. What do they care? None of them has papers and so they really have nothing to lose.

This same worker went on to describe how his crew had been made up of undocumented workers:

> They take advantage of the union. Nobody asks to see your papers when you go to get a dispatch. . . . They just walk onto the job. The foremen find out and they try to squeeze those guys and it ends up making it rough for everybody in the crew. . . . You have to fight to stay up with them because if you don't you might not keep your job. I went to the union office and told them about it, too. I told them there were at least fifteen indocumentados in my crew. They said they would see about it, but they never did anything. . . . Now those guys are out there scabbing against the union.

Subsequent interviews with other low seniority workers, documented and undocumented, provided a similar picture. Green-cards complained of being pushed harder and having to compete with undocumented workers in an effort to keep their jobs. Undocumented workers, including some of the strikebreakers, described threats attached to foremen's assessments of their performance. For example, one worker repeated his foreman's warning: "The union won't do a thing to protect you." Several workers openly criticized the union for protecting *los veteranos* (the more senior workers) and overlooking the less senior lechugeros and what went on in the crews. Union officials refused to comment on these complaints when I approached them.

The two-tiered system depicted above reflects less a union betrayal of low seniority crews than it does (1) an attempt on the part of management at Verde to reassert control via the manipulation of citizenship, and (2) more fundamentally, the inability of the union to change a labor system imposed by management.

Reassertion of Managerial Control

For most of the period of unionization at Verde, the company's organizational position, as a subsidiary of a prosperous conglomerate, provided fertile soil for the kind of achievements gained by the UFW for more senior crews. The company's ability to absorb or pass along losses in its operation to the parent corporation provided a buffer that allowed the union to acquire and enforce considerable advances in crew strength and benefits. Virtually unencumbered by the restraints characterizing less financially secure enterprises, Verde sought accommodation with the union, as it had done with unions in other phases of production, while the union sought to establish a model for its other contracts.

A major overhaul of management in 1977–78, however, accompanied by what one new executive described as a warning "that the company had three years to turn things around," resulted in an offensive to curb the union. One of the opening salvos of the campaign was a threat to replace ground crews with wrap machines, a direct challenge to the core of the union's strength. "We made it clear," the head of personnel proclaimed, "that we weren't going to put up with their actions any longer. Either they began policing membership about productivity and quality or we started shipping more wrapped lettuce."

This campaign found its strongest expression in the recent lettuce strike. Negotiators for Verde and the other struck companies opened fire on the union's major achievements: the hiring hall, strengthening management's disciplinary procedures, and management's right to introduce new technology. Complaints about the inefficiency of the hiring hall, the union's discretion in disciplining workers, and declining productivity levels dominated industry pronouncements during the lengthy strike (see in particular, Salinas *Californian*, May 20, 1979). Threats of movement to wrap machines and even mechanical harvesters were woven into the negotiations.

In effect, this strategy represents an attempt on the part of Verde to make itself more like Miracle and other lettuce firms. As the vice president of Verde argued in a local newspaper interview in Salinas, "Restrictions in UFW contracts over management rights are worth a lot of money. Verde will match the pay and benefits given by Miracle Co., if the UFW will give Verde the same latitude in control over the work force that is maintained by Miracle."

The Union and the Labor System

The construction of a formal system of hiring, seniority, and grievance resolution has had the cumulative effect of increasing the integrity and cohesion of the more senior crews at Verde. However, the two-tiered organization of crews reflects a structural obstacle that severely limits the union's capacity to alter the relations of production. This is a problem, then, of the union trying to deal with a management-imposed labor system.

To suggest that the creation of a system of industrial justice (Selznick, 1969) has increased the organizational strength of the senior crews is far different from arguing that the crews themselves have acquired the means by which to control the work they do. While the union has succeeded in bargaining for higher wages and benefits for its members, it has not altered the structure of the labor system. The work continues to be organized around a highly destructive labor process, with occupational mobility being severely limited. Competition for jobs goes on unabated. Despite the increased wages and benefits brought about by the advance of unionization, the system continues to operate to the advantage of management because the union does not control the supply of labor available for work and because it alone cannot erase the political vulnerability associated with that labor.

Within agricultural industries, the United Farm Workers union has sought explicitly to use the communal characteristics of the labor force as the basis for organization. The remarkable success of the UFW, particularly in the lettuce and grape industries, has its roots in the stress laid on the common ethnicity, national heritage, needs, and social position of Mexican and Mexican-American, documented and undocumented workers. As Friedland and Thomas (1974:56) have noted:

> By serving genuine needs and developing organizations within which farm workers could develop trust in one another, Chavez also created a set of organizations within which farm members could develop modern organizational skills.

The bonds of solidarity created in satisfying common needs have reinforced the ethnic and cultural heritage shared by the membership.

In the lettuce campaigns, such efforts were augmented by tapping into the organization potential of the harvest crews themselves. As a union organizer described the UFW's strategy: "We have to rely on the organization of workers in the contract (piece-rate) crews to make any headway. . . . They already are very organized because of the way they work and the way they travel." As important as their role in pulling workers out on strike (and/or into the union), the UFW owes an additional historical debt to the crews: during the Teamster raids on UFW contracts in the grape industry (1971–1975), dues from the lettuce workers helped keep the union alive financially. Furthermore, lettuce workers still constitute the largest percentage of union members.

The union's very success in organizing lettuce workers has, ironically, put it in a very sticky position. On the one hand, it cannot seek to regulate the labor supply—in particular to seek curbs on the volume of undocumented workers. To do so would be to alienate itself from those workers who are undocumented *and* supporters of members of the union.

Though limiting jobs to workers who have some measure of legal protection through their immigrant visas would enable the union to better police work conditions and hiring practices, the creation of an internal division in membership would likely tear the organization apart. Such divisions already exist to some extent, especially as noted in the comments of workers in previous sections, but they have generally been muted by the union's unwillingness to take a public stand on the issue. Nonetheless, the issue of documented versus undocumented workers has periodically hampered relations between the union and other labor, political, and social organizations of Chicano and Latino groups. In particular, Chavez's decision to request increased Border Patrol raids during the height of the 1979 lettuce strike caused a storm of protest from independent farm worker union organizers in Arizona and Texas. In the letter to UFW president Chavez in April 1979, an organizer for the Maricopa County Organizing Project in Arizona argued:

> We must urge you to stop all actions that would create a greater division among documented and undocumented workers. If the United Farm Workers Union has problems with undocumented workers being brought in as scabs, the answer is to organize these scabs, like we do any other scab that comes in to break our strike. (Salinas *Californian*, May 1, 1979)

While Chavez and others within the union have argued that they will continue to organize and accept undocumented workers, dissension remains barely beneath the surface.

On the other hand, the union cannot attempt to regularize employment and create a modicum of job security without gaining control over access to employment. In an effort to do this, the union has two options: (1) to take unto itself the functions of recruitment and job allocation (in the hiring hall); or (2) to locate these functions in the individual crews themselves, bypassing a formal challenge to the organization of the labor process.

The former strategy has emerged as dominant in Verde. The union has sought to regularize employment through the establishment of seniority privileges and the hiring hall. While seniority has increased the job rights of some individuals (particularly high seniority workers), neither seniority nor the hiring hall are capable of altering the basis of wage determination. Rather, the economic rewards for seniority are largely restricted to vacation and pension benefits. Without increased differentiation in jobs and wages (such as would characterize an internal labor market) or the control over work organization (such as craft unionism), performance remains the sole determinant of earnings.

Although the seniority/hiring hall approach provides the union with a broader negotiating stance vis-à-vis management, it largely focuses the union bargaining strategy on increasing piece-rates. In order to compensate crews for the loss of control over recruitment and testing—factors instrumental in determining work pace and, therefore, wages—the union has sought to increase the payment for output. Thus, in theory, while productivity may increase through a change from speed to seniority, wages may remain constant (or even increase) for the membership as a whole.

A bitter irony faces the union should it succeed in thoroughly regularizing the seniority/hiring hall process in the lettuce industry: as the union succeeds in monopolizing access to employment and job allocation, it threatens to erode the advantages to management of the crew method. Such is the case at Verde. The investment of some workers with conditional rights in their jobs undermines the managerial strategy of control by competition and manipulation of citizenship status. Success in such an effort, as borne out at Verde, converts the crew method to a much more expensive enterprise. Thus, one alternative open for Verde's management is to attempt to reassert dominance through the recruitment and manipulation of undocumented workers.

Another alternative managerial strategy resides in the reorganization of the labor process. Following the experience of such conflicts in other industries, for example, the rationalization of automobile production, a likely strategy would involve circumventing craft-type labor through the introduction of machines. To some extent, this has already begun with the increasing volume of production from the wrap machines, which reorganize production into a set of unskilled activities coordinated by machine technology. In place of a piece-rate, workers are paid an hourly rate with the pace of work determined by the machine. In replacing the piece-rate crews with wrap machines, migrant male workers have been supplanted by women from local labor pools. Thus, gender replaces citizenship as the communal status characterizing that segment of the labor force.

The UFW walks a tightrope. If the union attempts to use monopoly access to employment as the basis for steadily increased piece-rates, while lowering the productivity of crews, it undermines the advantages of the labor system to capital. If the process of recruitment and testing are turned over to the crews, the employer strategy of competition and manipulation of citizenship will remain viable, thus reinforcing the extant characteristics of the labor system.

6

Gender, Labor Supply, and Commitment

In increasing numbers, large hulking machines resembling grounded World War II bombers are seen lumbering through the lettuce fields of California and Arizona. Groups of workers, some standing on the machine, others walking behind it, busily cut, wrap, and fill cartons with heads of lettuce.[1] Each head is individually wrapped in soft, clear-plastic film emblazoned with the logo of the company that produced it. The product of this labor process, commonly referred to as "wrapped" or "source-wrapped" lettuce, is transported to eventually grace the shelves of produce counters, looking (ironically) both antiseptic and farm fresh.

Though the wrap machine technology is not as sophisticated as an electronic tomato harvester or a robot welder in an automobile plant, it does represent a significant change in both the labor process and the labor system. Unlike the ground crew, wrap crew productivity is much less a function of crew regulation and skill and much more a function of mechanical coordination. And, in contrast to earlier production systems characterized by massive inputs of labor and individualized piece-rates, the wrap machine employs large amounts of labor *and* capital.

Like the process of capital intensification undertaken by the Ford Motor Company some fifty years earlier, these mobile "lettuce assembly lines" have transformed the social organization of production. But, as in the automobile industry in 1914, capital intensification has raised important issues in labor organization and utilization. In other words, the profitability of the investment in the machine and in the new technology is dependent on four factors: (1) the continuous use of the equipment; (2) the availability of a stable labor supply; (3) the appearance of the same worker on a regular basis; and (4) the continuing demand for wrapped lettuce (especially from institutional buyers), demonstrated in the premium price paid for it. That is, in order for the investment to be realized, labor turnover and training costs must somehow be minimized. In 1914, Henry Ford sought a resolution to this problem with the introduction of the $5.00 day. Faced with nearly 400 percent turnover annually and the threat of unionization, Ford more than doubled the prevailing wage rate (Sward, in Braverman, 1975:149–150). According to Braverman, Ford's move

> raised pay at the Ford plant so much above the prevailing rate in the area that it solved both threats for the moment. It gave the company a large pool of labor from which to choose and at the same time opened up new possibilities for the intensification of labor within the plants, where workers were now anxious to keep their jobs. (1975:149–150)

Though, ironically, hourly wages in the lettuce industry reached $5.60 an hour (in 1981),[2] employment in any one production area does not exceed six or seven months out of the year. Furthermore, the high costs of transportation and housing have made migrancy difficult even with the higher wage rates. Therefore, it would seem, changes in work organization and wage rates brought on by capital intensification have undercut the basis for worker commitment to crew and company. How, then, do lettuce firms resolve this problem? How is sufficient labor found? How is work force stability induced? In more general terms, what are the consequences of change in the labor process for the organization of the labor systems?

In comparing the ground and wrap crew situses, I will suggest that the elimination of the mutual coordination and

experience of the ground crew has simultaneously undermined the advantages to management of the use of undocumented labor. The replacement of crew skill by centralized
control has not, however, made the economics of production
impervious to the potential effects of low worker commitment
and work force turnover. Therefore, labor force stability remains an issue. Because of their disadvantaged labor market
status, subordinate family position, and sources of nonwork
support, women have been tapped as a more attractive, but
equally stable, labor pool over undocumented workers.

The analysis that follows is divided into two parts. The first
part examines the effects of change in work organization for
managerial control over production. In it I will argue two
major points. First, I will show that while the foreman's role
as "labor contractor" remains essentially unchanged, the
mechanical coordination of work pace has increased managerial control. And, second, I will suggest that the combined
negative effects of alien status and gender serve, like citizenship, to enhance employer control over wages and working
conditions. The second part of the chapter deals with the
construction of the labor market as a whole. There I will
demonstrate how gender is used to generate a reliable labor
supply and to increase work force stability.

WORK ORGANIZATION AND CONTROL
IN THE WRAP CREW

The most visible change in the physical organization of harvesting with the wrap process is the machine itself. Looking
like an airplane stripped of its skin, the wrap machine takes
the element of mutual coordination out of the hands of experienced crew members and reconstructs it as the physical
property of a set of conveyor belts. With that change alone,
the discretion and judgment of the ground crew has become
an instrument directly controlled by a force outside the crew.
Thus, the pace and direction of work has been further subordinated to managerial control.[3] Yet, as in the case of the
ground crew, considerable informal control is used to augment formal regulation. The exercise of informal control by

management is, at one and the same time, a product of the allocation of discretionary authority to lower levels of management in the organization and a product of the manipulation of the communal status of labor external to the organization. Where in the ground crew the latter derived from the political vulnerability of undocumented workers in particular, in the wrap crews it derives from the manipulation of women. In both cases, nonmarket statuses are used to enhance managerial control over productivity and over the supply of labor.

To elaborate on these points, I will now turn to a comparison of work organization and control in the ground and wrap crews.

THE LABOR PROCESS IN
COMPARATIVE PERSPECTIVE

For a stranger to the fields, a visual comparison of a wrap crew working alongside a ground crew would most likely focus on the relative speed and motion of the two groups. A ground crew, as one grower earlier described it, looks like a buzz saw in action: workers move at a rapid pace through the field, leaving in their wake a jumble of excess leaves and a straight line of packed cartons. A wrap machine, in contrast, lumbers slowly forward like an awkward airplane taxiing along a rutted runway.

Workers' movements on and around the machine appear no less methodical than in the ground crew, but they are much more constrained. Cutters trail closely behind the outstretched wings of the machine, standing and stooping like automatic pistons as they reach down to cut the heads and stand to place them on the machine. Cutters in the ground crew, however, move fluidly along in a bent position, pausing only occasionally to straighten their backs before returning to their work. Packers on the wrap machine stand with their feet firmly planted on the fuselage, extending only their arms to reach for the packaged heads as they travel by on the conveyor. Packers in the ground crew, stooped like the cutters, hurry along behind, deftly plucking the heads from the ground by twos and threes and squeezing them into bulging cartons. Closers walk slowly alongside the machine sealing and stapling shut the cartons that are slid down a short ramp by the packers. Closers in the ground crew follow on the heels of the packers sealing and then upending the cartons.

Wrappers, absent from the ground crews, are motionless from the waist down as they stand perched on the wings of the wrap machine. In one continuous movement they draw plastic film from a roll in front of them, individually diaper the lettuce stacked beside them, and toss the sealed product on an adjacent conveyor belt (see fig. 4).

The economy of movement in both crews, however, belies the means by which activities are structured and coordinated. Though fundamentally the same activities are carried out on the ground and around the machine, the high degree of coordination evolves from two different sources. On the ground, the crew of thirty-six workers carries out a set of activities in which the coordination of work is a product of the experience of workers with one another. Coordination of the disparate activities of the packers, cutters, and others is achieved through the collective skill of the crew unit. The level of coordination, in turn, directly affects the productivity of the crew and the earnings potential of the individual crew members.

On the wrap machine, however, the element of coordination is provided by the machine itself. Coordination has been reconstructed as a problem of mechanical engineering: the conveyor belts directing the flow of lettuce substitute for the social construction of mutual coordination. The individual activities of the ground crew remain, but the capacity of the crew to affect the pace of the work or its content is greatly diminished.

Formal and Informal Controls in Production

The organization of work in the wrap crew largely removes the incentive for crew coordination beyond that which is organized by the machine. Workers are paid on a flat hourly rate with an increment for overtime, in most cases, over nine hours a day. Small differentials in pay may be associated with different positions on the machine, but those differentials rarely exceed 40 cents an hour (see table 20).

The conversion from a piece-rate to an hourly pay scheme has the effect of making work pace a matter of greater managerial concern. Given the frequency of complaints about the machine "going too fast" which I heard while working on a wrap crew, it would be reasonable to assume that, left to themselves, workers would have slowed the pace of work in return for the same wages. Many workers were pleased (both openly and out of sight of the foreman) when workdays were disrupted by machine breakdowns or reduced demand from headquarters. Ground crew workers, by contrast, loathed shortened days because they meant reduced earnings. Ground crew workers arrived fieldside in the mornings anxious to get started; wrap crew workers, however, had to be prodded into action.

While the volume of complaints and gripes was greater in the wrap crew than in the ground crew, dissatisfaction never coalesced into organized job actions aimed at the foreman or the company. Rather, the most common expression of opposition took the form of leaving the crew—either temporary leave or quitting. The low level of organized action has

Table 20. Hourly Wage Rates by Activity for
Lettuce Wrap Machines

Activity	United Farm Workers	Teamsters
Cut, trim, lift, wrap	$5.10	$5.25
Pack	5.30	5.25
Close	5.45	5.25
Load	5.50	5.25
Drive	10.18*	10.18*

Source: Salinas *Californian*, 7/20/79 and 9/20/79.

*Drivers are covered by a Teamsters contract.

its roots, I will argue, in the individualizing effect of work organization.

The individualizing effect of assembly-line production has received considerable attention by sociologists concerned with industrial organization.[4] What is pointed to here is the effect of the detailing of the harvest labor process on control over production. Rather than trios of cutters and packers interacting with one another to determine the pace of work, the wrap crew cutters, wrappers, and packers carry out their tasks in isolation from one another. For example, the volume of lettuce to be cut appears to be determined external to individual or group control. For cutters, the adjustment of the work of other cutters, wrappers, and packers is less important than the individual performance of a singular set of activities. Thus workers come to interact with individual commodities as they present themselves and with the machine as the determinant of the volume of these commodities. Contention between human and machine would sometimes take the form of a physical attack on the machine or the commodity. When workers attempt to keep pace with the machine and fail, they may stop momentarily and give it a kick or slam it with an open hand as a symbol of frustration. Along with fellow cutters, I often mutilated acceptable heads of lettuce as a means by which to vent my anger with falling behind. Wrappers would occasionally bang the wrapping device viciously when it failed to operate correctly and thereby cause themselves to be swamped with lettuce heads.

Workers recognize that the machine and the lettuce are inanimate objects, but, at the same time, the form that the interaction takes tends to diffuse dissatisfaction and/or frustration. Thus, individuals struggle to keep pace with the machine or the flow of work confronting them rather than act in concerted fashion to oppose the foreman's authority.

An additional element contributing to managerial control is the physical separation of the different operations. In the case of the machine on which I worked, the cutters, wrappers, and packers all worked at different levels of the machine. Cutters walked on the ground. Wrappers rode on the wings and were elevated about four feet above ground (so that the wrappers' waists were at about eye level to the cutters). Packers, in turn, stood on a platform behind the wrappers and were separated from them by canvas curtains. Almost everything taking place on the machine is therefore above or out of sight of most workers. As a result, problems confronting one group of workers generally escape the attention of the others. The physical proximity in which the work is performed, however, enhances the foreman's capacity to observe most of the operations.

The separation of workers and the mechanical coordination of tasks thus acts to undermine the degree of interaction and interdependence of crew members. These factors facilitate centralization of control by the foreman directly. As a result, the somewhat disparate and worker controlled and coordinated activities of the ground crews (especially the trios) are eliminated by the mobile assembly line.

Beyond muttered complaints and occasional displays of anger, the most direct forms of response to managerial practice were absenteeism and quitting. Though absenteeism was most common among the cutters, whose job most workers agreed was the most difficult and onerous, many workers used a day or two off as a means by which to escape and cool off. On several occasions workers who acted particularly frustrated or angry were advised by fellow crew members to take a day's rest. As one older cutter (age 46) told me: "It's better to stay home one day than to risk getting in trouble." At times, workers were absent for other reasons, but among crew members a shared understanding existed about the purpose of time away from work. Foremen complained about the problem of absenteeism, but rarely took direct punitive action against the occasional dropouts.

Quitting stood as the strongest statement of opposition to the foreman or the organization of work. During the time of my fieldwork (approximately eight weeks with the crew), three workers quit in anger. All had come from other jobs outside lettuce and began as cutters. Two of the three left after several confrontations over the speed at which they had to work. The third left several days after I began work. According to other crew members, he had attempted to organize job actions (in the form of slowdowns) in response to the foreman's practice of working the crew until the last break. It was company practice to pay workers for the 15-minute breaks in the morning and midafternoon if they worked after 3:00 P.M. (the time of the afternoon break). Antonio, the wrap crew foreman at Miracle, however, made a practice of working the crew until 3:15 P.M. and then stopping for the day. Thus, almost every day the crew lost 15 minutes (about $1.10) of paid rest time. This worker's plan was to refuse to work the last 15 minutes, or to stop working at 3:00 P.M. even if the machine continued moving. Several cutters reportedly went along with the scheme. Each attempt failed, however, as the foreman either threatened to fire the participants or slowed the machine temporarily and then gradually increased its speed. The plan failed because other crew members did not go along. Later, after the dissident left, several workers rumored that he had actually been a UFW organizer.

Formal and Informal Controls

The foreman on the wrap machines has a variety of devices for controlling the pace and organization of work. The most important device, as well as the most direct, is adjusting the forward speed of the machine itself. The foreman can instruct the driver (a Teamster whose pay rate is double that of the wrap workers) to speed the machine up or slow it down, depending on field conditions and the flow of work on the machine.

Such adjustments in speed operate within limits. Running the machine too slow results in a sparse flow of lettuce from one work station to the next. A common practice among cutters, in particular, when the machine ran too slow was to attempt to appear busy by remaining stooped. The lack of heads waiting to be wrapped by the wrappers, however, will spur the foreman to give a thumbs-up signal to the driver, an indication that the speed should be increased. Running the machine too fast, however, overloads the cutters, wrappers, and packers. If cutters fall back farther than an arm's reach of the platform on which trimmed lettuce is to be placed, they must either cut the lettuce, walk forward to place it on the platform, and then run back to cut more, or stay within reach of the platform and cut as much as possible, while leaving a percentage of mature heads behind. Furthermore, when the machine is going too fast, lettuce tends to pile up on the platforms in front of the wrappers. In such situations, attempts by cutters to further stack the heads are frustrated by their roundness, that is, they tend to fall to the ground and get bruised or dirty. For packers, a surfeit of lettuce clogs the conveyor belts. When this happens, the machine must either be stopped or slowed in order to allow the packers to catch up.

By contrast to the ground crew, however, the adjustment of work pace in the wrap crew need not require overt coercion or manipulation of workers by the foreman. Rather, since most workers (especially the wrappers and packers) ride on the machine, they can neither escape their tasks nor the foreman's action. And, because wrappers and packers tend to work around the same conveyor belts, they cannot shirk their own individual responsibilities during a speedup without causing others to work harder.

As an indirect adjustment of work pace, many foremen attempt to locate individuals in the jobs they do best. Such actions generally discourage the rotation of workers between jobs. For example, women who show themselves to be particularly adept at wrapping are assigned to the wrapping positions most likely to receive the largest volume of lettuce. Similarly, an experienced cutter will most often be teamed with an experienced wrapper. Several weeks after I had begun work as a cutter in a wrap crew, the foreman, Antonio, paired me with a new wrapper. However, when it became clear that I was cutting faster than Margarita, the wrapper, could handle, I was moved to work with a faster wrapper.

As in the case of the ground crews, however, informal devices are used to supplement the foreman's control over the pace of work. I will refer to three in particular: (1) the foreman's discretionary authority; (2) kin networks; and (3) the manipulation of gender roles.

The Foreman's Discretionary Authority

As in the ground crews, foremen exercise considerable influence in the recruitment and placement of workers in the wrap crews. Foremen mediate most interaction between workers and the company and are therefore in a position to grant favors to crew members. Given the physical isolation of crews and machines during the daily work process, the workplace comes to be dominated by the presence and authority of the foreman. They can excuse absences, okay short vacations, hire friends or family of crew members, and, in so doing, accrue substantial personal debt from crew members. As I found out from my own experience, such debts cannot be entirely repaid if this form of control is to be maintained.

A perplexing situation can develop for the foreman if one refuses to incur a debt. In my case, I began to realize after several weeks' work that the foreman's iciness toward me was not so much a result of my ethnicity or uniqueness (being the only Anglo in the fields). Rather, I had performed according to what I had initially believed to be the norm: punctually showing up for work, not complaining, and not bothering the foreman. In conversation with other workers, however, it became clear that owing something to the foreman was the norm. I experimented by asking for two days off. Though Antonio granted permission reluctantly, he warmed visibly when I returned and announced that now I "owed him" for that favor. On several occasions in subsequent weeks, he reminded me of my debt as a spur to get me to work harder. "Other foremen," he chided, "aren't so easy to get along with. You're lucky."

Kin Networks

Family networks provide a ready means of labor recruitment on the machines, as well as in other agricultural employment.[5] Foremen for the wrap machines often enlist their own family networks as well as those of crew members to fill empty spaces in the crews. One advantage of this recruitment technique is that it allows the foreman to exert control over the work indirectly through the family structure. Two examples of this situation will help illustrate.

An older woman, Señora Sandoval, and her two teenage daughters worked in my crew. The mother was a packer and both daughters wrapped. Complaining about her arthritis during lunch one day, she told me that she wanted to go back to live in Mexico with her son (she lived in Salinas at the time) but that her daughters wanted to stay and work in the United States. In order to work with them, Señora Sandoval had struck a deal with Antonio: in return for her job, she would see to it that her daughters worked well. Thus, she cracked the whip on her daughters. When they talked or allowed work to pile up in front of them, a sharp look or a stern command issued from Señora Sandoval and their errant behavior ceased.

A somewhat different example of family control centered on the foreman's and driver's wives. The wives of both Antonio and Jose (the driver) worked as wrappers on my crew. These women were good friends, worked side by side, and shared lunch and rest breaks with their husbands. They were also the fastest wrappers in the crew. But, beyond that, they often acted as subforemen. For example, at times when certain wrapping positions were busier than others, they would order their fellow wrappers to either pick up the slack or work harder. Most workers saw them as extensions of management and, as such, they were an unpopular pair in the crew. They were also capable of exerting leverage with Antonio: they could jeopardize workers with whom they did not get along and they were the only nonmanagement employees capable of getting Antonio and Jose to slow the work pace. With regard to the latter, on several occasions Luisa (Antonio's wife) convinced Jose to slow the machine while Antonio was away and the crew had begun to fall behind. The presence of Luisa and the driver's wife had the effect of tripling the amount of surveillance and supervision on the machine.

Manipulation of Gender Roles

The informal manipulation of women's status in the wrap crew situs resembles that found in other situations where male supervisors oversee women employees (Kanter, 1977; Tepperman, 1970). However, the capacity of the male foreman to exercise greater control over women is accentuated by the highly traditional sex roles characteristic of Mexican society. In the wrap crews this takes several forms. First, some foremen attempt to intimidate women workers through overt displays of anger or physical force. These are usually accompanied by threats of firing (i.e., abandonment) if correct behavior is not forthcoming. Incidents of this sort occurred infrequently in my crew, but when they did, they evoked embarrassment on the part of the chastised women. Men were never subject to such assaults. Several male workers commented after one of Antonio's verbal barrages that they would not stand for that kind of abuse if it were aimed at them. But they would not intervene on behalf of the women. As Armando, a fellow cutter, explained: "To a man, that would be a challenge to fight. To a woman, it is not right . . . but women are treated that way."

The other side of the same coin is flirtatious behavior. While there are limits to how far this can go[6] (as in the case with intimidation), flirting by foremen can evoke some degree of cooperation. Several women workers I interviewed complained that foremen flirted with younger women in an effort to get them to work in one job or another or to increase their cooperation with the foremen's rules. For example, a wrapper from Verde complained that foremen attempted to undercut job rotation (described as a way for wrappers and cutters to beat the boredom of the work) in order to speed up production. The foremen, she explained, would flirt with or differentially attend to the needs of young unattached women in order to convince them to stay in one position and not rotate. Flirting or attention-giving is not limited to younger, unmarried women; on several occasions Antonio attempted to placate the complaints of older, married women with charming behavior and compliments.

These devices—discretionary authority, family networks, and manipulation of gender roles—are all elements of control manipulated by the foreman and management to affect the level of productivity and effort of the wrap crew. Together they indicate quite clearly that informal mechanisms of control are at least as important as formal organizational rules and regulations.

On the whole, the reorganization of harvesting into the wrap crew acts to enhance managerial control over the labor process. The structuring of work into isolated activities diffuses the potential for substantive response to speedups or other managerial directives. Formal measures of control are augmented through the manipulation of statuses produced external to the organization. These factors in combination serve to enable the wrap crew's harvest to compete with the ground crew's.

GENDER AND LABOR SUPPLY

The preceding discussion showed that the transformation of the harvest labor process has had a number of important consequences for the organization and utilization of labor. The shared experience, commitment, and coordination of the ground crew has been replaced by a system that minimizes group interaction, individualizes skill acquisition, reduces skill requirements, and enhances managerial control over work. For workers, wages are less a function of crew skill than they are of the total number of hours worked in any given period.

The reorganization of harvesting has re-created the traditional conditions of agricultural employment: a high demand for low skill labor, low (hourly) pay, restricted occupational mobility, and little or no incentive for employment stability. Yet the change in harvesting techniques has been accomplished by means of a substantial increase in fixed capital investments.[7] The combination of high demand for labor with an increase in fixed costs raises a major organizational question: how are capital investments protected and the cost competitiveness of the technique maintained through the employment of what is generally considered to be unstable or casual labor? Asked a little differently, how is an abundant and stable supply of labor created and maintained?

Firms have been able to simultaneously increase capital intensity and labor demand through recruitment from another low status labor pool: women. While the costs associated with turnover have not been eliminated, they have been reduced by means of recruitment from large local, stable pools of women workers. The advantage of this system resides in the disadvantaged social, political, and economic status of women, especially noncitizen and Mexican-American women. The concentration of women in the wrap crews, in turn, represents an effort on the part of the industry to translate the low status of women into stability in the labor supply.

Through an analysis of data collected from survey, interview, and field research, I will demonstrate how gender is used to generate labor supply and to enhance labor commitment.

Gender and Labor Force Characteristics

The effects of gender on labor market organization are demonstrated quite clearly by the survey data. In comparing the demographic and organizational characteristics of men and women in the wrap crews, three major differences are important.

First, as summarized in table 21, men and women differ considerably in terms of their demographic characteristics. Men tend to be either younger or older, at the beginning or near the end of their work careers. Women, by contrast, are drawn from across the age distribution. In terms of marital and family status, the differences between men and women again are clear. Women tend much more often than men to be married and to have children young enough to need some sort of daily care. The combination of younger and older men results in a relatively small percentage who are married and/or with dependent children. Finally, among those who are married, women are much more likely to have a working husband in the family unit. In addition, as at the bottom of table 21,

Table 21. Demographic Characteristics of Wrap Crew
Workers by Gender (N = 82)

	Men (N = 22) (%)	Women (N = 60) (%)
Age		
17 – 23	36.0	25.0
24 – 30	37.0	17.0
31 – 37	0.0	26.0
38 – 44	0.0	24.0
45 – 51	5.0	6.0
52 and over	22.0	2.0
Total	100.0	100.0
Marital status		
Married	31.8	75.0
Other	68.2	25.0
Total	100.0	100.0
Dependent children		
Yes	36.4	66.7
No	63.6	33.3
Total	100.0	100.0
Spouse's employment		
Full- or part-time	13.6	78.9
Unemployed outside home	86.4	21.1
Total	100.0	100.0
	(22)	(57)
Spouse's average weekly income	$125.00	$186.00
Ratio of respondent's average income to spouse's	1.2	.62

women's spouses earn on average much more than they do. Though only rough figures are available, women in the sample earn about 62 percent of what their husbands earn.

Second, women working the wrap crews tend to be much more stable in terms of residence and employment than men (see table 22). Among workers surveyed in the Salinas Valley, 60 percent of the women and only 13.6 percent of the men made their permanent residence in the United States. Men were much more likely to move with work than women were; nine out of ten men worked in two major production areas or more in 1978, while less than two out of ten women migrated.

Third, women appear much more stable than men with respect to type of employment (job), company, and crew. As table 23 shows, women generally have greater experience in the kind of work they do—working in the wrap machine harvest—than men. The much higher percentage with three or more years' experience in the harvest (70 percent of women vs. 45.3 percent of men) suggests that women are much

Table 22. Residence and Migrancy in Work
by Gender (N = 82)

	Men (%)	Women (%)
Permanent residence		
United States	13.6	60.0
Mexico	86.4	40.0
Total	100.0	100.0
Migrant*		
Yes	91.0	18.2
No	9.0	81.8
Total	100.0	100.0

*Migrancy is defined by working in two or more major production areas during 1978. Production areas are listed in figure 1 in chapter 3.

Table 23. Years of Experience in Type of Current Work
by Gender (N = 82)

Years of experience in work	Men (%)	Women (%)	% Difference (women-men)
Less than 1	32.0	1.6	−30.4
≥1, <3	22.7	23.4	0.7
≥3, <5	22.7	40.0	17.3
≥5, <7	13.6	25.0	11.4
≥7	9.0	10.0	1.0
Total	100.0	100.0	
	(22)	(60)	

more likely to remain in their type of work than men. The median number of years' experience for women is 4.2 but for men the median experience is 2.6 years.

With respect to company tenure, again women are more stable than men. The outstanding feature of table 24 is the very high percentage of men who have worked with their present company for less than one year (half the sample). Women, on the whole, tend to have worked for the same company, though not necessarily in the same job, much longer than men. The median company tenure for women is approximately 3.6 years, whereas for men it is something less than one year.

The data for crew tenure mirrors that of company tenure (see table 25). The overall lower crew tenure among women suggests that they have moved or been moved between crews in the same company.

What remains a question, however, is why women, especially local and citizen women, should constitute such a large portion of the labor force. The issues of stability and commitment, generally reflected in the data on employment tenure, are important elements of the answer. To understand how and why women show up in these positions, I will now

Table 24. Years of Employment with Present Company
by Gender (N = 82)

Years with present company	Men (%)	Women (%)	% Difference (women-men)
Less than 1	50.0	15.0	−35.0
≥1, <3	13.6	25.0	11.4
≥3, <5	27.2	35.0	7.8
≥5	9.2	25.0	15.8
Total	100.0	100.0	
	(22)	(60)	

Table 25. Years of Work with Present Crew
by Gender (N = 81)

Years with crew	Men (%)	Women (%)	% Difference (women-men)
Less than 1	57.2	15.0	−42.2
≥1, <3	38.0	68.3	30.3
≥3	4.8	16.7	11.9
Total	100.0	100.0	
	(212)	(60)	

turn to an examination of the factors that affect women's
employment chances.

LABOR MARKET STATUS, FAMILY POSITION,
AND EMPLOYMENT

The greater overall stability of women in terms of work,
company, and crew is itself a product of the factors that serve

to segregate women into a separate labor market. Two major
constraints operate on women's labor market chances: those
imposed by women's status vis-à-vis all over labor market
participants, and those imposed by women's family roles. Together these constraints reduce the range of job opportunities
for women and, in turn, make women highly accessible as a
pool of labor for low paid, low status employment. It is not
possible here to discuss sex segregation in employment in
great detail.[8] It is important, however, to show how it is that
women come to constitute the primary source of labor for
wrap crew production and how those jobs come to be defined
as "women's work." The type and duration of employment
experienced by women workers is strongly influenced by their
disadvantaged status as women, as (frequently) noncitizens,
and by their family roles.

Labor Market Status

Many of the women I interviewed in the course of this study
were acutely aware of the range of jobs open to them. For
example, Juana, a nineteen-year-old wrapper born in Texas,
who attended high school in Salinas, described her own employment outlook:

> I got two more years of school if I want to get a diploma. Even
> if I do, what difference would it make? I want to do something
> like be a hairdresser, you know? But there's no work. So, what
> have I got but to work out there [in the fields]? Maybe after a
> while I'll go to work someplace else.

When asked why she did not work in some other job in town,
she replied:

> You mean like at Penney's or Mervyn's [department stores]? I
> make better money out here! Anyway, those jobs are no better.
> All the men have the good jobs. . . . If you're a woman, nobody
> wants to hire you. Everybody says that they don't want to train
> you to do a job because you'll just run off and get married. If
> you're a woman, that's one strike against you. If you're a woman
> and Mexican, forget it.

Another wrapper had gone back to work at age thirty-four after ten years of rearing children. She described her reasons for working the fields this way:

> When we got married, my husband didn't want me to work. But he lost his job last year and we don't have any money. It hurts him to see me work, but we need it. . . . If I could work someplace else, I would. But there aren't any jobs anywhere for women unless you got an education. So, I went to work here. I didn't know where to look so I called one of my *comadres*. She already worked here, so I came out, too.

For other women, the fields represent the only source of employment. A recent immigrant to Salinas told me, "I've always worked in the fields. I don't know anything else." Another wrapper, a forty-year-old woman named Manuela who commutes across the border to work in the Imperial Valley, commented straightforwardly, "Women can thin, weed, and work on the machines. Maybe sometimes there is work in the canneries. Sometimes there is work transplanting. But, mostly women work in the fields."

Even when women seek work outside the fields, they are often steered back there. In an interview with a male counselor at a state employment office in Salinas, I was told:

> Most Mexican-American women who come in here are given the names of employers who need field help. We have one woman who all she does is handle those calls. When a Mexican woman comes in, we just send her right over to talk to Dolores. It saves us a lot of time . . . especially if they don't speak English.

The barriers to nonfarm employment are real ones for women and, within agriculture, work opportunities are restricted. In a study of women farm workers in California, Barton (1978) shows that even when women workers seek to acquire more skills or higher skilled jobs, they are often met by hostile employers and insufficient training programs.

Compounding the constraints imposed by nonmarket statuses, employment in many heavily agricultural production areas offers little opportunity for higher earnings or status. Among women in the survey sample, less than 10 percent had held jobs outside agriculture in the preceding five years. In the Salinas, Imperial, and San Luis valleys, where the bulk of lettuce production is located, the only real alternatives to work in the fields are the canneries and packing sheds. These jobs, however, bear remarkable resemblance to wrap harvest employment, that is, work is seasonal, low paid and, for the most part, unskilled. Yet the canneries and the packing sheds have thrived historically on the availability of local supplies of female labor—particularly the wives of farm workers and other local workers.[9] Thus, the appearance of large numbers of women in the wrap crews represents, in part, an extension of employment practices (and assembly lines) from the canneries to the fields.

Women's Role in the Family

The position of women in the family acts as the other major factor influencing employment tenure and opportunities. Two elements of family organization are important here: the division of labor between husband and wife, and the economic position of the family.

The division of labor in the family is often cited as a major obstacle to the working careers of married women (Brown, 1977; Gubbels, 1977; Jones, 1970). The obligation to perform household labor and childrearing has traditionally fallen to women farm workers, even those who migrate (Barton, 1978). The women interviewed in this study were no exception. Of the sixty women interviewed in the survey, forty-five were married and/or had children. Of that number, over three-fourths had children who needed some sort of daily attention while their mother worked. Nearly all these married women reported that they performed all the major household chores on a regular basis. The remainder said they divided that labor between themselves and older children, in most cases older daughters. All this work is carried out in addition to working

in the fields during the harvest season. As one of the women
with whom I worked explained methodically:

> Every morning in the summer, I get up at 4 to make my lunch,
> his lunch, and the children's breakfast. At 5 I take the kids to
> my mother's house down the street. At 6 I leave for work. Then
> at 3 in the afternoon he gets home and takes a nap . . . he works
> real hard. . . . I am usually home by 4. I start dinner and then
> get the girls [daughters]. After dinner I do the dishes and
> maybe some cleaning. . . . If I'm lucky I get to bed around 8 or
> 8:30.

While many of the women complained about the tremendous amount of daily and weekend work to be done, the dual
roles of housewife and wage earner are most often accepted
(willingly or unwillingly) as a condition of their employment
and the family's well-being.

The subordinate position of women in the family is also
reflected in the practice of determining whether or not a wife
will work. In almost all instances, women reported having to
secure their husband's *permission* prior to taking a job; 93
percent of the women lettuce workers surveyed said that their
husbands held veto power over their employment.

According to data collected in interviews, the extent to
which the husband's objections result in actual refusal to let
his wife work is strongly affected by the economic position of
the family. Beyond the husband's employment, the most important factor affecting family economic position, and therefore the wife's employment, is the residential location of the
family itself. Whether the family lives in the United States or
in Mexico has considerable influence on the decision about
employment, even to the extent that economic necessity may
override traditional objections. To wit, married women living
in the United States or near the border are much more likely
to work (in lettuce or some other industry) than are married
women living in the interior of Mexico.

In this regard, two major components of residential location
emerge: the relative cost of living in the United States and
Mexico and the proximity of the family to work. For many

lettuce workers living in the United States, the added income for a second paycheck is necessary for the family to stay afloat financially. As one woman explained:

> With the inflation and all the bills here [in Salinas], I have to work, too. My husband makes good money, but it's just not enough. . . . Back in Mexico, we could get along with less. Here it's harder.

In this regard farm worker men and women share in the common plight of many working-class families in the United States.

Economic necessity can overcome even the staunchest of opposition from men, particularly among those families committed to living or remaining in the United States. The husband of a wrapper who himself worked in the packing sheds argued:

> We have lived here [in the U.S.] for almost five years. I want my kids to get an education and to do better than I have. . . . If that means my wife has to work, she works. Sometimes I feel like I'm doing all a man should do. You know, taking care of his family? But I let her work because the kids have to have a chance.

For some families, both spouses working is a precondition for settling in the United States. A common explanation among permanent immigrants sounded like the one given by a young woman with two children:

> I have two sisters who live nearby in Chualar. They have lived there with their husbands for almost six years. My brother-in-law told my husband that if we wanted to move, we'd have to both work. My husband told me that he would get me a job in the sheds or in the fields. That was the only way we could live here. . . . I don't like working on the machines . . . but that's what he wants. We can afford to stay only if I work too.

Among residents of Mexico, there is a decided split between those families in which wives do not work and those in which they do. Mexican men were the most openly opposed to their wives working, on traditional grounds. A common response to questions about wives' employment was a blank stare. Many of these men believed that either women should not work outside the home or that they should do so only under the most extreme circumstances. A smattering of representative comments echoes these conclusions:

> A woman cooks, sews, and cares for the children. That is woman's work.

> A man is less of a man if he has to make his wife work.

> If I get sick, maybe I will have my wife work. . . . I would rather borrow money first.

Even for the most traditional/chauvinistic men, the lower economic standards and the lesser availability of employment in Mexico acted against wives' working, as well. Several of the migrant ground crew workers explained that their income alone was sufficient to support their families. Using the standard of living in Mexico as the relevant criterion for comparison, one loader explained:

> We are not rich, but we have enough to get along. We live better than most of our neighbors. None of them has a car or a TV. . . . As long as I can make money this way, she should not work.

Another lechugero, from deep in the interior of Mexico, added that his wife's work at home was important economically:

> She takes care of our few chickens and goats when I am away. If she worked, who would do that?

The restricted character of employment opportunities in Mexico also reduces the likelihood of a wife working. A typical explanation went like this:

> If we lived near the border, maybe she could work in the fields. We live near Hermosillo [over 100 miles from the border] and

there's no work. . . . She stays with our family and cares for the
children while I work.

At the extremes, therefore, the economic conditions of the
United States and Mexico have different effects on the employment behavior of married women. The higher cost of
living in the United States compels women to seek work, even
over the initial objections of their husbands. The specific conditions of that employment must, however, mesh with wives'
dual role as wage-earner and housekeeper/babysitter. In contrast, the lower cost of living and lack of alternative employment in Mexico bolster husbands' traditional objections to
wives' employment.

To summarize briefly, the type and duration of employment experienced by married farm worker women is strongly
influenced by their generally disadvantaged status, by their
role in the family, and by the economic position of the family.
In almost all instances, women's work careers are organized
in such a way as to carry out the traditional duties of wife and
mother, in addition to that of wage earner. A wife's wage may
represent an integral part of the family budget, particularly
in the case of families living in the United States and border
areas, but the range of work opportunities and the duration
of employment are limited by her subordinate status in the
family. Thus, the availability of work in low skill, seasonal
production allows women to carry out the dual roles of wife
and wage-earner. At the same time, however, the availability
of this attractive labor pool facilitates expansion of those jobs.

THE CONSTRUCTION OF MEN'S
AND WOMEN'S WORK

The forces that restrict the employment opportunities of
women also act to stabilize that labor pool residentially. The
role of wife and mother, the subordinate status of a woman's
work to that of her husband, and the various family earnings
strategies severely limit the geographic mobility of married
women. In some instances, migrancy is a feature of the work
career, but only under the condition that the family migrates
as a unit. In the majority of cases, married women remain in

one location whether or not their husbands have jobs that require seasonal relocation.

According to interviews with personnel offices, union staff, and workers, the majority of women working on the wrap machines are drawn from labor pools in the separate production areas. In other words, most of the labor for the Salinas harvest comes from the Salinas Valley; likewise labor for the Arizona harvest comes from southwestern Arizona and the area directly across the border (e.g., San Luis, Mexico). The same sources also indicate that the localization of employment has increased in recent years.

The major indications of this trend were revealed in interviews with growers and union staff. First, employers reported that, in contrast to their ground crews and skilled maintenance labor, very few wrap crews migrate as units with the companies. The vice president of Salad Giant reported that only parts of two wrap crews (out of a total of 14 employed by the company) worked in more than one production area. The president of Miracle estimated that only 10 percent of his company's nearly 600 wrap workers followed the crop in any given year. Second, the increased localization of wrap and thinning crews, along with harvest workers in other crops, has spurred the UFW to press for seniority by geographic region in addition to company seniority (interviews with union staff; see UFW contracts, 1975, 1979).

The availability of women from local labor pools offers distinct advantages for employers. The most important advantage derives from the increased likelihood of a stable and returning labor force in successive seasons. The survey data presented earlier provides evidence for the relationship between localization and stability in company and crew employment among women. For employers, recruitment from localized labor pools thus provides one means by which to reduce the costs of training labor to work on the wrap machines. This factor is particularly important with regard to the wrapping jobs, the positions that have the greatest potential for creating bottlenecks in the labor process. As the personnel director at Miracle explained:

> Stability is the most important thing. If we have to spend time
> training our crews every year or season, we lose money because
> we slow down. It's very important that the people know what
> they're doing and that they know how to do it the Miracle way.

Though few employers or their staff would speak explicitly
about their recruitment techniques in this context, the vice
president of Salad Giant did provide some illustration. His
remarks are instructive with respect to the relationship between labor stability and productivity.

> Turnover is still a problem in our wrap crews. We, like everyone
> else involved in wrapping, feel like we've trained everyone who
> works in the industry. . . . At first, we expected all of our people
> to move with the company through the loop. But we found that
> just wasn't feasible. So we now make a practice of keeping
> contact with our workers in the different [production] areas.
> We just call them up when we get into their area and they come
> to work.

Beginning around 1974, Salad Giant began concentrating on
maintaining contact with local workers through the circulation of a company newsletter to all permanent and seasonal
employees. According to the Salad Giant official, the newsletter was designed to "bring the employees and managers closer
together." More important, however, the newsletter provided
a bulletin for production in the different regions. Coupled
with this effort was the development of an elaborate phone
network intended to inform workers of start-up dates for
harvesting.

Despite efforts such as those undertaken at Salad Giant and
other companies, turnover in the wrap crews remains a major
issue. Like most low paying seasonal jobs, work on the
machines is not rewarding financially or aesthetically. Thus,
some workers find the pay too low or the working conditions
unacceptable and leave. Though the rate of turnover among
women is decidedly lower than among men, the subordination
of women's employment to that of their husbands sometimes
means that they will withdraw from work for childbearing,

trips out of the area, or relocation. The greatest turnover, however, takes place among men who work on the machines.

There are several reasons why men are less stable. First, especially among the younger men, working in the wrap crews is designed as a means by which to gain entry into a ground crew or other better paying work. In the wrap crew in which I worked, the consensus among cutters was that wrap crew jobs provided both the training and the networks necessary to join the ground crews. As one young cutter remarked: "You can't make enough money in this work. The thing to do is learn how to cut or pack and then keep your ears open for jobs in the [ground] crews."[10] During the time I worked on the wrap crew, the turnover among men was about 75 percent; among women the turnover was only 20 percent. Most of the men joined company piece-rate crews in lettuce, broccoli, or celery; the remainder took off in search of work in other companies.

Second, the companies themselves often use the wrap crews as recruitment centers for their piece-rate operations. Company-sponsored tryouts for new crews often draw upon men already working on the wrap machines. For example, three days after I joined my crew, 8 of the 16 men on my machine (7 cutters and 1 packer) left to try out for positions in a newly formed ground crew. Though such "raiding" of the wrap crews provides a convenient internal recruitment device for the company, it does act in a counterproductive fashion as far as machine output is concerned; with each successive raid or defection, new workers have to be trained.

Finally, turnover among men is partially a product of the expectation of workmates that able men will attempt to find better paying work. The effect of peer pressure is considerable. First, peer pressure is exerted when new or replacement ground crews are in the process of formation. The move from working on the hourly wrap crews to the ground crews is more than an attempt to increase one's earnings. It also involves an attempt to take part in the mystique of the ground crews themselves—they are the hard-working, fast-living "champagne of farm workers." Trying out for the ground crew represents more than a test of skill: it is often equated with a test of manhood. As one worker described, it's a test of whether one has "the balls to work like a madman and survive." The fear and apprehension brought on by that mystique is so great that, especially among the younger workers, the friendships created during work on the wrap machines are used to pressure groups of workers to try out together. Friends and even passing acquaintances are used as the supports for deciding to try out and then remaining in the new situation once the decision has been made. Thus, I was urged almost insistently by fellow workers to join them in a tryout when new openings were announced.

The other way in which peer pressure is manifested is the attitudes of women workers. Though I will discuss the relations between men and women on the machine shortly, women can, in an indirect way, exert influence over the job tenure of men. Several women in my crew asked me and some of the other cutters when we were going to "move on" on the ground crews. Their expectation was that men would naturally seek better paying jobs. Though such expectations did not differ from those of the men, the fact that they came from women made the ground crews look like "men's work."

Older men, by contrast, are much more likely to remain in jobs on the wrap crew. In large part, this derives from the fact that they, like women, are more residentially stable. Most of the older men I interviewed were trying to keep working after long and arduous careers in the fields. Work in the wrap and thinning crews provided the only real opportunities for employment. However, this group in particular is the most likely to be plagued with physical ailments developed over the years.

Thus, by and large, locally based women have proven to be the most stable and predictable supply of labor in the reorganized harvest. What remains to be considered is the means by which female concentration in the crews is perpetuated.

Making It "Women's Work"

The ratio of women to men found in the wrap crews differs from company to company and sometimes from crew to crew.

However, the numerical predominance of women in that segment of the harvest labor process is clear. Evidence from the
survey data, my own fieldwork and observations shows that,
with the exception of jobs that require considerable physical
strength, women are represented in all occupational
categories, in wrapping, cutting, and packing positions.

A search for the origins of the concentration of women on
machines yields little illumination of the present situation.
More important are the processes by which certain jobs (and,
to some extent, all jobs) become "women's work." There are
three related processes taking place: (1) employers actively
recruiting women; (2) men reacting to the negative status
attached to the work; and (3) efforts on the part of women
to monopolize access to those jobs.

For most employers the actual recruitment of women is
taken more as a matter of standard procedure than as an
innovative technique. The fact that in certain situations
women are more attractive labor is not constantly rediscov-
ered. Employers instead simply look around and see that
women have been continuously employed in canneries, packing sheds, and harvesting in other industries (the mechanical harvest of canning tomatoes) and follow suit. Said one
grower: "So far we haven't found anything better or faster
than women doing the wrapping. They're fast and efficient"
(Packer, May 14, 1977, 16C).

The recruitment and job allocation process, however, is an
active part of making and perpetuating women's work. Here
employers intervene directly in an attempt to ensure that the
same category of labor continues to show up where it is most
advantageous. This takes two forms in the wrap crews. First,
wage reductions eliminate the economic basis for men working in those jobs because they are neither sufficient to encourage migration nor high enough to support the single family
paycheck. Second, women are actively recruited through a
variety of networks to occupy positions on the machines. The
utilization of foremen's networks and those of women crew
members enables firms to perpetuate identification of gender
with occupation.

The successful construction of enclaves of production as

women's work also acts to discourage the voluntary entry of men into those positions. As in most organizations where women are concentrated into an occupational category (e.g., secretarial and clerical work), the occupation comes to reflect the status of the occupants, not the requisite skills or aptitudes of the work they perform. There is nothing feminine about the job of wrapping, for example, though most employers assert that women are better suited to do the work (women are "more patient" or are capable of doing "mindless chores"). Nonetheless, workers and managers both respond to the status associated with the occupants and internalize it as a condition of employment.

Two illustrations from my fieldwork help elaborate this point. On six separate occasions when one or more wrappers were absent from work, the foreman shifted women from their packing jobs and made them wrap, or did the job himself. This took place even when male cutters could have been more easily spared than packers. No union rules or pay differentials between jobs prohibited men from being put temporarily in the wrapping jobs. When I asked the foreman why he did not use the cutters, he replied simply: "It's a woman's work." The brevity of the explanation assumed that enough was said.

The foreman's remark proved an understatement in comparison with the view held by many male workers. After the incidents described above, I pursued the issue among my workmates. Several workers told me straightforwardly that men who wrap are usually suspected of being homosexual (*maricon*). An incident that took place near the end of my work on the machine provided evidence of those sentiments. A seventeen-year-old Mexican working his second day on the machine volunteered to take over the wrapping position of a woman who had taken ill. Though a few derisive comments were made quietly among the cutters, nothing was said overtly. The following morning, however, when the sick wrapper failed to appear, the same young man climbed on the machine to replace her. Before he could settle in, he was met by a chorus of hoots and by vicious jokes questioning his sexuality. Confused and embarrassed, he climbed down and resumed his cutting position behind the machine. Afterward, one of the older male workers took him aside and explained the "facts of work." Nothing further was said and the cutter did not volunteer again. Interviews with men and women from other crews and companies confirmed that similar stereotyping takes place throughout the industry.

Finally, the construction of women's work is a process in which women themselves take a hand. Though certainly not intending to further management's purpose, women may organize around their communal status for the purpose of monopolizing access to jobs defined as women's work. For example, Felicia, a 32-year-old wrapper, explained that her crew was entirely female with the exception of the closers and loaders. That situation, she argued, "is much better than having some men and some women. The women all get along together. We can talk and work and not worry what the men think." Any time an opening occurs in cutting, wrapping, or packing, kinship networks are used to fill it:

> We don't have any agreements . . . that men shouldn't be hired. It's just that we like having all women together. . . . Nobody's ever tried to bring a man in.

On the one hand, the making of women's work involves purposive activity on the part of management and, to some extent, women; on the other hand, it involves the reaction of men to the sexual identification of the occupations in which women are concentrated.

CONCLUSION

Gender differences are used to create and enforce the distinction between crews. Like citizenship, gender is a communal status that, while socially constructed external to the labor process, has considerable consequences for the organization of work and wages. The status of women external to economic organizations, such as the lettuce firms described in this chapter, enables employers to use their labor in particular ways.

The severe restriction of women's labor market opportunities is seized upon by employers as a means for recruiting large quantities of low-skilled labor.

But, additionally, the enforced geographic stability of farm worker wives and children enhances the availability of women's labor on a regular, seasonal basis. Thus, employers can avail themselves of this element of an internal labor market without having to pay wages sufficiently high to encourage labor migration with the firm. Put slightly different, women's geographic stability, a product of their subordinate family and economic position, makes their labor available on a regular, seasonal basis. Employers, therefore, are ensured that at least a portion of the labor they trained (at an earlier juncture) will be available in local labor pools in each production area. As a result, the high costs of regularly training new workers are reduced through the attachment of local women to the firms.

7

Conclusion

By contrast to the characterization of agricultural labor markets as "competitive" or unstructured, I have shown that those markets have been severely structured historically. A core feature identified in the process of labor market construction has been the political intervention of employers and the state in matters of labor supply. But, as I argued in chapter 2, the politics of labor supply have been directly affected by structural changes taking place internal *and* external to the agricultural economy. In particular, differentiation in the structure of agricultural enterprises—a product of the uneven development of different segments of the agricultural sector—resulted in a differentiated demand for labor. For some firms an undifferentiated labor supply continued to be most attractive, in part because of the constraints imposed on them by their subordination to larger firms placed between the farm and the market. In those cases, the lack of direct access to markets, and blocked opportunities for expansion via forward integration, made the availability of a low wage, unskilled, and seasonal labor force quite important. For other firms, however, organizational expansion and product diversification suggested new ways to organize production and, subsequently, new demands for labor. Few of these firms reorganized production so dramatically as to open themselves to the influx of domestic workers and unions; instead, they sought out the same workers but imposed new conditions of employment. As was shown in the case of the lettuce industry, the bracero program proved incapable of providing the kind of labor attractive to employers. But, instead of hiring domestic workers, employers sought foreign workers (especially indocumentados) who could be used in new ways. Thus while political intervention continued unabated, its form has been partially shaped by structural change internal to agriculture.

External structural changes also shaped the politics of labor supply. In particular, the broader struggles taking place in manufacturing industries following World War II and in the civil rights movement in the 1960s brought the political and economic rights of citizenship to the forefront of political debate. Efforts by organized labor to cement legal protections for their members and strengthen such basic guarantees as the minimum wage meshed directly (though not always openly) with the demands by civil rights proponents for extended guarantees of citizenship entitlements for blacks and other minorities. These forces provided an important grounding for both the national and the local political opposition to state intervention on behalf of agricultural employers. The demise of the bracero program at the hands of these forces directly influenced the strategies undertaken by employers to meet their demands for labor. Some firms moved rapidly in the direction of labor displacement through harvest mechanization; others, like the lettuce industry, expanded the use of politically vulnerable labor. The availability of that supply of labor, undocumented workers, continued to rest on a process of political intervention in the labor market—one now characterized not by direct regulation of individual workers but by the denial of access to citizenship for an entire category of workers. The achievement of broader guarantees of rights and entitlements to citizens therefore simultaneously acted to increase the vulnerability of noncitizens and to make noncitizens more attractive as a source of labor to agricultural and nonagricultural employers.

In combining the analyses of structural changes internal and external to agriculture, I have attempted to argue against the notion of unidirectional determination of labor market structure by capitalist enterprises. I have argued instead that labor market structure is affected by factors directly related to employers' demands for labor *and* by factors and processes external to the industry and the workplace. In contrast to the thrust of the literature on segmented labor markets (Edwards et al., 1975; Edwards, 1979; Gordon et al., 1982), I have tried to combine analyses of the ways in which enterprises and industries structure job and career opportunities through the way they organize production, with an analysis of how social and political processes acting on labor markets can themselves influence the organization of production. In this sense, this study has tended much more in the direction of a split labor market explanation. While it shares with split labor market theory an emphasis on the ways in which fractions of the working class (especially organized labor and noncitizen labor) have interacted to influence employers' recruitment strategies, the approach undertaken here has made much more problematic the processes through which those fractions are produced and reproduced over time. Thus, in contrast to both the segmented and the split labor market theories, I have tried to call into question: (1) *why* certain identifiable groups have proven attractive or useful for employers, and (2) how those "attractive" characteristics have been produced and reproduced over time. In the following discussion I will show how these facets are linked and use them to argue for a more systematic analysis of the relationship between class, citizenship, and gender as systems of inequality.

CITIZENSHIP AND UNDOCUMENTED IMMIGRATION

This study of the lettuce industry has shown that an employment system built around citizenship and gender inequalities has provided considerable advantage for employers. The construction of a system of labor recruitment around noncitizen workers has made possible satisfaction of a particular demand for labor: skilled and stable, but also politically vulnerable; capable of carrying out tasks that require considerable group experience and mutual coordination, but competitive as well. The employment system built around gender inequality has served to satisfy another particular demand for labor: large in supply and largely unskilled, but also stable in its availability and in its attachment to individual firms. The principal dimensions of advantage accruing to employers through the utilization of these two particular categories of labor are found in: (1) labor productivity; (2) labor stability; and (3) control over the labor process. Each of these will be considered in turn.

Productivity of the Labor Process

In the ground crew harvest, in particular, the recruitment of noncitizen workers enhances managerial control over the productivity of the labor process. The lack of political protections or avenues for redressing grievances for undocumented workers and the incapacity of workers generally to stem the flow of labor into the industry severely limit claims for higher status and reward. These two factors act to create an intense competition among workers to find employment and, once employed, to keep their jobs. Thus, the channeling of undocumented workers into the ground crews, as demonstrated in chapter 4, leads not only to competition but to differing employment strategies on the part of documented and undocumented workers. While documented workers attempt to "stretch out" their work careers, undocumented workers seek to maximize their short-run earnings. Because employers seek to sustain high levels of productivity, the decentralization of recruitment to the level of the foreman enables indocumentados to fulfill their employment strategies while at the same time undermining those of the documented workers.

Beyond the pace of work, the organization of the labor system also serves to undercut the organizational potential of the crews themselves. The recruitment of undocumented workers makes it possible for a labor process built on mutual coordination and collective skill to be highly productive without being subject to control by worker organizations. In the case of unionized workers at both Miracle and Verde, differences in citizenship status severely hamper efforts to translate crew skill into a more traditional career. At Verde, where union organization has been most aggressive, the only real achievement has been the tying of seniority to job security. Senior workers may enjoy greater security in employment, but the result has been the construction of a two-tiered system in which greater demands are made on low seniority workers. Within the industry as a whole, the availability of a highly elastic and politically vulnerable labor supply enables employers to use workers in a physically destructive labor process without being held accountable for its effects. This was clearly evidenced in the sloping age-earnings profile (fig. 3), in short work careers, and in the high rate of physical disability among workers.

In the ground crew, the recruitment of undocumented workers serves as a form of insurance for the organization's investment in training individual workers and crews. The nonmarket control exercised by employers over undocumented workers virtually prevents that skill (acquired within the organization) from being appropriated by labor and withheld from the firm for the purpose of wage negotiation or control over the work itself. The political vulnerability of undocumented labor—especially with regard to petitioning state regulation of occupational attainment or certification of skill—prevents skill from showing up as the property of the worker independent of the organization. Political vulnerability and the availability of competitive labor also prevent crews, the larger unit of skill, from effectively bargaining with employers. Even when skills are acquired external to the organization that purchases them, that is, in the event that individuals or crews are trained in another firm, workers cannot use that skill as the basis of wage negotiation.

In the wrap crews, by contrast, the pace of work is much less influenced by the skills or coordination of workers than it is by the technology of the machine. Thus the value of undocumented workers in the ground crews, their vulnerability to political coercion over work pace, is less important in the wrap crew. However, the recruitment of women (both citizen and noncitizen) enables firms to reorganize production without having to make concessions or compensation to the labor force. At the same time, the concentration of women in the crews creates a gender identification with key positions in the crews, especially in wrapping, and acts to enhance external control over production.

Stability in the Labor Force

In both the ground and wrap crew harvests, the recruitment of noncitizens and women enhances the stability of the labor force. That stability, measured as a function of turnover in the labor force, translates into savings in production costs: it reduces the number of workers who have to be trained to carry out the tasks associated with the harvest.

In the wrap crews, the recruitment of women and older workers enables firms to turn labor's vulnerability to the organization's advantage. The disadvantaged status and the restricted labor market position of women serve to severely limit occupational opportunities, especially for women with children. The division of labor in the family constrains women's choice of occupations: the dual role of wife and mother removes many career options from women's grasp. Beyond that, women's status as the secondary wage earner means that most women are limited in terms of the geographic area they can cover occupationally (e.g., as migrants). Thus, women can be employed seasonally. Citizen women, in particular, can be supported financially by an alternative set of institutions—the family or the state—when they are not employed. In other words, the highly restricted occupational opportunities for citizen and alien women and, in turn, the availability of alternative sources of support ensure the creation of an abundant and stable supply of wrap crew labor.

Control Over the Labor Process

The distinctive legal and political disadvantages imposed on farm workers have been used to isolate agricultural employment as an enclave for immigrant workers. The manipulation of ascribed characteristics has further been used to drive a wedge between groups of workers: citizens and noncitizens, men and women. The efforts of organized labor unions to gain a foothold in agricultural labor markets have suffered from the ability of employers to stimulate conflict and competition between domestic and foreign workers, as well as between different ethnic groups making up the alien labor force. These kinds of tactics have been cited in numerous other settings as well (Castles and Kosack, 1975; Castells, 1975; Burowoy, 1976; Paige, 1975).

Efforts by organized labor to extend into agriculture have demonstrated the difficulties inherent in overcoming both the political power of agricultural employers and the conflict generated between protected and unprotected labor (Galarza, 1971; McWilliams, 1971; Friedland and Thomas, 1974). While the major labor unions and the AFL-CIO consistently opposed the importation of alien labor, forays into actual labor organization were scattered and largely unsuccessful. Differences in the structure of agricultural and industrial work practices and employment, on the one hand, and differences in legal status of agricultural workers, on the other, acted to diminish the progress and the persistence of union organizing drives. In the case of the AFL, minimal returns on investment led to diminished efforts in organizing. In the case of the Teamsters, a strategy of containment—where the union sought to prohibit the expanded use of alien labor—was developed to protect nonfield workers. As a result, the conditions and earnings associated with agricultural labor remained under the control of employers.

The irony of the most successful of farm worker unions—the United Farm Workers—is that its organization around the common national and cultural heritage and employment situation of farm workers has made it subject to severe whipsawing by employers. The political and social divisions in the membership along the lines of citizenship and gender have blunted the union's ability to challenge the organization of work and has forced it to pursue two restricted and costly strategies. One strategy, the pursuit of political protections through state extension of labor legislation to include farm workers, has limited the union's ability to carry on extensive organizational campaigns. Time and organizational resources that might otherwise be devoted to membership campaigns at the local level have had to be focused on legislative and electoral battles on a state-by-state basis instead. The other strategy, admittedly a last resort, has focused union efforts to negotiate the highest possible wage settlements for workers, with secondary emphasis on the conditions or organization of work. This strategy, prevalent in the lettuce industry, has demonstrated the implicit notion that many of the workers presently covered will eventually be displaced through mechanization (Thomas and Friedland, 1982).

CITIZENSHIP AND IMMIGRATION POLICY

The economic and organizational attractiveness of noncitizens as labor market participants has been heightened by the increased political and economic claims associated with citizenship. Of the general category of noncitizens, undocumented immigrants offer the most significant contrast with persons who have some claims to make on either economic or political citizenship. Undocumented immigrants are politically unenfranchised labor whose presence in the nation-state is almost totally dependent upon their participation in economic organizations. As nonmembers of the community, undocumented immigrants can make no claims against the collectivity for politically mediated transfers or support payments. When employed, they are severely restricted in their ability to make claims against employers/economic organizations for higher status or reward. They cannot make claims on the state to regulate or enforce their occupational, labor market, or organizational position; skill or training certification is either denied or devalued as the basis for negotiation over the price of labor power. Furthermore, undocumented immigrants are denied the capacity to use citizenship entitlements—unemployment compensation or general assistance aid—as the basis for establishing geographical stability. Thus, they cannot draw welfare to make up for periods of seasonal disemployment or industrial relocation in order to sustain a stable residence. Undocumented workers are forced to be more mobile and, subsequently, more "responsive" to economic conditions.

The lack of protection, political or economic, associated

with this labor pool makes it particularly vulnerable to manipulation by employers. Undocumented workers may be paid less than their enfranchised counterparts in the domestic labor force—though they cannot be paid less than what is necessary to sustain them at a given level of skill. Undocumented workers represent cheaper labor in price terms. Beyond pay levels, however, undocumented workers can be used to sustain more labor-intensive production processes because they are less able to reproduce skill as higher status or reward. Undocumented workers, if not used directly to undercut the bargaining position of citizen and documented labor, can be used to politically and organizationally fragment labor at several levels. First, they can be brought into competition with negatively privileged citizen labor, most particularly blacks, Latinos, women, and youths. As competitors for the same category of jobs (e.g., in service and retail trade), undocumented workers provide the equivalent of a decrease in the overall wage levels associated with those jobs or a diminution of minimum wage laws in that sector. The latter strategy provides the equivalent of a reduction in the guarantees of citizenship without directly expressing the battle in those terms.

Second, undocumented workers can be used to politically fragment ethnic organizations. In particular, the question of strategy regarding the undocumented worker has strained organizational efforts in the Hispanic community (Thomas, 1981). In this case, common ethnic and national heritage draws undocumented workers and citizens together but differences in political protection/vulnerability pull them apart. Third, and at a more general level, the emphasis on "illegality" as portrayed in the popular press and political debate focuses organizational strategies among trade unions on the characteristics of undocumented workers as nonmembers of the community, not as members of a common class. Thus, undocumented workers have been viewed by leading figures in the labor movement as an "external" explanation for the deteriorating position of American labor. Although unemployment due to economic decline has captured national attention most recently, it was not so long ago that George

Meany and colleagues in the AFL-CIO were decrying the illegal alien menace as the principal cause for increased urban unemployment. Caught up in the worsening national economic situation, Meany, and others far to his left, focused on the supposed threat to the national community posed by the alleged invasion of Mexican and Latin American workers.

The capacity of employers to manipulate undocumented workers politically, using communal status as the lever, depends on the reproduction of the distinctive negative privileges associated with noncitizenship. Not only does the supply of labor have to be perpetuated but labor's distinctive quality must also be sustained. It is not surprising, therefore, that efforts to deal with the illegal alien/undocumented immigrant issue focus not on employer involvement in the recruitment of labor but on regulating the flow and restricting the claims available to noncitizens.

In recent years two major directions for immigration policy have been developed to perpetuate political manipulation and reproduction of political vulnerability. The first has focused most directly on regulation of the flow of labor across the borders. Greater efforts to monitor border crossings and to apprehend and deport border violators have had the effect of sensitizing the public to the alleged threat of unchecked immigration and, at the same time, has increased the circulation of labor across the border. This "enforced circulation of labor" (Burawoy, 1976) has not proven any more successful in curbing the flow of labor between Latin America and the United States. But that was not its intention. Rather, increased surveillance and apprehension has served to prevent the stabilization of undocumented labor in the United States and, in the process, has increased the risk for individual migrants. That increased risk has redounded to the advantage of employers: fear of apprehension and deportation makes workers that much more committed to employment where they can find it, especially when employers offer a form of protection against apprehension. A proposed program to further regulate the flow of labor, though not to eliminate it, has been offered in various circles: something on the order of a revised bracero program (Craig, 1971, and Galarza, 1964, for detailed discussions of the bracero program, Public Law 78) or an American version of the "guestworker" (*gastarbeiter*) system found in West Germany. Such a program would directly involve the government in the licensing or certification of noncitizen workers for employment in the United States for a limited duration. Both these systems create a semi-caste system of labor. Both provide for political mediation of labor market processes where the denial of access to citizenship entitlements provide the equivalent of a denial or (at least) an abridgment of economic citizenship (i.e., formal market freedom).

Equally important, efforts to "distribute the burden" of blame for employment of undocumented workers, such as that proposed by recent legislation (the Simpson-Mazzoli bill), do little more than push Hispanic groups into an uneasy alliance with employers. The approach suggested by the Simpson-Mazzoli bill would impose financial penalties for employers who hire undocumented workers—a goal long advocated by organized labor in the United States. Enforcement of such provisions, however, would require an effective means for employers to screen potential employees, something less easily counterfeited than a Social Security card, driver's license, or green card. Job applicants of Hispanic descent or appearance would be immediately suspect unless they provided adequate proof of their legal immigrant status or citizenship. To avoid overt discrimination against Hispanics, the only workable solution would be to require some universal form of identification for all citizens. Since civil rights advocates have long argued against universal identification papers for U.S. citizens and Hispanics have argued vehemently against a restricted version, civil rights activists, liberal politicians, and Hispanic leaders find themselves temporarily standing alongside employers in the fight to quash such programs. Even with the creation of a somewhat less objectionable identification system, the current legislation provides few concrete clues as to how efforts to police employers (and the border) will prove any more effective than past attempts to regulate illegal border entry.

The other major direction for immigration policy has been

one of total exclusion of noncitizen labor. This approach would be tantamount to the creation of a Berlin Wall at the border—or, alternatively viewed, a Great Wall of Mexico—sufficiently well protected to deny access to any but the most qualified immigrants. While the content of those qualifications themselves are the topic of important debate, the past experience of efforts to seal off the border only alert us to the fact that restrictions increase the utility of undocumented labor to employers and the vulnerability of undocumented labor to political manipulation. The refusal to sanction employers for hiring undocumented workers or to provide sufficient funding to make such sanctions enforceable reinforces the representation of the issue as one in which indocumentados "steal" jobs. The circulation of labor across the border (whether as a category or as individuals) effectively reproduces the distinctive political inequalities associated with noncitizenship. The insistence on the integrity of the border and national economic health (i.e., the representation of noncitizens as a threat to citizens) increases the utility of undocumented labor to employers. As long as enforcement of immigration laws is located at the level where it cannot work, at the level of the individual, then the rhetoric of an "invasion" of illegal aliens sustains employer advantage while appearing to be a threat to the entire community.

CITIZENSHIP, GENDER, AND CLASS

To this point, I have argued that the maintenance and reproduction of the nonmarket statuses attached to indocumentados and women have granted to employers significant advantages. Undocumented workers and women in the lettuce industry are paid less than equally skilled workers in other sectors and can be employed in physically destructive and arbitrary ways. Yet employers do not create those statuses; they purchase labor power and seek to transform workers' activity into products and profits. How, then, do we account for the production of those debilitating statuses?

At the outset I argued that neo-Marxian analysts of labor markets and labor processes generally explained citizenship status and gender as either functional aspects or ideological distortions of underlying class relations. In this, the concluding section, I will argue that citizenship and gender must be understood as systems of inequality which are parallel to and interactive with class inequality.

Citizenship Broadened

Serious consideration of the role played by undocumented labor in agriculture and other sectors of the economy necessarily leads to questions about how citizenship is to be understood both as an analytic category and as a feature of social organization in capitalist society. In this study, the abridgment or denial of citizenship has served as a central feature conditioning the use and the compensation of labor. But, as I pointed out in chapter 4, noncitizenship has nothing to do with the quality of indocumentado laborers or their capacity to work. Rather, it applies to their position in the national polity, to the kinds of claims they can make on the state and/or the economic organizations in which they are employed. If undocumented workers are active economically (indeed, they have to be in order to remain in the country) but can make no political claims on the basis of that activity, how then are we to characterize the political and economic claims of citizens? Are they homogeneous or are there different claims or levels of qualification for citizenship among those acknowledged to be members of the national polity?

What makes citizenship something of a peculiar concept is that it is often viewed as nonproblematic. For some sociologists (especially those concerned with the formation of nation-states, Weber, 1954; Bendix, 1969; Skocpol, 1979; Tilly, 1975; Moore, 1966) citizenship has been used as an important indicator of social development—particularly as regards the creation and generalization of certain kinds of reciprocal rights and obligations that tie individuals to a national community. However, in the study of social inequality and social organization, citizenship is not often considered a crucial defining characteristic distinguishing one set of actors from another. This is particularly true when individual nations are taken as the unit of analysis. In that sense, national boundaries are taken for granted and are only considered of central importance when exchanges or relations between states affect the object of study. In much political economy, the focus is on the movement of capital, commodities, or organizations (e.g., transnational corporations) across national boundaries, even in the case of migrant flows of highly skilled technical and managerial labor. Most demographers who study population flows do pay more attention to issues of national origin and destination but fail to develop a rigorous conceptualization of citizenship and, thus, often underemphasize the political and economic consequences of differences in citizenship status among those migrants. In some cases, the issue of workers or immigrants with different citizenship statuses is taken into account; however, those studies have more often focused on the isolated or regional significance of those differences, for example, the general argument that undocumented workers or noncitizens show up in southwestern agriculture because agriculture needs certain kinds of labor and Mexicans happen to be nearby in search of jobs.

With the discovery of large numbers of undocumented immigrants working in the United States, however, the meaning of citizenship both as a symbol and as a concrete practice has become much more a problem for sociological analysis. At the most general level, I would argue, citizenship refers to a relationship between the individual and the collectivity. National citizenship, by extension, refers to membership in a national collectivity. Though individuals may claim or be granted a number of citizenships—municipal, regional, and state—I am most concerned with national citizenship. National citizenship represents a form of membership unmediated by intervening levels of organization or allegiance in its most extreme form: a higher order of responsibility or obligation between the individual and the state. While an individual may claim a variety of citizenships, the defining characteristic of national citizenship is its use as a status that *transcends* all other, intervening memberships in particular areas. Thus, to be a citizen of the United States entails a more general set of rights or obligations than, for example, to be a citizen of Michigan, Detroit, or the Poletown neighborhood.

Beyond the ascriptive sense, citizenship also represents a reciprocal relationship between the individual and the collectivity—in this case, the nation-state. To be a citizen is to (consciously or unconsciously) undertake certain responsibilities or obligations to the collective. The nature of these obligations may vary; from the payment of taxes as a rent on membership to some further and more directly continuous participation in state-directed activities, such as military service. At the same time, citizenship entails certain rights or entitlements that individuals may claim against the collectivity and collective resources; again, these may vary, but usually include some claims against state activity such as military protection and state services (e.g., education, welfare, etc.). Most often, the nature of these resources or services will be described as social goods—goods that represent the benefits of participation in the national collectivity. They may also be represented as symbols of participation: life, liberty, and the pursuit of happiness, to cite one common reference.

Citizenship, in its most universal form, represents a *symbol of equality* among members of a given collectivity, a symbol that represents equality of obligation and equality of entitlement. In the United States and other Western democracies, citizenship represents a category of claims for formal equality in the political life of the community. This goes beyond the more popular notion of citizenship—or, perhaps more correctly, generalizes that notion—in that it includes more than what are conceived to be the "obligations" of citizens to be politically active—to vote, to take an interest in national affairs, to write to Congressional representatives—or the "rights" of citizens to run for public office, to publicly address or seek redress of grievances, and so on. Citizenship in the United States stands opposed to a system in which status or class differences are associated with unequal claims on the polity. In particular, I refer to differential access to political power based on criteria such as land ownership, sex, race, or occupation. In the formal sense at least, citizenship is available to all who meet certain criteria. In the United States the major criteria for acquisition and exercise of citizenship are age, mental competence, residence and, for immigrants, some visible means of support. Though these criteria can be manipulated to serve certain purposes for certain groups, at the most general level citizenship is at least identified with political equality.

Citizenship is also an important status with respect to economic activity, though it is generally not associated with the operations of a market economy. In the United States, citizenship represents a guarantee of formal market freedom, that is, the freedom to enter into the economic arena (market) and economic relations (economic exchange) and to do so on an equal footing with fellow participants. The polity acts to guarantee that formal equality through legal enforcement of contracts and regulation of market exchanges such that contract partners are held accountable for performance of their respective obligations. But, in contrast to the political dimension of citizenship, where equality of claims and outcomes are supposed to be guaranteed, freedom to enter into the market does not bring with it an assurance or guarantee of equality of outcome in market transactions or economic activity. In other words, the political features of membership in the collectivity (citizenship) are detached from, or only effective within limits on economic activity and economic outcome.

These two aspects or dimensions of membership in the collectivity come to confront one another as opposing principles in capitalist society: political and economic citizenship clash as competing symbols of participation in the collectivity. Political citizenship represents political equality and equality of access to the marketplace while economic citizenship represents formal market freedom and inequality of outcome. In other words, political equality is confronted by a division of labor between social groups (workers and capitalists) and between economic organizations that are built around unequal access to the means of production.

This conflict has been dealt with by T. H. Marshall in his essays on social class and citizenship. Marshall (1977) argues that the conflict between these two principles of social organization—of political equality and economic inequality—gives rise to *citizenship* as an important social category and to the *welfare state* as an effort to overcome the contradictory features of citizenship and class. The welfare state operates, according to Marshall, in two ways: first, it operates to facilitate the "fair fight," that is, to ensure that contestants in the marketplace (the fighters in this analogy) are properly prepared to contest. Such action is carried out through educational activities and through regulation and enforcement of contracts. However, the welfare-state acts ameliorate the negative outcomes of the "fair fight." It offers ice packs in the form of state-mediated support and transfer payments to those who lose in the market. The welfare state may be either reactive—reacting to the conditions of the economy—or it may be proactive—responding to the demands made upon political citizenship in the area of equality of access (responding to historical inequalities in access by such measures as Affirmative Action or the Equal Rights Amendment).

But because the welfare state notion (as espoused by Marshall, in particular) does not coincide with total state intervention in the economy, it does not pose a direct challenge to the principles of private property or economic (class) inequality. Thus the exercise of citizenship is conditioned by individual and group position in the economy and economic organizations. That is to suggest that citizenship ought to be conceived of as something of a continuum: *a variable instead of an invariant characteristic.* Political citizenship constitutes rights and entitlements associated with the welfare functions of the state and the criteria for exercise of that status is intermittent, unstable participation or nonparticipation in economic organizations or value-producing labor processes. In particular, the exercise of political citizenship is conceived of as the making of claims on state-mediated transfers and services such as welfare aid, aid to dependent children, disability payments, old age aid, and state-supported food allocation programs. These claims are based on membership in the collectivity and are claims against collective resources.

Economic citizenship, by contrast, constitutes rights and entitlements associated with economic activity and rewards for participation in the economy and economic organizations. The exercise of economic citizenship is conceived of as the making of claims on transfers mediated by economic organizations (health and medical benefits, pensions, and low-interest loans) and state-mediated transfers based on past participation in the economy (Social Security, federally guaranteed loans, tax benefits, and incentives). These kinds of transfer payments are sometimes referred to as welfare to the middle and upper classes, though broadly conceived they are also to be found in the wage and benefit packages that form the core of many union contracts.

To summarize to this point, the exercise of political citizenship is the exercise of rights associated with membership and participation in the community. It is associated with claims that form a "floor" level of existence in the society. In Marxian terms, this can be roughly equated to the social determination of the floor cost for reproducing labor at the lowest level of skill. The exercise of economic citizenship is the exercise of rights associated with both membership in the community *and* participation in the economy: where membership in the community facilitates a set of rights and entitlements in economic organizations and where participation in economic organizations facilitates a distinctive set of claims on the state. Most important, within a class analysis of economic organizations, citizenship for those who are economically active provides the potential for negotiation over the price of their labor, the ability to push the price of labor above the cost necessary to reproduce it at a given level of skill by means of enforcement of market position.

The thrust of this theoretical discussion can now be stated in much simpler terms. The rise of citizenship and the welfare state are related directly to conflict between the nation-state as a collection of politically equal individuals and the capitalist organization of the economy as the locus of inequality. The extension of the political rights of citizenship (especially into the area of welfare aid to those who are not economically active) has simultaneously created a floor level of existence (a guarantee against starvation) and has bolstered the market position of those who are economically active.

This conceptualization of citizenship in capitalist society incorporates the basic assumption of Marxian theory of the formal market freedom of labor but questions its applicability to all members of society. By drawing attention to the distinctions between participation in economic organizations and participation in political organizations (in a broad sense, the welfare state), I seek to highlight the material base and the ideological consequences of differences in citizenship status. Marxian theory focuses our attention on the ways in which the capitalist labor process and the drive to accumulate capital construct a social structure appropriate to the reproduction of surplus value (what Gordon et al. refer to as a "social structure of accumulation," 1982:22–25). Yet, as I have attempted to illustrate here, political citizenship is rooted in a labor process in which *no new value* is produced; it is *transferred*. Thus, the welfare recipient makes nothing; but, through the exercise on claims associated with political citizenship, he or she participates in a labor process in which the physical activity of living in a tenement "unlocks" values stored in that building, values that, logically, would not be realized if the exchange were market-mediated, and transfers them to its owner—in the form of rent paid by the state. Similarly, a visit to the hospital by the same welfare recipient produces nothing; but the fact that he/she is acted upon by a doctor or technician results in a transfer of value to the medical care industry. Equally important, participation in this peculiar labor process confers a specific status on those who exercise political citizenship: that of "deadbeat" or parasite (for a similar argument, see Piven and Cloward, 1971). And, to the extent that an identifiable category of citizens (disproportionately black, minority, and female) participate in that labor process, the status is generalized to all members of that category.

The point here is not to suggest that the assumption of formal market freedom of labor is entirely inapplicable; it is instead to argue that the assumption does not apply to all members of society. This does not constitute a reversion to the Marxian concept of an industrial reserve army of labor because at least some portion of that army of labor will remain outside participation in economic organizations. They remain outside participation in economic organizations for two reasons: first, because a growing segment of the economy—most notably medical care and urban real estate—has developed on the basis of transfers of resources through the welfare system; and, second, because the advantages accruing to economic citizens—particularly unionized labor in core industries—have been built on the bedrock of a welfare system that serves as their lever for claims for a larger portion of the surplus they produce.

Thus citizenship in capitalist society stands apart from but necessarily interacts with economic class inequality. It is offered here as part of a theory of political inequality which seeks to account for the three phenomena surfaced in this study: (1) the integrative functions of membership in a national polity, that is, the ideology of a community of equals which acts to obscure differential access to wealth and property; (2) the manner in which political rights and entitlements associated with membership are themselves products of efforts by different class fractions to create relatively privileged positions in the polity and the economy, that is, different citizenships; and (3) how these different citizenships have altered the operations of the capitalist economy, that is, between those engaged in value-producing and value-transferring labor processes.

GENDER AND CLASS

If citizenship conditions the expenditure and the compensation of labor and exists as a status external to the labor process, gender shares many of those qualities. As was demonstrated in chapter 6, the unique disadvantages associated with being a woman provide distinct advantages to employers seeking to rationalize production. But, if gender is not the product of the organization of the labor process, then where do we find its source?

This problem has been posed in recent years by a number of feminist scholars seeking to remove the study of gender from the shadows of both Marxian and bourgeois theory. Heidi Hartmann (1979:3), in particular, has suggested that

> Most Marxist analyses of women's position take as their question relationship of women to the economic system, rather than that of women to men, apparently assuming the latter will be explained in their discussion of the former.

Beyond simply raising a question of relations among men and women, however, she is correctly concerned that the explanations for gender inequality not be reduced to an analysis of the functions of gender for class:

> The categories of Marxist analysis, class, reserve army of labor, wage labor, do not explain why particular people fill particular places (in the structure of production). They give no clues about why *women* are subordinate to *men* inside and outside the family and why it is not the other way around. *Marxist categories, like capital itself, are sex blind* [emphasis added]. (1979:10–11)

The clues for the subordination of women to men, Hartmann argues, reside in the interaction between capitalism and patriarchy (1976:208). Under capitalism, employers purchase labor power and, through the labor process, arrange its transformation into commodities and profit. Where possible, they will endeavor to increase their control over the labor process and often do so by recruiting workers whose social position affords them less protection from direct exploitation or forced competition in the market for jobs. Women, like undocumented workers, have been viewed historically as a source of labor vulnerable enough to be used to undercut the established positions of male laborers. But, as Hartmann and others point out, arguing that women are capable of being used in this fashion does not explain the source of their disadvantaged status. Thus, patriarchy, as a system of hierarchical relations between men and women, is employed as a structure parallel to capitalist social relations to explain the coincidence of class and gender as organizing principles of stratification. Patriarchy, according to Hartmann (1979:18), is

> a set of social relations which has a material base and in which there are hierarchical relations between men and solidarity among them which enable them in turn to dominate women. The material base of patriarchy is men's control over women's labor power.

Patriarchal stratification, according to this argument, predates the development of capitalism but the two have come to structure one another over time. Capitalism strips from patriarchy the all-encompassing control of men over women through the creation of a "free" market for labor. Yet patriarchy persists (albeit in altered form) in its effect on capitalism: capitalists, managers, and organized labor are overwhelmingly composed of men, and women's disadvantaged labor market positions are very much a product of men *as* men attempting to protect their privileged positions in the economy and society. Capitalism acts to reduce the capacity of families to sustain themselves independent from the market or wage labor (Braverman, 1975:271–283), but patriarchy and patriarchal ideologies of male superiority sustain men's control over their wives' labor in the family. This latter point is attested to quite strongly in the discussion of decisions about wives' working and women's double day in farm worker families (see chap. 6). The persistence of men's dominance in the family and in labor market positions enforces the dependence of women on men through the combined activities of gender-role socialization and job segregation. Thus capitalism and patriarchy, through their interaction, create the basis for an alliance among men as men, despite their hierarchical arrangement as capitalists, managers, and workers.

In conclusion, this study of citizenship, gender, and work has shown that the capacity of workers to organize to make claims for higher wages or to gain closure over entry into their occupations (in order to accomplish the same end) can be undermined by the vulnerability attendant on them as unenfranchised labor. While the cost of producing skill is equivalent across categories of citizenship and gender, I have tried to demonstrate that the ability of workers to force up the price of labor is affected by their political status. The elements of labor cost—the factors associated with producing and reproducing labor of a particular intensity—are not reduced but the potential price of labor is. Therefore, the utility of a migrant labor system, particularly one dominated by undocumented immigrants, is evident. Undocumented labor, and the labor that must compete with it, can be employed effectively in a highly skilled production process because first, it cannot translate into an organizational basis for bargaining over price, and second, its vulnerable political position makes high wages only attainable through higher levels of productivity.

The construction of this type of labor system depends heavily on the ability of employers to exert leverage in the market for labor. To the extent that domestic workers can exert and enforce claims to some level of closure over entry into the market, then the appearance of this form of labor system is unlikely. However, where political and organizational forces can be mobilized to counter that closure, the recruitment and utilization of undocumented labor becomes increasingly likely.

This study has sought to provide an explanation for the organization of work and wages in industrial agriculture. In it, I have attempted to show how nonmarket statuses are used to influence labor market and wage determination processes. Rather than argue that the disadvantaged status of Mexicans or women is a product of ethnic, national, or biological differences (characteristics inherent in the workers themselves), I have argued that the division of labor in production, the political intervention of employers, and the system of stratification external to the workplace together produce and maintain that status. Thus the organization of the labor process, while distinctly capitalist, is nonetheless intimately linked to the form the labor market takes. In the case of the lettuce industry, the communal organization of work in skilled crews is linked to the perpetuation of a labor system built around noncitizen and undocumented workers. In the case of the wrap crews, the capacity of firms to successfully reorganize production and avail themselves of abundant and stable labor is linked to the disadvantaged status and labor market restrictions upon women and noncitizens.

This is not to argue that people who harvest lettuce are any less engaged in a capitalist system of production than are, for example, carpenters or machinists. Nor is it to suggest that the study of capitalist relations of production should forsake analysis of the labor process. It is to argue, however, that the status of labor external to the labor process has a direct effect on how that work is organized. To understand how lettuce firms are able to acquire skilled labor at a low price, one must also account for the practices that attach a particular status to labor. The analysis of industrial organization, agricultural and nonagricultural, must take into account the construction of labor *supply* as well as demand.

Notes

1: Citizenship and Labor Supply

1. The role of union organizations will be considered in some detail, especially in relation to efforts to control access to employment. However, this is not a study of farm worker unions per se (the United Farm Workers Union, AFL-CIO). While a thorough study of the UFW remains to be done, there are recent works that address the history and the dynamics of farm worker movements; see, for example, Thomas and Friedland, 1982; Friedland and Thomas, 1974; Majka and Majka, 1982; Jenkins and Perrow, 1977; and Thomas, 1981. The UFW and other unions will be drawn into this analysis where their inclusion is crucial for historical or analytic purposes.

2. The impetus for this research design came from both the nature of the problems being studied and from the inspiration provided by three other works that attempted to combine structural and interactional analysis, i.e., Becker, Geer, Hughes, and Strauss (*Boys in White*, 1961); Lipset, Trow, and Coleman (*Union Democracy*, 1956); and Burawoy (*Manufacturing Consent*, 1979).

3. This name and the name given to the other major companies studied (Miracle Vegetable, Verde Lettuce, and Salad Giant) are fictitious. The real names are masked in order to protect the identities of individuals who are employed by these companies and who feared reprisal should their remarks be exposed. I have given the companies names that differ considerably from their real ones and have substituted pseudonyms for all respondents. The choice of Miracle Vegetable Company for fieldwork was somewhat arbitrary. During the course of the year's study, a strike among unionized lettuce workers began. To avoid the hazards associated with strikebreaking and the likely bias resulting from the influx of less experienced workers, I chose to work at a company still under contract with a union not participating in the strike. However, being in the

fields and in the labor camps during that time enabled me to monitor the strike and to interview workers who had walked out.

3: Economic Organization, Labor Force, and Labor Process

1. The bottom tier firms are not really competitive of course with the top tier firms in the case of contract production. Rather the significance of the relationship resides in the fact that it stands in contrast to the traditional alternative of marketing cooperatives for smaller firms. In this sense, a larger firm, not a cooperative, has centralized control over capital and thus determines the allocation of market returns. While the contract relationship does not allow the smaller firm to compete with the larger, in order for the relationship to be maintained the smaller firm must also be maintained. The smaller firms can, and most often do, use the rent to sustain themselves and to finance continued production of other commodities. Thus "yeoman" farmers are drawn into the structure of industrial production rather than being expelled from it. Granted, their subordinate position in the relationship seriously limits opportunities for further expansion, as was argued in chapter 2, but it also raises an important issue for further research. That is, if this kind of relationship is a durable one (as I suggest elsewhere [Thomas, 1977]), then one might rephrase the commonly asked question, "Why are small farms vanishing?" to ask instead, "Why are there so many small farms still around?"

2. For a more detailed organizational analysis of one of these firms, see Fredrick's study, "Agribusiness in the Lettuce Fields" (1979), and Friedland, Barton, and Thomas (1981).

3. Commuters, in contrast, are workers who have temporary passes to allow them daily entry into the United States. In the lettuce industry, these workers are of particular importance to production areas near the Mexican border, e.g., the Imperial Valley in California and the San Luis Valley in Arizona. Since these workers have limited access to work in the U.S., they are least likely to show up in production areas farther than 50–75 miles from the border.

4. These figures are based on data presented in chapter 6 in tables 24 and 25.

5. This is calculated on the basis of information supplied by the president of Miracle Vegetable Company. The company operates a total of 16 wrap machines valued at $125,000 each for a total investment of $2 million.

4: Citizenship, Earnings, and Work Organization

1. As continues to be the practice today, firms harvest and market lettuce under different labels. The label names correspond to the quality of lettuce packed. For example, Miracle Vegetable markets lettuce under three labels: Imperial, Prince, and Viceroy, in order of descending quality.

2. In company literature distributed to employees at this and other companies, the use of drugs and alcohol on the job are specifically prohibited. However, even at companies that prepare these employee booklets, most workers reported never having received the literature. In any case, only a small percentage of the workers I interviewed could read English or Spanish.

3. Despite persistent requests made of a total of eleven firms, none would allow access to such data. Many of the firms expressed fear that they would lose competitive advantage should such data be revealed—even when assured that records would remain anonymous. Others flatly refused or suggested that the union might find the information useful. Also, even if companies were to divulge production figures, there would be no way legally to obtain verification of citizenship status from workers for the purpose of comparison. Attempts were also made to gain access to blind earnings records of United Farm Workers members through the union's accounting apparatus. Citing the urgency of preparations for contract negotiations, the UFW declined to participate in the study. It was later revealed to me during consultation with union staff that the UFW did not keep track of production, even for developing contract proposals.

5: Comparative Case Studies

1. At the time of the interviews, Mondragon (whose name has been changed to protect his present position) worked for another lettuce producer in the Salinas Valley. His departure from Miracle came about as a result of the firm's having been raided by the Border Patrol in two consecutive months. The circumstances are recounted later in this section. However, Mondragon's testimony as to management practice was corroborated by former employees of the company.

2. In addition, I had decided during the course of the strike not to openly engage in research or discussion with the strikebreaking

workers. Given the turmoil and the emotions of the times, I felt it wise to pursue other avenues of data collection.

3. Verde executives reported that the company had had some financial problems but refused to elaborate. Annual reports of the parent corporation describe in vague terms the position of the subsidiary but mask the extent of losses by aggregating sales and income figures for Verde with other associated subsidiaries. Therefore it is impossible to give an accurate picture of the actual profit/ loss situation for the company.

4. Promotion at Verde is no less restricted in its scope, however, than other companies. As in other companies, upward occupational mobility is limited to the fields. Though in theory a worker could rise in the ranks from fieldwork to maintenance or other technical employment, organizational obstacles block such movement. Most higher level jobs require that applicants speak and read English. The training needed for technical certification, e.g., a welder's license, is not provided by the company. Finally, jurisdictional boundaries between unions act to create exclusive occupational ladders, e.g., the distinction between field and nonfield work is simultaneously a boundary between the UFW and the Teamsters.

5. Twenty-seven lettuce workers from Verde were interviewed at length during the course of the study. Fifteen had two or more years' seniority with the company while the remainder had less than two years. Because evidence of the two-tier system began to emerge only after a majority of the interviews had been conducted, I could not collect more specific data on earnings or work history for the entire group. Therefore, the material presented and the conclusions reached are based almost entirely on those interviews.

6: Gender, Labor Supply, and Commitment

1. See figure 2 in chapter 3.

2. Salinas *Californian,* 9/20/79, and table 20.

3. The use of technological change for the purpose of enhancing managerial control has been widely studied. For some recent examples, see Braverman (1975), Noble (1977), and Edwards (1979).

4. See, among others, Blauner (1964), Chinoy (1955), Roy (1952), Burawoy (1979), and Braverman (1975).

5. This sort of extended supervision through family members is by no means restricted to wrap machine crews. Examples can be found in small family businesses and other industries in which family labor is employed. In an earlier study of work organization on the

tomato harvesting machines, I found that some of the companies employed husbands as machine drivers and their wives as "foreladies"; see Thomas (1977) and Friedland and Barton (1975).

6. This is not to deny that some foremen flirt in order to pick up women in their crew. One foreman at Miracle, in particular, had a reputation for such behavior. As a result, women who worked on his crew were often suspected by others of sleeping with him.

7. See the discussion of machine cost in chapter 3.

8. For example, see Tepperman (1970); Balu and Jusenius (1976); U.S. Department of Labor (1975); Gubbels (1977); and Glazer and Waehrer (1977).

9. I am grateful to Anne Fredricks for sharing this insight gained from her fieldwork in Wisconsin canneries.

10. During the early morning hours when workers assembled in the company parking lot waiting for the buses to arrive, most conversation among the men was centered on the availability of work in other crews and companies and on the earnings of the ground crew workers. Not unlike the network-building described by Lipset et al. (1956:194–197) in *Union Democracy*, wrap crew workers attempted to strike up conversations and friendships with ground crew members in the hope of finding an "in" to those jobs.

Bibliography

Aronowitz, Stanley
   1973   *False Promises: The Shaping of American Working Class Consciousness.* New York: McGraw-Hill.
Averitt, Robert T.
   1968   *The Dual Economy.* New York: Norton.
Bach, Robert
   1978   "Mexican Immigration and U.S. Immigration Reform in the 1960s," *Kapitalstate* 7:63–80.
Baran, Paul, and Paul Sweezy
   1968   *Monopoly Capital.* New York: Monthly Review Press.
Baron, James N., and William T. Bielby
   1980   "Bringing the Firm Back In: Stratification, Segmentation and the Organization of Work," *American Sociological Review* 45:737–765.
Barton, Amy
   1978   "Campesinas: Women Farmworkers in the California Agricultural Labor Force." Sacramento: Calfornia Commission on the Status of Women, State of California.
Beck, E. M., Patrick Horan, and Charles Tolbert
   1978   "Stratification in a Dual Economy: A Sectoral Model of Earnings Determination," *American Sociological Review* 43:704–720.
Becker, Gary
   1964   *Human Capital.* New York: National Bureau of Economic Research.
Becker, Howard S., Blanche Geer, Everett Hughes, and Anselm Strauss
   1961   *Boys in White: Student Culture in Medical School.* Chicago: University of Chicago Press.
Bell, Carolyn
   1977   "Economics, Sex and Gender," in Nona Glazer and Helen Y. Waehrer, eds. *Woman in a Man-Made World,* pp. 30–38.

Bendix, Reinhard
    1969   *Nation-Building and Citizenship.* Garden City, N.Y.:
            Doubleday.
Bibb, Robert, and William Form
    1977   "The Effects of Industrial, Occupational and Sex Stratifi-
            cation on Wages in Blue Collar Labor Markets," *Social
            Forces* 55:974—996.
Blau, Francine, and Carol Jusenius
    1976   "Economists' Approaches to Sex Segregation in the
            Labor Market: An Appraisal," *Signs: Journal of Women in
            Culture and Society* 1:181–199.
Blauner, Robert
    1964   *Alienation and Freedom.* Chicago: University of Chicago
            Press.
Bluestone, Barry
    1970   "The Tripartite Economy: Labor Markets and the Work-
            ing Poor," *Poverty and Human Resources* 5:15–35.
Boas, Max, and Steve Chain
    1976   *Big Mac: The Unauthorized Story of McDonald's.* New York:
            New American Library.
Bonacich, Edna
    1976   "Advanced Capitalism and Black-White Relations in the
            United States: A Split Labor Market Interpretation,"
            American Journal of Sociology 41:34–51.
Braverman, Harry
    1975   *Labor and Monopoly Capital.* New York: Monthly Review
            Press.
Brown, Gerald
    1968   "The United Farm Workers Union and the Culture of
            Poverty." Ph.D. dissertation, Cornell University.
Burawoy, Michael
    1976   "The Functions and Reproduction of Migrant Labor:
            Comparative Study of California and South Africa,"
            American Journal of Sociology 81(5):1050–1066.
    1979   *Manufacturing Consent: Changes in the Labor Process Under
            Monopoly Capital.* Chicago: University of Chicago Press.
Bustamante, Jorge
    1977   "Undocumented Immigration from Mexico: Research
            Report," *International Migration Review* (1977):149–177.
Buttel, Fred, and Howard Newby (eds.)
    1980   *The Rural Sociology of the Advanced Societies.* Montclair,
            N.J.: Allanheld Osmun.

Buttel, Fred, Philip Ehrensaft, and William H. Friedland
Forth-   *Political Economy of Food and Agriculture in the Advanced*
coming   *Societies.* Ithaca, N.Y.: Cornell University Press.
Cain, Glenn
1976   "The Challenge of Segmented Labor Market Theories
           to Orthodox Theory: A Survey," *Journal of Economic Lit-*
           erature V, 14:1215–1257.
California Crop and Livestock Reporting Service
1979   *Annual Report (1978).* Department of Agriculture, Sac-
           ramento, California.
Cargill, B. F., and G. Rossmiller
1968   *Fruit and Vegetable Harvest Mechanization.* Rural Man-
           power Center Reports #16–18, East Lansing, Michigan
           State University.
Carman, Hoy
1980   "Coming: More Corporate Farms in California," *Califor-*
           nia Agriculture (January 1980):9–10.
Castells, Manuel
1975   "Immigrant Workers and Class Struggles in Advanced
           Capitalism: The Western European Experience," *Politics*
           and Society 5(1):33–66.
Castles, Steven, and G. Kosack
1975   *Immigrant Workers and Class Structure in Western Europe.*
           London: Oxford University Press.
Chambers, Clark A.
1952   *California Farm Organizations.* Berkeley and Los Angeles:
           University of California Press.
Chinoy, Eli
1955   *Automobile Workers and the American Dream.* Boston:
           Beacon Press.
Collins, Orvis, Melville Dalton, and Donald Roy
1946   "Restriction of Output and Social Cleavage in Industry,"
           Applied Anthropology 5:1–14.
Cornelius, Wayne
1976   "Mexican Immigration to the United States: The View
           from Rural Sending Communities," Center for Interna-
           tional Studies, MIT.
Craig, Richard
1971   *The Bracero Program.* Austin: University of Texas Press.
Dobb, Maurice
1963   *Studies in the Development of Capitalism.* New York: Inter-
           national Publishers.

Doeringer, Peter, and Michael Piore
  1975   *Internal Labor Markets and Manpower Analysis.* Lexington,
          Mass.: Heath.
Drossler Associates
  1976   *Results of the Distribution Research Study Conducted for
          California Iceberg Lettuce Advisory Board.* San Francisco:
          Drossler Research Corporation.
Dunlop, John
  1948   "The Development of Labor Organization: A Theoreti-
          cal Framework," in Richard Lester and Joseph Shister,
          eds. *Insights into Labor Issues.* New York: Macmillan.
Edwards, Richard C.
  1975   "The Social Relations of Production in the Firm and
          Labor Market Structure," *Politics and Society* 5(1):83–108.
  1979   *Contested Terrain.* New York: Basic Books.
Edwards, Richard, Michael Reich, and David Gordon, eds.
  1975   *Labor Market Segmentation.* Lexington, Mass: Heath.
Federal-State Market News Service
  1980   *Marketing Lettuce from Salinas-Watsonville-King City and
          Other Central California Districts.* Sacramento: Department
          of Food and Agriculture, Annual Reports.
Federal Trade Commission
  1976   *Commission Decisions: Findings, Orders and Opinions,* "In
          the Matter of United Brands Company," Vol. 83.
          Washington, D.C.: Government Printing Office.
Fellmeth, Robert
  1973   *The Politics of Land.* New York: Grossman.
Finiay, William
  1980   "The Occupational Community as a Labor System: The
          Case of Pacific Coast Longshoremen," Master's Thesis.
          Northwestern University.
Fisher, Lloyd H.
  1953   *The Harvest Labor Market in California.* Cambridge: Har-
          vard University Press.
Forbes Magazine
  1982   "Top 500 Corporations," May 1982.
Fredricks, Anne
  1979   "Agribusiness in the Lettuce Fields," *Food Monitor* 10:12–
          15.
Friedland, William H.
  1979   "Who Killed Rural Sociology?" Paper presented to the
          1979 meetings of the American Sociological Association,
          San Francisco.

Friedland, William H., and Dorothy Nelkin
1972 "Technological Trends and the Organization of Migrant Farm Workers," *Social Problems* 19(4):509–521.
Friedland, William H., and Robert J. Thomas
1974 "Paradoxes of Agricultural Unionism in California," *Society* II(4):52–60.
Friedland, William, and Amy Barton
1975 "Tomato Technology," *Society* 13(6).
Friedland, William H., Amy Barton, and Robert J. Thomas
1981 *Manufacturing Green Gold: Capital, Labor and Technology in the Lettuce Industry.* New York: Cambridge University Press.
Friedmann, Harriet
1981 "The Family Farm in Advanced Capitalism: Outline of a Theory of Simple Commodity Production in Agriculture." Paper presented to meetings of the American Sociological Association, Toronto, August.
Frundt, Henry
1981 "The Forces and Relations of Food Processing in the United States." Paper presented to the Conference on the Political Economy of Food and Agriculture in the Advanced Societies, Guelph, August.
Fuller, Varden
1955 *Labor Relations in Agriculture.* Berkeley: Institute of Industrial Relations, University of California.
Galarza, Ernesto
1964 *Merchants of Labor.* Santa Barbara: McNally and Loftin.
1971 *Spiders in the House and Workers in the Field.* Notre Dame: University of Notre Dame Press.
1977 *Farmworkers and Agri-Business in California, 1947–1960.* Notre Dame: University of Notre Dame Press.
Gamio, M.
1930 *Mexican Immigration to the United States.* Chicago: University of Chicago Press.
Glaser, Barney, and Anselm Strauss
1967 *The Discovery of Grounded Theory.* Chicago: Aldine.
Glass, Judith C.
1966 "Conditions Which Facilitate Unionization of Agricultural Workers: A Case Study of the Salinas Valley Lettuce Industry," Ph.D. dissertation, University of California, Los Angeles.
Glazer, Nona, and Helen Y. Waehrer
1977 *Woman in an Man-Made World.* Chicago: Rand-McNally.

Gordon, David M.
    1972   *Theories of Poverty and Underemployment.* Lexington, Mass.:
             Heath.
Gordon, David M., Richard Edwards, and Michael Reich
    1982   *Segmented Work, Divided Workers.* New York: Cambridge
             University Press.
Gouldner, Alvin
    1954   *Patterns of Industrial Bureaucracy.* New York: Free Press.
Gubbels, Robert
    1977   "The Supply and Demand for Women Workers," in
             Nona Glazer and Helen Y. Waehrer, eds. *Woman in a
             Man-Made World.* Pp. 320–331.
Hartmann, Heidi
    1976   "Capitalism, Patriarchy and Job Segregation by Sex,"
             Signs: Journal of Women in Culture and Society 1
             (Spring):137–169.
Hartmann, Heidi
    1979   "The Unhappy Marriage of Marxism and Feminism," in
             Lydia Sargent, ed. *Women and Revolution.* New York:
             Monthly Review Press.
Hartmann, Heidi and Ann Markusen
    1980   "Contemporary Marxist Theory and Practice: a Feminist
             Critique," *Review of Radical Political Economics* 12 (Sum-
             mer):87–94.
Hawley, Ellis
    1966   "Politics of the Mexican Labor Issue: 1950–1965," *Ag-
             ricultural History* 40(3):1570–1576.
Haynes, Sue
    n.d.   "Farm and Non-farm Wages and Farm Benefits, 1948–
             77." Cooperative Extension Service, University of
             California, Berkeley.
Hightower, James
    1972   *Hard Tomatoes, Hard Times.* New York: Schocken.
Hobsbawm, Eric
    1964   *Laboring Men: Studies in the History of Labor.* London:
             Weidenfeld and Nicolson.
Jamieson, Stuart
    1945   *Labor Unionism in American Agriculture.* Washington, D.C.:
             Government Printing Office.
Jenkins, Craig
    1978   "The Demand for Immigrant Workers: Labor Scarcity
             or Social Control," *International Migration Review* 12:514–
             535.

Jenkins, Craig, and Charles Perrow
1977 "Insurgency of the Powerless: Farm Worker Movements, (1946–1972)," *American Sociological Review* 42(2):249–267.

Johnson, S. S., and M. Zahara
1976 "Prospective Lettuce Harvest Mechanization: Impact on Labor," *HortScience* 101(4):378–381.

Jones, Beverly
1970 "The Dynamics of Marriage and Motherhood," in Robin Morgan, ed. *Sisterhood is Powerful.* Pp. 46–61.

Kalleberg, Arne, and Aage B. Sorensen
1979 "The Sociology of Labor Markets," *Annual Review of Sociology* 5:351–379.

Kanter, Rosabeth Moss
1977 *Men and Women of the Corporation.* New York: Basic Books.

Kerr, Clark, and Abraham Siegel
1954 "The Balkanization of Labor Markets," in E. Wight Bakke et al., eds. *Labor Mobility and Economic Opportunity.* New York: Wiley.

Kiser, George C., and Martha Woody Kiser
1979 *Mexican Workers in the United States: Historical and Political Perspectives.* Albuquerque: University of New Mexico Press.

Lamb, Helen B.
1942 "Industrial Relations in the Western Lettuce Industry," Ph.D. dissertation, Radcliffe College.

Lappe, Frances Moore, and Joseph Collins
1977 *Food First: Beyond the Myth of Agricultural Efficiency.* Boston: Houghton-Mifflin.

Larrowe, Charles P.
1972 *Harry Bridges.* New York: Lawrence Hill and Company.

Levy, Jacques
1975 *Cesar Chavez: Autobiography of La Causa.* New York: Farrar, Straus & Giroux.

Lipset, Seymour Martin, Martin A. Trow, and James S. Coleman
1956 *Union Democracy.* New York: Free Press.

London, Joan, and Henry Anderson
1970 *So Shall Ye Reap.* New York: Thomas Y. Crowell.

McConnell, Grant
1977 *The Decline of Agrarian Democracy.* New York: Atheneum.

McWilliams, Carey
1971 *Factories in Fields.* Santa Barbara: Peregrine.

1976   *California: The Great Exception.* Santa Barbara: Peregrine.
Majka, Linda, and Theo Majka
1982   *Farmworkers, Agribusiness and the State.* Philadelphia: Temple University Press.
Mandel, Ernest
1968   *Marxist Economic Theory.* Vol. I. New York: Monthly Review Press.
Mann, Susan, and James A. Dickinson
1980   "State and Agriculture in Two Eras of American Capitalism," in Buttel and Newby, eds. *The Rural Sociology of the Advanced Societies.* Montclair: Allanheld Osmun.
Marshall, T. H.
1977   *Class, Citizenship, and Social Development.* Chicago: University of Chicago Press.
Marx, Karl
1975   *Capital,* Vol. I. New York: International.
Merrill, Richard
1976   *Radical Agriculture.* New York: Harper.
Mines, Richard, and Ricardo Anzaldua
1982   *New Migrants vs. Old Migrants: Alternative Labor Market Structures in the California Citrus Industry.* Program in U.S.-Mexican Studies, University of California, San Diego.
Miracle Vegetable Company
1972   *Preliminary Prospectus.* Miracle Vegetable Company, May 1972.
Monterey County
1979   *Annual Crop and Livestock Report—1979.* Monterey County Agricultural Commissioner's Office, Salinas, California.
Moore, Barrington, Jr.
1966   *The Social Origins of Dictatorship and Democracy.* Boston: Beacon.
Moore, C. V., and Herbert J. Snyder
1969   "Risk and Uncertainty in Lettuce Production in the Salinas Valley, California." Davis: California Agricultural Experiment Station, Giannini Foundation Report No. 300.
Morgan, Robin, ed.
1970   *Sisterhood is Powerful.* New York: Random House.
Noble, David
1977   *America by Design.* New York: Oxford University Press.

North, David S.
  1970   *The Border Crossers: People Who Live in Mexico and Work in the United States.* Washington, D.C.: Linton and Company.
North, David S., and Marion Houstoun
  1976   *The Characteristics and Role of Illegal Aliens in the U.S. Labor Market.* Washington, D.C.: Linton and Company.
O'Connor, James.
  1973   *Fiscal Crisis of the State.* New York: St. Martin's Press.
Oster, Gerry
  1979   "A Factor-Analytic Test of the Theory of the Dual Economy," *Review of Economics and Statistics* 62 (March):33–39.
Padfield, Harlan, and William Martin
  1965   *Farmers, Workers and Machines.* Tucson: University of Arizona Press.
Paige, Jeffrey
  1975   *Agrarian Revolution.* New York: Free Press.
Perelman, Michael
  1976   "Efficiency in Agriculture: The Economics of Energy," in Richard Merrill, ed. *Radical Agriculture.* New York: Harper.
Pfeffer, Max
  1980   "The Labor Process and Corporate Agriculture: Mexican Workers in California," *Insurgent Sociologist* X(2): 25–44.
Piore, Michael
  1975   "Notes for a Theory of Labor Market Stratification," in Richard Edwards, Michael Reich, and David Gordon, eds. *Labor Market Segmentation.* Lexington, Mass.: Heath. Pp. 125–150.
  1979   *Birds of Passage: Migrant Labor and Industrial Societies.* New York: Cambridge University Press.
Piven, Frances Fox, and Richard Cloward
  1971   *Regulating the Poor.* New York: Pantheon.
Portes, Alejandro
  1977   "Labor Functions of Illegal Aliens," *Society* 14:31–37.
  1978   "Migration and Underdevelopment," *Politics and Society* 8:1–48.
Roy, Don
  1952   "Quota Restriction and Goldbricking in a Machine Shop," *American Journal of Sociology* 57:427–442.

Samora, Julian
   1971   *Los Mojados: The Wetback Story.* Notre Dame: University
             of Notre Dame Press.
Scheuring, Ann, and Orville Thompson
   1978   *From Lug Boxes to Electronics: A Study of California Tomato
             Growers and Sorting Crews.* Davis: University of California
             Agricultural Policy Seminar Monograph No. 3.
Scruggs, Otey
   1960   "Evolution of the Mexican Farm Labor Agreement of
             1942," *Agricultural History* 34(3):140–149.
Segur, Hub
   1973   "From Seed to Supermarket: Study of the Lettuce Indus-
             try," Master's thesis, University of California, Davis.
Selznick, Philip
   1969   *Law, Society and Industrial Justice.* New York: Sage.
Skocpol, Theda
   1979   *States and Social Revolutions.* New York: Cambridge Uni-
             versity Press.
Smith, Francis J.
   1961   "The Impact of Technological Change in the Marketing
             of Salinas Lettuce." Ph.D. dissertation, University of
             California, Berkeley.
Sosnick, Stephen H.
   1978   *Hired Hands.* Santa Barbara: McNally and Loftin.
Soule, Whitman T.
   1979   "Inequality Among Organizations and the Historical
             Construction of Industries." Unpublished paper, North-
             western University.
State of California
   1964,   *Economic Report of the Governor.* Office of the Governor,
   1977   Sacramento.
Stinchcombe, Arthur
   1959   "Craft and Bureaucratic Administration of Production,"
             Administrative Science Quarterly 4:168–187.
Stomberg, Ann, and Shirley Harkess
   1978   *Women Working.* Palo Alto: Mayfield.
Sutherland, E. H.
   1977   "White Collar Criminality," in G. Geis and R. Meier, eds.
             *White Collar Crime: Offenses in Business, Politics and the
             Professions.* New York: Free Press.
Sward, Keith
   1948   *The Legend of Henry Ford.* New York: Harper.

Taylor, Paul S., and Tom Vasey
1936a "Historical Background of California Farm Labor," *Rural Sociology* 1(3):281–295.
1936b "Contemporary Background of California Farm Labor," *Roral Sociology* 1(4):401–419.
Taylor, Ronald B.
1975 *Chavez: A Study in the Acquisition and Use of Power.* Boston: Beacon Press.
Tepperman, Jean
1970 "Two Jobs: Women Who Work in Factories," in Robin Morgan, ed. *Sisterhood is Powerful.* New York: Random House.
Thomas, Robert J.
1977 "Political Economy of a Salad: Comparative Analysis of the Lettuce and Tomato Industries." Master's thesis, Northwestern University.
1980 "Framework for the Study of Agricultural Industrialization." Paper presented to the meetings of the Midwest Sociological Society.
1981 "Social Organization of Industrial Agriculture." *Insurgent Sociologist* X(Winter):5–22.
Thomas, Robert J., and William H. Friedland
1982 "The United Farm Workers Union: From Mobilization to Mechanization?" Working paper #269, Center for Research on Social Organization, University of Michigan.
Tilly, Charles
1975 *The Formation of National States in Western Europe.* Princeton: Princeton University Press, chapters 1, 6, and 9.
U.S. Bureau of Census
1974, *Census of Agriculture, 1940–1974.* Vol. 1, California.
1978
U.S. Department of Agriculture
1978 *Farm Labor 1948–77.* Statistical Research Service. Washington, D.C.: Government Printing Office.
U.S. Department of Labor
1975 *1975 Handbook on Women Workers.* Washington, D.C.: Government Printing Office.
U.S. Senate
1941 Committee on Education and Labor, Hearings before the Subcommittee on Violations of Free Speech and the Rights of Labor, 76th Congressional 2d Session,

Washington, D.C., 1940.

Villarejo, Don
1980   *Getting Bigger: Large Scale Farming in California*. Davis: California Institute for Rural Studies, Inc.

Watson, Don
1977   "Rise and Decline of Fruit Tramp Unionism in the Western Lettuce Industry." Paper presented to Southwest Labor Studies Conference, March 1977, Tempe, Arizona.

Weber, Max
1954   *Law in Economy and Society*. Cambridge: Harvard University Press, chapter 5.

Weiner, Merle
1978   "Cheap Food, Cheap Labor: California Agriculture in the 1930's," *Insurgent Sociologist* 2:181–190.

Western Grower and Shipper
1979   *1979 Yearbook*. Newport Beach, Calif.: Western Grower-Shipper Association.

Whyte, William F.
1961   *Men at Work*. Homewood, Ill.: Dorsey Press.

Wright, Erik, and Luca Perrone
1977   "Marxist Class Categories and Income Inequality," *American Sociological Review* 42:32–55.

Zahara, M., Stan Johnson, and Roger Garrett
1974   "Labor Requirements, Harvest Costs and the Potential for Mechanical Harvest of Lettuce," *Hortscience* 99(6):535–537.

Zwerdling, Daniel
1980   "The Food Monsters," in J. Skolnick and E. Currie, eds. *Crisis in American Institutions*. Boston: Little, Brown. Pp. 38–53.

Index

Designer:	U.C. Press Staff
Compositor:	Prestige Typography
Printer:	Edwards Bros., Inc.
Binder:	Edwards Bros., Inc.
Text:	10/12 Baskerville
Display:	Palatino